Full Stack Web Development with Remix

Enhance the user experience and build better React apps by utilizing the web platform

Andre Landgraf

‹packt›

BIRMINGHAM—MUMBAI

Full Stack Web Development with Remix

Copyright © 2023 Packt Publishing

All rights reserved. No part of this book may be reproduced, stored in a retrieval system, or transmitted in any form or by any means, without the prior written permission of the publisher, except in the case of brief quotations embedded in critical articles or reviews.

Every effort has been made in the preparation of this book to ensure the accuracy of the information presented. However, the information contained in this book is sold without warranty, either express or implied. Neither the author, nor Packt Publishing or its dealers and distributors, will be held liable for any damages caused or alleged to have been caused directly or indirectly by this book.

Packt Publishing has endeavored to provide trademark information about all of the companies and products mentioned in this book by the appropriate use of capitals. However, Packt Publishing cannot guarantee the accuracy of this information.

Group Product Manager: Rohit Rajkumar
Publishing Product Manager: Jane D'Souza
Senior Editor: Aamir Ahmed
Book Project Manager: Sonam Pandey
Technical Editor: K Bimala Singha
Copy Editor: Safis Editing
Proofreader: Safis Editing
Indexer: Hemangini Bari
Production Designer: Aparna Bhagat
DevRel Marketing Coordinator: Nivedita Pandey

First published: October 2023

Production reference: 2301023

Published by
Packt Publishing Ltd.
Grosvenor House
11 St Paul's Square
Birmingham
B3 1RB, UK.

ISBN 978-1-80107-529-9

www.packtpub.com

Foreword

Andre and I first met over Zoom in March 2022, while the world was still in the grip of the global COVID-19 pandemic. During that meeting, we discussed the possibility of Andre joining our software engineering team at LinkedIn. While Andre's qualifications clearly met the bar, what struck me most was his passion and dedication to Software Engineering, which shone through even amid the Zoom fatigue that had become all too familiar during those days.

Since then, I have had the pleasure of collaborating with Andre on numerous projects, each varying in product focus, complexity, and definition. In every one of these collaborations, I was consistently impressed by Andre's principled approach, his consistent implementation of best practices, and his ability to create scalable software that not only delivers results but can also be leveraged by other teams and products. At the core of this capability is Andre's knack for breaking down complex problems, developing technical opinions based on fundamental principles, and effectively communicating this process to his collaborators.

Andre's approach to addressing real-world problems by relying on timeless principles has also allowed him to effectively present technical topics at LinkedIn and international Remix conferences, a noteworthy feat given the rapid pace of evolution in the frontend landscape.

This book encourages readers to delve into theory beyond the framework by solving real, modern technical problems. While focusing on either of these aspects in isolation can be beneficial, it's the synergy between them that provides the most enduring sense of gratification. I hope that by focusing on both, as this book does, you will be inspired by the same passion and dedication that left such an impression on me during that initial Zoom call years ago.

Enjoy.

Dor Solomon

Software Engineering Manager, LinkedIn

Contributors

About the author

Andre Landgraf is a web developer from Germany. He graduated with an MS in information systems from the Technical University of Munich and was awarded an MS in computer science from Sofia University in Palo Alto.

Andre lives in Cupertino, California, and works as a software engineer at LinkedIn. He loves learning, writing, and speaking about all things web. In his free time, he tutors aspiring developers, organizes tech meetups, and builds cool websites.

For Andre, Remix has been an amazing learning journey packed with opportunities, such as speaking at Remix Conf 2023 and writing this book. The Remix community has been welcoming and wonderful to engage with at tech meetups, conferences, and online.

I want to thank my partner in life, Alessandra, my parents, Beate and Tilo, and my sister, Leoni, for all their love, support, and endurance.

Thanks to Brooks for his honest and constructive feedback and to the team at Packt for this opportunity.

About the reviewer

Brooks Lybrand is a software engineer, community builder, and amateur educator. Starting in the field of data science, Brooks switched to web development to be closer to the end user.

Brooks' engineering experience has led him to a place where he is able to mentor and provide opportunities for other engineers in the industry. He founded and runs the Remix Austin meetup group, as well as many internal company meetups and educational workshops and opportunities.

Brooks started learning Remix before it was open source software and has been engaged with the community ever since. To him, Remix is more than just a web framework; it's a framework that teaches you better web fundamentals, which is why he so enthusiastically supports and promotes it.

Table of Contents

Preface   xi

Part 1 – Getting Started with Remix

1

The Era of Full Stack Web Frameworks   3

Introducing Remix 4	**Remix behind the scenes** 10
Remix is a web framework 4	Remix is a compiler 11
Remix is a full stack framework 5	Remix is a router 11
Understanding the philosophy behind Remix 7	Remix is a runtime 12
	What Remix is not 12
Primitives, conventions, and levers 9	**Summary** 13
Primitives 9	**Further reading** 13
Conventions 9	
Levers 10	

2

Creating a New Remix App   15

Technical requirements 15	Client and server code 25
Creating a "Hello World!" Remix app 16	**Troubleshooting Remix applications** 27
Understanding Remix's file and folder structure 18	A Remix troubleshooting process 27
	Looking for answers 31
Exploring the client and server environments 22	**Summary** 32
	Further reading 33
The two bundles of your Remix application 23	

3

Deployment Targets, Adapters, and Stacks — 35

Technical requirements	35	Using Remix Stacks	45
Picking a deployment target	36	Working with Remix official stacks	45
Picking a JavaScript runtime	37	Working with custom templates	46
Picking a hosting environment	38	**Working with BeeRich**	**47**
Making the final decision	40	Summary	48
Switching between adapters	42	Further reading	48

4

Routing in Remix — 51

Technical requirements	52	Sharing layouts	65
Working with Remix's route module API	52	Using parent layout routes	65
		Using pathless layout routes	67
Route file-naming conventions	52	Handling navigations in Remix	69
Working with file-based routing	52	Navigating with Remix's link components	69
Creating route modules	54	Indicating page transitions	73
Available route module exports	56	Redirecting a user from the server	75
Composing pages from nested routes	57	Summary	78
Using route parameters for dynamic routing	63	Further reading	79
Parameterized route segments	63		

Part 2 – Working with Remix and the Web Platform

5

Fetching and Mutating Data — 83

Technical requirements	83	Fetching data at the route level	84
Fetching data	84	Fetching dynamic data in parameterized routes	89

Table of Contents   vii

Loading data in parallel   92
Mutating data   **97**
Mutating data without JavaScript   97
Mutating data with JavaScript   103
Summary   **105**
Further reading   **106**

6

Enhancing the User Experience   107

Technical requirements	**107**
Understanding progressive enhancement	**108**
Progressive enhancement in Remix	108
Making it work without JavaScript	108
Making it worse before making it better	109
Testing on slow networks	110
Prefetching data	**111**
Working with action data	**114**
Handling concurrent mutations	**117**
Adding a form to a list	117
Supporting multiple pending states	120
Summary	**124**
Further reading	**125**

7

Error Handling in Remix   127

Technical requirements	**127**
Dealing with unexpected errors	**128**
Invoking client and server errors	128
Handling errors with the root error boundary	130
Nested error handling	134
Handling thrown responses	**137**
Throwing responses	138
Handling exceptions with error boundaries	138
Creating a resilient experience	140
Handling page-not-found (404) errors	**142**
Summary	**144**
Further reading	**144**

8

Session Management   145

Technical requirements	**145**
Working with search parameters	**146**
Reading search parameters in loader functions	146
Updating search parameters with form submissions	148
Programmatically submitting forms	151

Creating user sessions with cookies	153	Authenticating access to user data	162
Working with Remix's session helpers	153	Accessing cookie data on the server	162
Adding a user registration flow	155	Working with user data on the client	164
Adding a user login flow	158	Enforcing authentication on the server	166
Deleting a session during logout	160	**Summary**	**171**
		Further reading	**172**

9

Assets and Metadata Handling — 173

Technical requirements	173	Managing links in Remix	181
Using meta tags in Remix	173	Styling in Remix	184
Declaring global meta tags	174	Working with images in Remix	187
Exporting the meta function	174	**Exposing assets with loader functions**	**187**
Nesting meta exports	176		
Using loader data in meta functions	177	**Summary**	**188**
Using matches data in meta functions	178	**Further reading**	**189**
Handling fonts, images, stylesheets, and other assets	**180**		
Working with static assets	180		

10

Working with File Uploads — 191

Technical requirements	191	Authorizing access to assets with resource routes	208
Using multi-part form data in Remix	192		
Processing files on the server	197	**Forwarding files to third-party services**	**210**
Loading files into memory	197		
Using Remix's upload handler helper functions	199	**Summary**	**210**
		Further reading	**211**

Part 3 – Advanced Concepts of Full Stack Web Development with Remix

11

Optimistic UI — 215

Technical requirements	215	Adding optimistic UI updates in Remix	217
Considering optimistic UI	216	Creating an expense	217
Communicating rollbacks	216	Updating an expense	218
Synchronizing client and server states	216	Deleting an expense	220
Synchronizing client and server states in Remix	217	Removing an attachment	222
		Summary	223
		Further reading	224

12

Caching Strategies — 225

Technical requirements	225	Caching immutable data responses	231
Working with HTTP caching	226	Caching dynamic data responses with entity tags	233
Adding HTTP headers in Remix	226		
Caching public pages in shared caches	226	Exploring in-memory caching	235
Understanding Remix's built-in caching	228	Summary	236
Caching personalized pages in private caches	230	Further reading	237

13

Deferring Loader Data — 239

Technical requirements	239	Understanding HTTP streaming requirements	242
Streaming data to the client	239		
Motivating server-side data fetching and streaming	240	Deferring loader data	243
		Summary	249
		Further reading	249

14

Real Time with Remix — 251

Technical requirements	251	Understanding WebSocket	252
Working with real-time technologies	251	Building real-time UIs with Remix	253
Understanding polling	252	Summary	259
Understanding SSE	252	Further reading	259

15

Advanced Session Management — 261

Technical requirements	261	Summary	269
Managing visitor sessions	261	Further reading	269
Implementing pagination	265		

16

Developing for the Edge — 271

Living on the edge	271	Understanding the edge's benefits and limitations	274
Computing at the edge	271	Summary	276
Running web apps on the edge	272	Further reading	277
Remixing the edge	273		

17

Migration and Upgrade Strategies — 279

Migrating to Remix	279	Working with a backend application	283
Migrating non-React apps to Remix	280	Keeping Remix apps up to date	285
Migrating from a React app	280	Summary	286
Migrating from React Router	282	Further reading	287

Index — 289

Other Books You May Enjoy — 296

Preface

Welcome to *Full Stack Web Development with Remix*. We live in exciting times for web development. Modern web apps are complex, and they operate on intricate business logic. As web developers, it's our job to deliver great user experiences, using the latest web development advancements and tackling the complexities of today's business requirements.

React is the de facto standard for building modern web applications, but it draws clear lines where its responsibilities end. It allows you to compose your UI from reusable components, but React doesn't cover other key elements of your app. This is where React is supplemented by a full stack web framework. Today's web frameworks offer abstractions for routing, data fetching and mutations, caching, session management, progressive enhancement, optimistic UI, and many other aspects crucial for building state-of-the-art web experiences. This is where Remix comes into play.

Remix is a full stack web framework for React applications. It is built with different deployment targets in mind and utilizes web standards to unlock the full potential of the web platform. Remix provides great primitives, conventions, and levers to let us build modern applications and great user experiences faster. Most importantly, Remix operates on a simple mental model that lets us build complex user interfaces with reduced complexity by leveraging the philosophy of progressive enhancement. Building pending, optimistic, and real-time user interfaces has never been easier. Personally, I have never felt more productive building for the web, and I also never had more fun doing so!

This book follows a real-world project that goes beyond what can be found in Remix's documentation, tutorials, and workshops. By the end of this book, you will be able to apply and articulate many best practices to work with Remix. You will further work with web standards and learn how to unlock the full potential of the web platform with Remix. Finally, you will understand the advantages of utilizing a web server environment in your application architecture. Let's dive into *Full Stack Web Development with Remix* and learn how Remix can make us more productive in building better user experiences faster.

Who this book is for

This book is for React developers looking to use a full stack framework to unlock the full potential of the web platform. This book will also come in handy to evaluate and justify a migration to Remix.

This book is for you if you are the following:

- A web developer who wants to utilize web standards to build fast, slick, and resilient user experiences.
- A React developer who is curious to learn more about full stack web development and the benefits of adding a web server environment to the frontend.
- A tech lead evaluating a migration from a single-page application to Remix, looking to learn more about today's full stack web frameworks.

What this book covers

Chapter 1, The Era of Full Stack Web Frameworks, introduces Remix as a full stack web framework and highlights the advantages Remix provides you as a React developer. The chapter further discusses Remix's philosophy and establishes the mental model of primitives, conventions, and levers. Finally, the chapter explains how Remix works under the hood.

Chapter 2, Creating a New Remix App, kicks off your Remix development journey. The chapter guides you through creating a new Remix application using Remix's `create-remix` CLI script. The chapter also provides an overview of Remix's file and folder structure and Remix's two environments – the client and the server. Finally, the chapter offers a troubleshooting guide for Remix projects.

Chapter 3, Deployment Target, Adapters, and Stacks, offers an overview of Remix's different deployment targets and discusses considerations to select the right target for your application. The chapter further details how to switch between adapters and how to use Remix Stacks to use an existing application template. Finally, the chapter introduces you to BeeRich, the demo application of this book.

Chapter 4, Routing in Remix, reviews Remix's file-based routing convention. The chapter guides you through creating standalone pages, nested routes, parameterized routes, pathless layout routes, and other routing concepts. The chapter also discusses page navigations in Remix.

Chapter 5, Fetching and Mutating Data, dives deep into data fetching and mutations with Remix. The chapter documents Remix's request-response life cycle and provides detailed practices to work with Remix's server-side `loader` and `action` functions. The chapter also explains Remix's built-in data revalidation.

Chapter 6, Enhancing the User Experience, formalizes how progressive enhancement works in Remix. The chapter then focuses on advanced data fetching and mutation concepts, such as prefetching and handling concurrent mutations.

Chapter 7, Error Handling in Remix, provides an overview of handling expected and unexpected errors in Remix to develop resilient user experiences.

Chapter 8, Session Management, guides you through implementing a search feature and a login and signup flow in BeeRich. The chapter provides a practical deep dive into managing UI and session state, using web standards and Remix's primitives.

Chapter 9, Assets and Metadata Handling, focuses on meta tags and static assets in Remix. The chapter includes practices to expose static assets and work with custom fonts. Finally, the chapter discusses how to manage images with Remix.

Chapter 10, Working with File Uploads, introduces you to Remix's file upload helpers. The chapter guides you through the implementation of uploading user files in BeeRich and emphasizes limiting access to the uploaded files to authorized users only.

Chapter 11, Optimistic UI, discusses the trade-offs of the optimistic UI. The chapter further lets you work with optimistic UI in BeeRich using Remix's primitives. Finally, the chapter highlights how Remix eases the implementation of optimistic UI through its primitives and built-in data revalidation.

Chapter 12, Caching Strategies, provides an overview of different caching strategies to improve the performance of a Remix application. First, the chapter reviews different HTTP caching strategies before discussing in-memory caching. The chapter offers practical examples using the BeeRich demo application.

Chapter 13, Deferring Loader Data, introduces you to Remix's concept of deferring loader data. The chapter further explains HTML streaming and motivates its usage and use cases to use streaming to defer data requests.

Chapter 14, Real-Time with Remix, examines popular real-time technologies and allows you to implement real-time data updates in BeeRich, using a Remix resource route and Server-Sent Events.

Chapter 15, Advanced Session Management, explores additional session and UI state management use cases. The chapter provides an overview of Remix's cookie helper primitives compared to its session helpers. The chapter further guides you through the implementation of pagination in BeeRich.

Chapter 16, Developing for the Edge, defines the term *edge* in detail and considers the advantages and disadvantages of deploying Remix applications to an edge environment.

Chapter 17, Migration and Upgrade Strategies, wraps up the learning journey of this book and offers an overview of different strategies to migrate to Remix. The chapter also explains Remix's future flags and how they can be used to ease major version upgrades.

To get the most out of this book

This book guides you through the development of a full stack web application with Remix. Each chapter introduces new concepts and includes practical examples to gain hands-on experience. You will get the most out of this book if you have some experience building web applications with React or a similar frontend framework or library. Since this book's demo application is written in TypeScript, previous TypeScript exposure will also be helpful to follow along with the code examples.

To follow the hands-on exercises in this book, you will need a computer with Node.js and npm installed. We advise using the latest LTS version of Node.js (currently v18). You can download Node.js and npm here: `https://nodejs.org/en`. An editor such as VS Code is also recommended.

Each chapter is accompanied by one or more `README.md` files in the book's GitHub repository. The `README.md` files contain additional guidance and set-up instructions for each chapter if necessary.

If you are using the digital version of this book, we advise you to type the code yourself or access the code from the book's GitHub repository (a link is available in the next section). Doing so will help you avoid any potential errors related to the copying and pasting of code.

Download the example code files

You can download the example code files for this book from GitHub at `https://github.com/PacktPublishing/Full-Stack-Web-Development-with-Remix`. If there's an update to the code, it will be updated in the GitHub repository.

We also have other code bundles from our rich catalog of books and videos available at `https://github.com/PacktPublishing/`. Check them out!

Conventions used

There are a number of text conventions used throughout this book.

`Code in text`: Indicates code words in text, database table names, folder names, filenames, file extensions, pathnames, dummy URLs, user input, and Twitter handles. Here is an example: "The root of the `routes` folder maps to the `/`-path."

A block of code is set as follows:

```
import { H1 } from '~/components/headings';

export default function LoginPage() {
  return (
    <main>
      <H1>Login!</H1>
    </main>
  );
}
```

When we wish to draw your attention to a particular part of a code block, the relevant lines or items are set in bold:

```
<Routes>
  <Route file="root.tsx">
    <Route index file="routes/index.tsx" />
    <Route path="demo" file="routes/demo.tsx" />
  </Route>
</Routes>
```

Any command-line input or output is written as follows:

```
npx remix routes
```

Bold: Indicates a new term, an important word, or words that you see on screen. For instance, words in menus or dialog boxes appear in **bold**. Here is an example: "Notice that one route is flagged as **index**, while the demo route has a **path** property, which matches its filename."

> **Tips or important notes**
> Appear like this.

Get in touch

Feedback from our readers is always welcome.

General feedback: If you have questions about any aspect of this book, email us at `customercare@packtpub.com` and mention the book title in the subject of your message.

Errata: Although we have taken every care to ensure the accuracy of our content, mistakes do happen. If you have found a mistake in this book, we would be grateful if you would report this to us. Please visit `www.packtpub.com/support/errata` and fill in the form.

Piracy: If you come across any illegal copies of our works in any form on the internet, we would be grateful if you would provide us with the location address or website name. Please contact us at `copyright@packt.com` with a link to the material.

If you are interested in becoming an author: If there is a topic that you have expertise in and you are interested in either writing or contributing to a book, please visit `authors.packtpub.com`.

Share Your Thoughts

Once you've read *Full Stack Web Development with Remix*, we'd love to hear your thoughts! Scan the QR code below to go straight to the Amazon review page for this book and share your feedback.

`https://packt.link/r/1-801-07529-8`

Your review is important to us and the tech community and will help us make sure we're delivering excellent quality content.

Download a free PDF copy of this book

Thanks for purchasing this book!

Do you like to read on the go but are unable to carry your print books everywhere? Is your eBook purchase not compatible with the device of your choice?

Don't worry, now with every Packt book you get a DRM-free PDF version of that book at no cost.

Read anywhere, any place, on any device. Search, copy, and paste code from your favorite technical books directly into your application.

The perks don't stop there, you can get exclusive access to discounts, newsletters, and great free content in your inbox daily

Follow these simple steps to get the benefits:

1. Scan the QR code or visit the link below

https://packt.link/free-ebook/9781801075299

2. Submit your proof of purchase
3. That's it! We'll send your free PDF and other benefits to your email directly

Part 1 – Getting Started with Remix

In this first part, you will be introduced to Remix. You will get to know Remix's philosophy and understand how Remix works under the hood. You will then create your first Remix app and discover how Remix can be deployed to different environments and runtimes. Finally, you will kick off your development journey with BeeRich – the example application of this book – and learn about Remix's routing convention.

This part has the following chapters:

- *Chapter 1, The Era of Full Stack Web Frameworks*
- *Chapter 2, Creating a New Remix App*
- *Chapter 3, Deployment Targets, Adapters, and Stacks*
- *Chapter 4, Routing in Remix*

1
The Era of Full Stack Web Frameworks

"The only constant in life is change."

– Heraclitus

We live in exciting times for web development. The landscape is changing at an astonishing pace. There have never been more technologies to choose from to develop for the web. It feels like a new framework or library is published every other month. Existing frameworks and libraries release new major versions with new features, breaking changes, and new conventions. The industry's fast pace can feel overwhelming, but it is also fascinating to see such a high level of innovation.

The larger web development community moves at a much slower pace than the cutting edge does. Most enterprises and developers are waiting to see what technologies stick around before adopting them – creating something we can consider the industry standard. I would count React as part of this standard. However, moving fast and adopting a new technology can be a competitive advantage if it moves the needle far enough. I believe Remix is such a technology.

Since you bought this book, you've decided to try Remix – awesome! As a React developer, Remix provides you with many benefits, such as the following:

- A backend environment for your frontend
- A full stack data mutation story
- A declarative approach to error handling
- Simplified client-side state management
- Server-side rendering
- The latest advancements in React, such as streaming
- An app runtime that can run anywhere, even on the edge
- Progressive enhancement through an embrace of web standards

With Remix, you can tap into the full capabilities of the web. This book guides you through the process, starting with the basics and progressing to more advanced techniques. In this first chapter, we will go over the following topics:

- Introducing Remix
- The philosophy behind Remix
- Primitives, conventions, and levers
- Remix behind the scenes

First, we will introduce Remix as a full stack web framework. After that, we will investigate the philosophy behind Remix and introduce a mental model to categorize the different tools Remix provides. Finally, we will look under the hood and learn about the different responsibilities that Remix takes on.

The goal of this first chapter is to introduce you to Remix. Most importantly, we want to showcase the advantages of Remix to your React development. We hope this will motivate you to get going. Therefore, this chapter touches upon several advanced concepts. But fear not; everything mentioned will be studied in detail later in this book.

Introducing Remix

It's intuitive to think of Remix as another React framework. Still, the team behind Remix stresses that Remix is not a React framework but a **full stack web framework** – an important distinction.

In this first section, we will summarize what it means that Remix is a full stack web framework. First, we will look at the web framework part and explain why Remix is genuinely a framework for the web. After that, we will highlight why Remix is full stack.

Remix is a web framework

The main reason Remix is a web framework is its deep embrace of the web platform. Remix aims to enable a "fast, slick, and resilient user experience" by using web standards. HTML forms and anchor tags, URLs, cookies, meta tags, HTTP headers, and the **Web Fetch API** are all first-class citizens in Remix. Remix's conventions, levers, and primitives are thoughtfully designed abstraction layers of existing web APIs and standards. This sets Remix apart from other popular frameworks that feel more decoupled from the web platform.

The **Open Web Platform** is the collection of standards defined by the **World Wide Web Consortium (W3C)**. This includes JavaScript web APIs, HTML and CSS, accessibility guidelines, and HTTP. The web standard moves at a much slower pace than the industry standard does. New web standards take a long time and go through many iterations before being released, and it's even longer before all browsers support them.

As a web developer, your resources are limited. To make the most of your time and energy, it's essential to focus on learning the core principles of the web, which will be applicable regardless of the tools you choose. Learning the foundations of the web is transferable knowledge that benefits you regardless of what frameworks and libraries you use. When using Remix, you will often refer to the MDN Web Docs instead of the Remix documentation. Learning Remix means learning standard web APIs.

React plays a vital role in Remix. Remix leverages the latest features of React where it makes sense. With React 18, React is becoming more sophisticated. React's latest features are more tailored to framework authors than app developers. Remix provides necessary abstractions to take advantage of these latest advancements.

When paired with React, Remix utilizes client-side routing and data fetching, creating a similar experience to building **single-page applications** (**SPAs**) with React. However, Remix has a broader scope than React and addresses additional concerns in web development, such as caching, user sessions, and data mutations. This makes Remix a web framework.

Remix is a full stack framework

Let's see why Remix is full stack. Remix embraces the client/server model of the web platform. It orchestrates both the frontend and the backend of your web application:

- On the server, Remix acts as an HTTP request handler
- On the client, Remix orchestrates a server-side-rendered React application

Remix acts as a frontend and a backend framework. These two frameworks are independent pieces executed in different environments (the browser and the server environment). During your app's runtime, the two frameworks communicate over the network.

During development, you create one Remix application where the client and server code is nicely co-located in one /app directory. We can even write client and server code in the same files.

The following code example showcases what a page/route file looks like in Remix:

```
// The route's server-side HTTP action handler
export async function action({ request }) {
  // Use the web Fetch API Request object (web standard)
  const userId = await requireUserSession(request);
  const form = await request.formData();
  const title = form.get("title");
  return createExpense({ userId, title });
}

// The route's server-side HTTP GET request data loader
export async function loader({ request }) {
  const userId = await requireUserSession(request);
```

```
    return getExpenses(userId);
}

// The route's React component
export default function ExpensesPage() {
  // Access the loaded data in React
  const expenses = useLoaderData();
  // Simplify state management with Remix's hooks
  const { state } = useNavigation();
  const isSubmitting = state === "submitting";

  return (
    <>
      <h1>Expenses</h1>
      {expenses.map((project) => (
        <Link to={expense.id}>{expense.title}</Link>
      ))}
      <h2>Add expense</h2>
      <Form method="post">
        <input name="title" />
        <button type="submit" disabled={isSubmitting}>
          {isSubmitting ? "Adding..." : "Add"}
        </button>
      </Form>
    </>
  );
}
```

In the code example, we use Remix's route module API to define a `loader` function for server-side data loading, an `action` function for mutating data, and the route's React component for rendering the UI.

Remix co-locates server-side request handlers and the app's route components. This makes sharing code between the client and server way easier and provides full visibility and control over how our app's frontend and backend work together.

On the server, we handle incoming HTTP requests and prepare responses using Remix's `action` and `loader` functions. In the code example, the server-side request handlers manage user sessions and load and mutate data. We use web standards such as the Fetch API, `FormData`, and HTTP cookies.

In the route component, we access the server-side-loaded data and read transition states with Remix's React hooks. We further use Remix's `Form` component to define a data mutation declaratively. On the client, Remix runs JavaScript to enhance the browser's default experience. This is where we utilize the power of React to compose dynamic UIs.

Remix is a web framework that lets you take advantage of the full stack. Remix truly allows you to unlock the full potential of the web platform for your React development.

Now that we have introduced Remix, let's dive into its philosophy.

Understanding the philosophy behind Remix

Remix's mission is to let you build fast, slick, and resilient user experiences. The vision is to let you deliver software that people love. In this section, we will have a closer look into the philosophy behind Remix. You will learn about the creation of Remix and the values that the team promotes.

Remix was created by Ryan Florence and Michael Jackson (`@ryanflorance` and `@mjackson` on Twitter and GitHub). Ryan and Michael are React veterans and the authors behind React Router – the most popular routing library for React applications with over 1 billion downloads on `npm`. Remix's philosophy is heavily influenced by the lessons Ryan and Michael learned by building and maintaining React Router.

Initially, Remix was intended to be a license-based framework. But in October 2021, the development team behind Remix announced that they had secured seed funding and would make Remix open source. In November 2021, the team released v1 of Remix after 18 months of development. A year later, in October 2022, Shopify acquired Remix. The Remix team is now fully focused on Remix's development while still pursuing the same mission and vision at Shopify.

Not only is Remix open source, but the Remix team also embraces open development. The team has made the roadmap and all **Requests for Comments** (**RFCs**) and proposals available to the public. They also live-stream roadmap meetings and actively encourage community participation and contributions. The goal is to open the development process to the community as much as possible while still fostering the philosophy that guided Ryan and Michael.

Over time, the team behind Remix has mentioned many of the things that are important to them. Above all, Remix is meant to push the web forward. Both Ryan and Michael stress that they want to see better websites. The mission is to provide you with the tools to build great user experiences. They want people to love using your stuff.

The Remix team did a great job summarizing its philosophy in the Remix documentation. Some of the points that the Remix team has emphasized are as follows:

- Remix aims to avoid over-abstraction. In Remix, APIs are meant to be a thin abstraction layer on top of the web platform. Simplicity is king. Remix does not reinvent the wheel.

- Remix looks both forward and backward. It mixes cutting-edge technologies and matches them with battle-proven web standards to create new approaches. Remix takes advantage of HTTP2 streaming and edge deployment but simultaneously embraces HTML forms, cookies, and URLs.

- Remix progressively enhances the user experience without straying from the browser's default behavior. The goal is to stay true to the browser's default behavior and be able to fall back to it whenever possible.
- Remix is about unlocking the full stack of the web platform – or, as the Remix team phrases it, the client/server model.
- The team behind Remix deeply cares about the network tab and your app's bundle size. The goal is to load less and load things as quickly as possible.

Frameworks provide the foundation and framing for your application code. The Remix team also refers to Remix as being center stack (instead of full stack). Remix is meant to be the core, reaching out to both the client and server sides of your application. It is meant to be the centerpiece.

For me, Remix is a powerful tool with great developer experience that lets me build for the web. I value the simplicity and utility of the APIs that Remix provides. I have learned a lot about the web since picking up Remix, all thanks to the emphasis on using the web platform. Remix combines new approaches with old ones. It is refreshing to use and has already started influencing the ecosystem around it. We now truly live in the era of full stack web frameworks.

The Remix team promotes the Remix way of thinking. For instance, Ryan suggests a three-step process for developing web experiences:

1. Make everything work without JavaScript.
2. Enhance the experience with JavaScript.
3. Move as much business logic as possible to the server.

In each step, we build upon the last step to enhance the experience:

1. First, we focus on building the feature without JavaScript. With Remix, we take advantage of the web platform. We use forms to mutate data and use server-side redirects to communicate feedback. After the feature works without JavaScript, we could possibly publish it and be done.
2. Next, we use JavaScript on the client to enhance the user experience. We may add optimistic UIs, deferred data loading, and real-time data updates.
3. Finally, we move as much business logic as possible to the server. This allows for graceful degradation in case client-side JavaScript isn't loaded. It also decreases the bundle size of your app.

By using Remix and engaging with the Remix community, you are exposed to Remix's philosophy. Applying Remix's philosophy to your development process will truly supercharge your React development.

Remix's philosophy can also be understood by the tools it provides you. In the next section, I want to introduce you to a mental model of framework features.

Primitives, conventions, and levers

In this section, we will categorize the different features Remix offers. A framework provides the foundation and framing for your application. It further exposes tools to you as a developer. We can divide these tools into three categories:

- Primitives
- Conventions
- Levers

Primitives, conventions, and levers can serve as a great mental model to map different features of Remix. Let's see how the three categories differ.

Primitives

Primitives are used in your application code to interact with the framework layer. They are the wiring that integrates your application into the foundation and framing provided by the framework. Common primitives are functions, hooks, constants, types, classes, and components. The framework exposes these primitives so you can use them in your code. The art is to make primitives easy to understand yet composable enough to enable powerful business logic. Remix has done just that.

Remix provides primitives for both your client and server code. Remix primitives are often just a thin abstraction layer of the web platform and offer similar APIs to the native primitives. For instance, Remix's `Form` component accepts the same properties as the native form element but also offers some additional properties to enhance the experience.

Also, Remix's primitives themselves expose standard web APIs. Most server-side code you write in Remix has access to a `Request` object that follows the Web Fetch API specification. Remix does not reinvent the wheel.

Conventions

Frameworks also introduce conventions. Common conventions are file and folder naming conventions. In the previous section, we showed a code example of a route file in Remix. Remix's route files (route modules) allow you to export specific functions that are part of Remix's route filenaming convention.

Conventions are meant to improve the developer experience. For instance, file-based routing lets you define your application's route structure as a file and folder hierarchy. Remix compiles your code and infers your route hierarchy, so you don't have to define your route hierarchy as code.

Intuitive conventions reduce the amount of configuration required to wire an application. They shift the burden toward the framework. Conventions make up the contract between the framework and your application and can significantly reduce the amount of boilerplate code you have to write.

The API of a framework is mainly composed of primitives and conventions. All frameworks include primitives, and many frameworks utilize conventions. However, Remix places a particular emphasis on a third category: levers.

Levers

Levers can be interpreted as options. Ryan coined the metaphor in one of his first conference talks about Remix. Ryan emphasizes that Remix is just a thin abstraction layer on top of the web platform. Remix lets you decide what web vitals to optimize for. **Time to First Byte (TTFB)** or **Cumulative Layout Shift (CLS)**? Loading spinners or slower page loads? Optimizing for different web vitals can be conflicting goals. Remix offers levers so that you can stir your web app in the direction that is right and important for you.

With levers comes utility but also responsibility. Remix provides the primitives, but you must decide how to design your application. I believe this power makes you a better web developer. But more importantly, it unlocks the full potential of the web platform. There are many things to optimize for, and Remix provides the levers. This sets Remix apart from other frameworks that don't give you the same kind of flexibility and control.

Now that we've prepared a mental model for how to categorize Remix's features, we will have a look behind the scenes. Remix offers many great features and comes with many quality-of-life improvements. This is because it takes on several responsibilities at once. Let's peek under the hood to understand what that means.

Remix behind the scenes

So, how does Remix work behind the scenes? Based on what we have learned so far, Remix seems to do quite a lot. In this section, we will have a look behind the curtain. This will help you understand some of the responsibilities Remix takes on.

Remix offers a fantastic developer experience but can also feel like magic. A bit of magic goes a long way, but it can also be overwhelming when one doesn't understand what is happening. Magic is also hard to troubleshoot if something goes wrong. That is why I want to reveal some of Remix's inner workings even before creating our first Remix project.

We can identify three distinct responsibilities that Remix takes on:

- Remix bundles your code
- Remix manages routing in your application
- Remix handles incoming HTTP requests

Based on the identified responsibilities, Remix can be broken down into three main components: a compiler, a router, and a runtime. In the following sections, we will examine each component. To start, let's take a closer look at how Remix operates as a compiler.

Remix is a compiler

Remix compiles your file-based route modules into code. It infers the route structure from the file and folder hierarchy. For each route module, Remix inspects what functions it exports and translates the routes folder into a data structure used during runtime. This makes Remix a compiler.

One thing you will notice while working with Remix is the speed of its build step. This is thanks to esbuild, the build tool used by Remix. Remix doesn't expose esbuild. Hence, Remix can adapt how it bundles your code and be competitive in the future by using the latest and greatest build tools. If an even faster, more powerful build tool is released, Remix could switch out esbuild tomorrow.

Remix builds on top of esbuild to bundle your JavaScript files into the following:

- A server bundle
- A client bundle
- An asset manifest

Remix's **command-line interface** (**CLI**) builds your code into a client and server bundle. The server bundle contains Remix's HTTP handler and adapter logic. This is the code that runs on the server. The client build contains client-side scripts that operate Remix's client-side React application.

Remix also compiles an **asset manifest** based on your route hierarchy. Both the client and server use the asset manifest, which includes information about the dependency graph of your application. The manifest tells Remix what to load and allows prefetching assets and application data for page transitions.

Speaking of page transitions…

Remix is a router

Remix implements a router for both your client and server code. This eases the server-to-client handoff. The deep integration between the frontend and backend makes Remix bridge the network gap. This allows Remix to do some neat things. For instance, Remix calls your route `loader` functions in parallel to avoid request waterfalls.

We can simplify things and say that Remix uses React Router under the hood. To be more specific, Remix uses both `react-router-dom` and `@remix-run/router`. `@remix-run/router` is a frontend library/framework-agnostic package used by React Router v6 and Remix. React Router and Remix have been aligned and share a similar API surface. In many ways, you can think of Remix as a compiler for its underlying routing solution.

Remix has a client-side and a server-side part, as does its routing solution. The React components exposed by Remix make sure your application feels like an SPA. Remix handles form submissions and link clicks. It prevents the browser's default behavior if JavaScript is loaded but can fall back to full page loads if necessary. All that is managed by Remix's router at runtime.

Speaking of runtimes…

Remix is a runtime

Remix runs on an existing server, such as an Express.js Node server. Remix provides adapters to create combability with different server-side JavaScript environments. This enables Remix's HTTP handler to be agnostic to the underlying server.

The adapter translates incoming requests from the server environment to standard `Request` objects and reverts the HTTP handler's responses back to the server environment's response implementation.

Remix receives HTTP requests via the JavaScript server and prepares the responses. Remix's router knows what route modules to load and render and which assets to fetch. On the client, Remix hydrates your React application and orchestrates the routing and data fetching. As a framework, Remix provides the foundation for your application and executes your application's code. Next, let's have a look at what Remix is not.

What Remix is not

Earlier in this chapter, we introduced Remix and explored many of the tools and features that it provides. Remix is a full stack web framework, but it is also essential to understand what Remix is not. Most importantly, Remix is not one of the following:

- A JavaScript server
- A database
- An **Object Relation Mapper** (**ORM**)
- A cloud provider
- A styling or theming library
- A magic crystal ball

Remix is neither a server nor a JavaScript engine. Remix runs on a JavaScript environment such as Node.js and uses adapters to communicate with a web server such as Express.js. Remix also provides no solutions for the data layer of your application. It helps you load and mutate data, but it is your job to implement those data loaders and actions. It is your job to select a database solution that fits your use case. Remix is also not an ORM. Hence, you must query your data in your actions and loaders, define your data types, or use third-party libraries for support.

The company behind Remix does not act as a cloud provider or offer a cloud hosting service. You can host your Remix application almost anywhere where JavaScript can be executed. Many cloud services support Remix out of the box, but Remix as a company does not offer any hosting services.

Remix is also not a styling or theming library. Remix is opinionated on how to work with CSS, but its solution is generic. Remix provides no tools for styling or theming other than utilities to load your stylesheets on a prefix route level.

Most things listed are out of scope for Remix, but some might be up for change in the future. For now, let's focus on the present. In this first chapter, we have learned a lot about the many features Remix has to offer. Most of the things mentioned happen behind the scenes. This book will guide you through each aspect of Remix step by step. Each chapter will focus on a specific topic, such as routing, data fetching and mutation, error handling, and state management. By examining these topics one by one, we will explore the significance of Remix. I am certainly excited to start coding!

Summary

In this first chapter, we introduced Remix as a full stack web framework. Remix promotes the usage of the web platform and lets you take advantage of standard web APIs. It bridges the network gap by tightly integrating the frontend and the backend. This allows Remix to do some cool things.

We also looked at the philosophy behind Remix. The team behind Remix emphasizes avoidance of over-abstraction. Its mission is to let you build fast, slick, and resilient user experiences. The vision is to let you deliver software that people will love.

We introduced the terms primitives, conventions, and levers to categorize Remix's different features. Primitives are the exposed utilities that can be imported and used in our code. Conventions are contracts such as file and folder naming conventions that are used to avoid tedious configuration. Levers are options provided by Remix that allow us to optimize our application for what's important to us.

You also learned more about what Remix does behind the scenes. Remix takes on three distinct responsibilities. It is a compiler, a router, and a runtime. Combining those three responsibilities in one framework enables great things, such as flattening request waterfalls and avoiding the frontend-backend split by co-locating client and server code.

In this chapter, we touched upon many concepts, such as server-side rendering, prefetching, and client-side routing. We will revisit all the mentioned concepts throughout this book. In the next chapter, we start our Remix development journey and create a "Hello World" Remix app.

Further reading

If you haven't looked through Remix's home page (`https://remix.run`), I encourage you to do so. The team behind Remix has done a great job of breaking down its value proposition and pitching its solutions. Also, it looks awesome.

The same goes for the Remix documentation. I encourage you to familiarize yourself with Remix's documentation as you work through the chapters of this book. For example, the team behind Remix has done a fantastic job of summarizing its philosophy. You can read more about it here: `https://remix.run/docs/en/v1/pages/philosophy`.

Are you interested in more in-depth explanations about Remix? You can find an in-depth technical explanation about Remix here: `https://remix.run/docs/en/2/pages/technical-explanation`.

You can find the official announcement of Remix joining forces with Shopify here: `https://remix.run/blog/remixing-shopify`.

The public roadmap and most other planning documents are located on GitHub. The roadmap can be found here: `https://github.com/orgs/remix-run/projects/5`.

If you want to learn more about Remix's approach compared to alternative technologies, check out this blog post: `https://remix.run/blog/remix-and-the-edge`. If you want more context around alternative solutions, I recommend the following blog post: `https://frontendmastery.com/posts/the-new-wave-of-javascript-web-frameworks`.

2
Creating a New Remix App

Getting started with a new framework means familiarizing yourself with its primitives, conventions, and levers. This book uses a demo application that we will build from start to finish. Each chapter focuses on one specific topic of full stack web development with Remix. In this chapter, we will explore explore the breadth of Remix's `create-remix` CLI script, introduce Remix's file and folder structure, and familiarize ourselves with Remix's runtime.

This chapter covers the following topics:

- Creating a "Hello World!" Remix app
- Understanding Remix's file and folder structure
- Exploring the client and server environments
- Troubleshooting Remix applications

First, we will walk through the setup of a new Remix project using the `create-remix` CLI script. The chapter then introduces you to Remix's folder structure. We will investigate each file and learn about its function. Next, we will discuss Remix's two environments: the client and the server. You will learn how to manage client and server code in Remix. Finally, we will introduce a troubleshooting guide that will help us debug Remix applications.

By the end of this chapter, you will know how to create a Remix project and will have familiarized yourself with Remix's file and folder structure. You will also learn more about Remix's client and server environments and how to troubleshoot Remix applications.

Technical requirements

To complete this chapter, you will need a computer that can run Node.js. All common operation systems should suffice. Please install both Node.js and npm on your machine. An editor such as VS Code is recommended.

You can download Node.js and npm here: `https://nodejs.org/en/download/`.

The solution for this chapter can be found here: `https://github.com/PacktPublishing/Full-Stack-Web-Development-with-Remix/tree/main/02-creating-a-new-remix-app`. Try to read through this chapter first before peeking at the final code.

Creating a "Hello World!" Remix app

This section walks you through the creation of a new Remix application using the `create-remix` CLI script. The script is maintained by the Remix team and used to bootstrap new Remix projects:

1. Open a new terminal window and run the following command:

    ```
    npx create-remix@2
    ```

    We use `npx` to execute the `create-remix` script. **npx** is part of npm and stands for **Node Package Execute**. The command lets us run remote node scripts locally on our machine – pretty nifty!

    Note that we specify to use the latest available version of `create-remix` v2. The examples in this book are based on Remix v2. By adding the `@2` postfix to the package name, we ensure that our first demo application installs a Remix v2 application.

    For projects outside of this book, we recommend using the following command instead to work with the latest stable version of Remix:

    ```
    npx create-remix@latest
    ```

2. If you are asked by `npx` to install `create-remix`, enter `y` to answer with yes.

3. After installing the `create-remix` script, we are prompted to provide a valid location for our Remix project:

    ```
    Where should we create your new project? ./my-remix-app
    ```

    Pick an install location on your machine or use the default install location offered by the CLI tool.

    After hitting *Enter*, the script informs us that it selected the basic template, also called **Remix App Server**. The script defaults to the basic template if no other template is specified. We will learn more about templates in the next section.

4. The script prompts us to initialize a new Git repository. Select **Yes**:

    ```
    Initialize a new git repository? ● Yes  ○ No
    ```

5. Now, we must decide whether we want to run `npm install`:

    ```
    Install dependencies with npm? ● Yes  ○ No
    ```

    Since we want to run the app, select **Yes**.

6. Wait until `npm install` has finished. Next, use the terminal to navigate into the newly created project folder:

    ```
    cd ./my-remix-app
    ```

    Congratulations on bootstrapping your first Remix project! Let's start the local development server.

7. The following command starts our Remix application locally:

    ```
    npm run dev
    ```

    Once the Remix application is running, it should provide you with a URL to open the running application in a web browser:

    ```
    > dev
    > remix dev

    ◉  remix dev

    info  building...
    info  built (204ms)
    Remix App Server started at http://localhost:3000
    (http://10.0.0.173:3000)
    ```

    Please note how fast Remix builds. Built in 204 ms – that is the power of esbuild. The exact number of milliseconds varies based on your system, but it's amazing that we can speak about build times in milliseconds!

8. Open the specified URL in your browser: `http://localhost:3000`. It should render a simple HTML page.

    Congratulations on running your first Remix application locally! However, it wouldn't be a "Hello World!" project without printing "Hello World" on the screen.

9. Open the Remix project in an editor of your choice. In the editor, open the `_index.tsx` file, located in `app/routes`. You will find it exports a React component. Remove the existing JSX code and replace it with the following:

    ```
    export default function Index() {
      return (
        <h1>Hello World!</h1>
      );
    }
    ```

    Note that Remix ships with TypeScript by default. Don't be worried if you haven't used TypeScript before. There are only a few instances where we will have to deal with TypeScript directly. Mostly, we can enjoy type inference and autocompletion without having to write types ourselves.

10. Save the file changes. Your browser tab should now automatically reload and display the updated HTML: **Hello World!**

The `create-remix` CLI script makes it easy to create new Remix applications. In this section, we bootstrapped a simple Remix application using the default template and rendered **Hello World!** to the screen. Next, let's inspect the bootstrapped folder structure. We will inspect each file and study its function.

Understanding Remix's file and folder structure

Remix takes on the responsibilities of a compiler, router, and runtime. It provides the foundations and framing for the application. As such, it proposes a skeleton folder structure for the application. Some files serve as entry points that you can hook into. Others can be used to configure Remix. Let's review our bootstrapped Remix app.

Which files and folders are present depends on the selected configuration options during the creation process. However, most files are part of all setups. Selecting the basic Remix App Server template yields the following file and folder structure:

```
my-remix-app
├── .eslintrc.js
├── .gitignore
├── README.md
├── app
│   ├── entry.client.tsx
│   ├── entry.server.tsx
│   ├── root.tsx
│   └── routes
│       └── _index.tsx
├── package.json
├── public
│   └── favicon.ico
├── remix.config.js
├── remix.env.d.ts
└── tsconfig.json
```

Let's have a look at each file and folder. Remix ships with a `.eslintrc` file, which configures ESLint to extend Remix's ESLint extensions. You can adapt or remove this file based on your linting and formatting preferences.

When initializing a new Git repository, Remix also creates a `.gitignore` file. It is set up to ignore Remix's build artifacts, temporary files such as the `.cache` folder, and other commonly ignored files and folders. You can update this file based on your application's requirements.

Every newly created project comes with a `README.md` file. The file contains important information on how to run and deploy your application. The documentation varies based on the selected template. Make sure to read through the `README.md` file whenever you bootstrap a new Remix application.

Next, let's continue with the `package.json` file. If you have worked with Node.js-based projects before, you will be familiar with the content. Remix's `package.json` file comes with all the sections you would expect:

- `scripts`
- `dependencies`
- `devDependencies`

The `scripts` section includes a set of scripts to run your Remix application locally, build your application, and run your application in production. Usually, those scripts are named `dev`, `build`, and `start`. Your application might come with additional scripts depending on the selected template.

Take a moment to investigate the `dependencies` and `devDependencies` sections. You might notice that Remix is split into several packages. Some are dependencies, and others are `dev` dependencies. One dependency to highlight is the adapter in use.

We learned in the previous chapter that Remix can run anywhere where JavaScript can be executed. Remix's server-side HTTP request handler uses adapters to run on different JavaScript runtime and server environments. Each Remix application uses an adapter that sits between Remix and the web server.

The basic template uses the `@remix-run/serve` package to run on a Node.js server environment. The package implements the Remix App Server, a production-ready Express.js server. In contrast to other templates, the Remix App Server does not expose the Node.js server setup. Perfect to get started.

Next, let's have a look at the `public` folder. The `public` folder contains static files and assets that are exposed over the internet. Currently, the folder includes a `favicon.ico` file.

After running the app locally (`npm run dev`), the folder should further include a `build` folder. The folder is one of two `build` folders that contain your bundled app code. To build your application, locate your terminal and run `npm run build`. This will generate the two bundles for production based on your latest code changes.

Remix includes a client and a server application. When writing your Remix application, you write code for two different environments, runtimes, and applications. The client-side application code is bundled into the `public/build` folder. These files are exposed over the internet and can be fetched from a browser.

If you peek inside the `public/build` folder, you can notice that each JavaScript module filename ends with a hash. The hash is referred to as the file's fingerprint. There cannot be two files with the same name and different content. This simplifies caching. Since a new version of a file means a new file is generated, we can cache each file forever without having to deal with cache invalidations. If the content of a module changes in a new version of your application, then it will have a different unique filename and will be freshly loaded.

Inside the `public/build` folder, you can also locate a manifest file (`manifest-*.js`). Remix compiles an asset manifest, which is used to route requests and locate assets. Since the manifest must be accessed by the client, it is also part of the `public/build` bundle.

Let's have a look at the `remix.config.js` file. This JavaScript file exports an `AppConfig` configuration object. This file can be used to configure Remix, enable future flags, and override Remix's default behavior. Normally, you won't need to touch this file. However, since its content might change depending on what template and adapter you choose, it may be relevant when switching between templates or adapters. We will learn more about switching adapters later in this book.

Next, let's inspect the `remix.env.d.ts` file. This file includes information for the TypeScript compiler. The file contains triple-slash directives that declare packages that the application is dependent on. The declarations tell TypeScript that your application is dependent on Remix's packages.

Finally, there is the `tsconfig.json` file – or `jsconfig.json` file if you picked a template without TypeScript. These config files contain configuration options for the TypeScript compiler and are used to bundle and compile your Remix application.

Now that we have visited all top-level files and folders, let's have a look inside the `app` folder. This is where the Remix application lives and where we write our application code. Remix populates the folder with a set of starter files. The `entry.server.tsx` and `entry.client.tsx` files serve as entry points for the client and server frameworks, respectively.

The `entry.client.ts` file contains the code that serves as an entry point for the client. Its responsibility is to hydrate React and, hence, initialize the SPA-like experience on the client. Remix exposes the entry file so that you can adapt it based on your use case. The file can serve as a great place for any code that has to be executed only once when the application first loads on the client. You can also delete the file, in which case Remix will fall back to the default implementation.

The `entry.server.tsx` file exports the `handleRequest` function as its default export. The `handleRequest` function is called on incoming requests and generates the HTTP response. The general flow of `handleRequest` looks as follows: `handleRequest` is invoked with a request object and some additional parameters. The function renders React on the server side. The rendered markup is returned, wrapped in a new `Response` object, and returned to the adapter code, which passes the response to the server to serve the response to the client.

Let's have a look at the `root.tsx` file and the `routes` folder. Remix utilizes a file-based routing solution. Every file inside the `routes` folder is considered a nested route module within the route tree. The file and folder hierarchy of the folder maps to the routing hierarchy. Every document/UI route must export a React component.

The `root.tsx` file contains the root document route module. As such, it also exports a React component as its default export:

```
export default function App() {
  return (
    <html lang="en">
      <head>
        <meta charSet="utf-8" />
        <meta name="viewport" content="width=device-width,initial-
          scale=1" />
        <Meta />
        <Links />
      </head>
      <body>
        <Outlet />
        <ScrollRestoration />
        <Scripts />
        <LiveReload />
      </body>
    </html>
  );
}
```

Note that Remix manages the full HTML document, including the `<html />` tag and the `<head />` tag in React. This gives us full control over the structure of our HTML document. With Remix, you can conditionally render meta tags, change the `lang` attribute, or add and remove client-side JavaScript (`<Scripts />`) conditionally.

The route component in `root.tsx` renders several of Remix's built-in components:

- `Meta`
- `Links`
- `Outlet`
- `ScrollRestoration`
- `Scripts`
- `LiveReload`

The `Meta` component adds meta tags defined in `meta` exports to the HTML document. Similarly, the `Links` component adds links defined in `links` exports. You will learn more about the `Meta` and `Links` components in *Chapter 9, Assets and Metadata Handling*.

Instead of `{children}` – which you might have expected – Remix provides an `Outlet` component to specify where to render the child route. You will learn more about the `Outlet` component and nesting of child routes in *Chapter 4, Routing in Remix*.

The `ScrollRestoration` component manages scroll positions for all client-side navigations. SPAs avoid full page reloads and instead render a new page with JavaScript on the client. The `ScrollRestoration` component is used to emulate the browser's default behavior and restore the scroll position when the browser's back and forward buttons are used.

The `Scripts` component might be one of the most fascinating components that Remix exposes. The component adds all script tags of the bundled Remix application to the HTML document. By removing the `Scripts` component, we can remove all client-side JavaScript from our Remix application.

The `LiveReload` component triggers page reloads during development whenever the development server detects any file changes. `LiveReload` is part of Remix's development server setup and is not used in production environments.

Notice that Remix offers us control over its inner workings by exposing when and how its built-in components are rendered. For instance, if we are not interested in live reloads during development, we can just remove the `LiveReload` component. If we want to develop static pages without client-side JavaScript, we can remove the `Scripts` component.

The `routes` folder contains all other routes of your Remix application. As of now, it only contains an `_index` route. An `_index` route is the default child of its parent route and shares the same URL. The present `_index` route maps to the `/` pathname. We will learn all about routing in *Chapter 4, Routing in Remix*.

That was quite a few files! Remix acts as your compiler, router, and runtime. As such, Remix must be aware of your compiler configurations and the location of your code. Remix must further know about all your route modules. As your runtime, it also must own the entry points of your application. Since Remix is not a server, it must expose these entry points to the server environment. Most of the time, you don't have to touch these entry points and configuration files. However, it is great that you can easily alter the content of those files and hook application logic into these places if needed.

Now that we have gone through Remix's folder structure and investigated Remix's configuration and project files, we will learn more about the two environments of your Remix application.

Exploring the client and server environments

In this section, you will learn about the two environments of every Remix application: the client and the server. First, we will learn more about how code is executed during runtime. Next, you will learn where to write your client and server code and how to help Remix's compiler recognize what belongs in the client bundle and what belongs in the server bundle.

The two bundles of your Remix application

The Remix App Server does not expose its server setup, but most other templates do. In this section, we will use the Express.js template to review how Remix interacts with the web server.

Follow these steps to bootstrap an Express.js Remix app:

1. Run the following `create-remix` command in a terminal:

   ```
   npx create-remix@2 --template remix-run/remix/templates/express
   ```

   This time, we don't use the basic template but Remix's Express.js template.

   Note that the `--template` flag points to a folder on GitHub.com, using the following pattern: `:username/:repository/:path-to-folder`. You can learn more about the different `--template` options by calling `npx create-remix@latest --help`.

2. Pick a new folder location for this Remix application and follow the prompts as practiced in the previous section.

3. Review the new Remix application. Compare the `package.json` file with the Remix App Server `package.json` file from the last section. How do the `dependencies` and `scripts` sections differ?

4. Next, open the `server.js` file. The file contains code to set up a new Express.js application. Let's go over the code together and discuss the most important aspects.

   Notice that `createRequestHandler` is imported from Remix's Express.js adapter (`@remix-run/express`).

   Next, the server build of the Remix application is dynamically imported:

   ```
   const BUILD_PATH = path.resolve("build/index.js");
   const initialBuild = await reimportServer();
   ```

   The server `build` folder contains the bundled server code of the Remix application. Among other things, it contains the `entry.server.tsx` file and the content of the `handleRequest` function that we reviewed in the last section.

   In the next step, the Express.js application is created:

   ```
   const app = express();
   ```

   The express app is further configured to expose static files from the `public/build` folder:

   ```
   app.use(
     "/build",
     express.static("public/build", { immutable: true, maxAge: "1y" })
   );
   ```

Every request to `/build` is mapped to modules in the `public/build` folder. This is how we expose the content of the client bundle.

Similarly, the rest of the `/public` folder is also exposed by the web server:

```
app.use(express.static("public", { maxAge: "1h" }));
```

Anything put into the `/public` folder is accessible over the internet. All other requests to the web server are then forwarded to Remix's HTTP handler:

```
app.all(
  "*",
  process.env.NODE_ENV === "development"
    ? createDevRequestHandler()
    : createRequestHandler({
        build: initialBuild,
        mode: initialBuild.mode,
      })
);
```

We pass the content of the server `build` folder to the `createRequestHandler` function, using the `initialBuild` object we defined earlier.

The `createRequestHandler` function acts as an **adapter** between Remix and the underlying server environment. It returns a wrapper function around the request handler (`handleRequest`) found in `entry.server.tsx`. The wrapper function handles requests according to the underlying server environment and translates incoming requests into a format understood by Remix. The wrapper function also translates Remix's `Response` into instructions understood by the server environment.

Finally, we start the Express.js application by calling `app.listen`. All incoming requests are mapped from our Express.js app to Remix.

Note that the server environment is informed about both the client and server bundle of the Remix application. The client bundle is exposed over the internet. The server bundle is passed to the Remix adapter and called on incoming requests.

> **Remix is an HTTP request handler**
>
> Remix is not a web server but an HTTP request handler that runs on a server environment. Remix uses adapters to communicate with the underlying server.

Remix's adapter code is used within the server environment. The adapter passes requests from the server environment to our Remix application and manages our HTTP handler's response using the primitives of the server environment. Depending on the selected template and deployment target, the server code differs.

With Remix, we have full control over the `server.js` file. If necessary, we can hook into the server code and add additional logic. For instance, we could add a WebSocket server to our Express.js application and let it run next to our Remix application. Remix's architecture offers full control over the runtime of our application.

Next, let's write some application code inside the `app` folder.

Client and server code

With Remix, you can take advantage of the full stack of the web platform. In this section, we will learn more about how to write client and server code in Remix.

Earlier in this chapter, we printed **Hello World!** on the home page of our first Remix application. We used the following code to render a React component onto the screen:

```
export default function Index() {
  return (
    <h1>Hello World!</h1>
  );
}
```

Let's investigate Remix's client and server runtimes:

1. Open your `Hello World!` Remix application in an editor and add a `console.log` statement into the `function` component in `app/_index.tsx`:

    ```
    export default function Index() {
      console.log("Another hello to the world!");
      return (
        <h1>Hello World!</h1>
      );
    }
    ```

    The `console.log` is executed anytime our React component renders.

2. Start the Remix application locally. In your terminal window, execute `npm run dev` at the root of the project. Can you guess how many times the `console.log` statement will be run?

3. Open the application in a new browser tab.

4. Next, review the terminal where you executed npm run dev. You will see that Another hello to the world! is printed in the terminal.

    ```
    Remix App Server started at http://localhost:3000
    (http://10.0.0.37:3000)
    Another hello to the world!
    GET / 200 - - 66.536 ms
    ```

The terminal is connected to our server-side environment. Visiting the web page in a browser tab creates a `GET` request for the web server. `GET  /  200` – the `GET` request to the `/` – path is responded to with status code `200`.

First, the request is received by the underlying server environment. The web server calls Remix's adapter callback and the adapter forwards the request to Remix's `handleRequest` function. Remix then renders the React application on the server. While our `Index` React component is executed, the `console.log` statement is called, printing the statement to the terminal. Conclusively, `console.log` is executed once on the server. But is that all?

5. Navigate to your browser window and open the developer tools in the tab that shows the Remix application. In the developer tools, navigate to the **Console** tab. You should see **Another hello to the world!**.

    Your browser downloads the rendered HTML document from the server and loads the linked JavaScript modules. The browser then executes the code inside the `entry.client.ts` file. Here, Remix rehydrates your React application. React re-renders on the client and renders the `Index` component again. Hence, the `console.log` statement is run once on the server and then also on the client.

The React code of your Remix application is run on the server and on the client. However, some code should only ever run on the server or the client. For instance, the `entry.client.tsx` module should only run on the client, and the `entry.server.tsx` module should only ever be executed on the server.

It is also important that no server-side code makes it into the client bundle. The code in the client bundle is exposed over the internet. Think about your API tokens and other secrets that may be present in your backend logic. Moreover, the browser and server environments differ. Node.js APIs are not available on the client, and the browser's global `window` object is not available in Node.js. Server-side code may throw errors when executed on the client, and vice versa.

Remix is your compiler and bundles your code into a server and a client bundle. But how do we tell Remix what to bundle for the server and what to bundle for the client? Most of the time, Remix can figure it out by itself. Remix uses "tree shaking" to filter your code and aims to infer which code belongs to which bundle. However, you can also explicitly tell the compiler – and developers working on your project – that code should only be executed in one of the two environments.

Remix offers a convention to mark files as purely server-side or client-side modules. Adding `.client.` or `.server.` to the end of the filename tells Remix's compiler to avoid including these files in the server or client bundle, respectively. For instance, you can name your database setup file `db.server.ts` to explicitly exclude it from the client bundle. Similarly, you can name a file that imports client-only libraries `libs.client.ts` to explicitly avoid importing these packages on the server.

You might have noticed that both entry files (`entry.server` and `entry.client`) follow this convention. Feel free to add `console.log` statements to both entry files and recognize where each statement is executed – the terminal window or the browser **Console** tab.

Note that some files cannot be declared as server or client files. For instance, route modules in the `/routes` folder must not be declared as client or server files as they may include both client and server code.

In this section, you learned more about the code flow of a `GET` request through your Remix application. You learned that Remix receives `GET` requests on the server and renders your React application on both the client and the server. Some code in your Remix application is run on both environments, while other code should only run on one environment.

Remix runs on both the client and the server. Learning how to troubleshoot across the two environments is crucial. In the next section, you will learn more about how to interpret error messages in your Remix application and where to get help.

Troubleshooting Remix applications

In this section, you will learn more about debugging Remix applications. First, we will provide you with a general process to approach issues while developing with Remix. Next, we will document how to best search for answers and get help from the community.

A Remix troubleshooting process

Remix is not a server but runs on top of a web server and an underlying server runtime environment. Remix acts as an HTTP request handler, orchestrates your routes, executes your code during runtime, and acts as your compiler. Quite a few things can go wrong. That's why it's important to practice the process of debugging in Remix.

In the last section, we learned more about Remix's two environments, the client and the server. Remix runs on the server and then executes logic inside the browser. Hence, when debugging your Remix application, we must investigate both the client and the server environment. Let's break the `Hello World!` App:

1. Add the following troublesome code to the `app/routes/_index.tsx` file in your `Hello World!` app:

    ```
    export default function Index() {
      const userAgent = navigator.userAgent;
      console.log(`Another hello to ${userAgent}!`);
      return (
        <h1>Hello to {userAgent}!</h1>
      );
    }
    ```

    The code uses the browser's `navigator` interface to access user agent information. Our goal is to greet the user based on their user agent.

2. Run `npm run dev` to start the app if it is not already running.
3. Visit the Remix app in a new browser window or refresh an existing one. Unfortunately, you will notice that the application throws an error. The page should show the headline **Application Error**. Snap! Let's start debugging.

1. Trust the error message

If something goes wrong, the first thing you should do is inspect the terminal that is running Remix locally. You should be able to see the following error message in the terminal:

```
ReferenceError: navigator is not defined
```

You might have to scroll a bit to find the relevant line above the stack trace. Additionally, the error message should also be rendered in the browser tab. Remix displays a fallback error page in case something goes wrong. The error message on the page is more readable than on the terminal, but consider the terminal the source of truth when it comes to troubleshooting. In this case, both errors are matching. It seems like the `navigator` object is undefined.

2. Locate the line

Let's investigate the error message in the terminal in more detail. We can utilize the stack trace to learn which file threw the error and follow the stack trace downward across the stack of function calls. You should be able to see that the `app/routes/_index.tsx` file threw the error. Seems like that's an application error and not an error with Remix or a dependency since it's our code that broke.

3. Build time or runtime

Next, note that the error occurs only after we request a page from the web server. As `npm run dev` succeeded without throwing any errors, this is a runtime issue, not a build time issue. The server also started without throwing errors. This indicates that the error occurred within the request handlers and not in the server startup code.

4. The Console and Network tabs

Let's open the developer tools in the browser window. Click on the **Console** tab to view any logged client-side errors. The following error should show up:

```
GET http://localhost:3000/ 500 (Internal Server Error)
```

A `GET` request failed with an internal server error. We investigate further by navigating to the **Network** tab, as shown here:

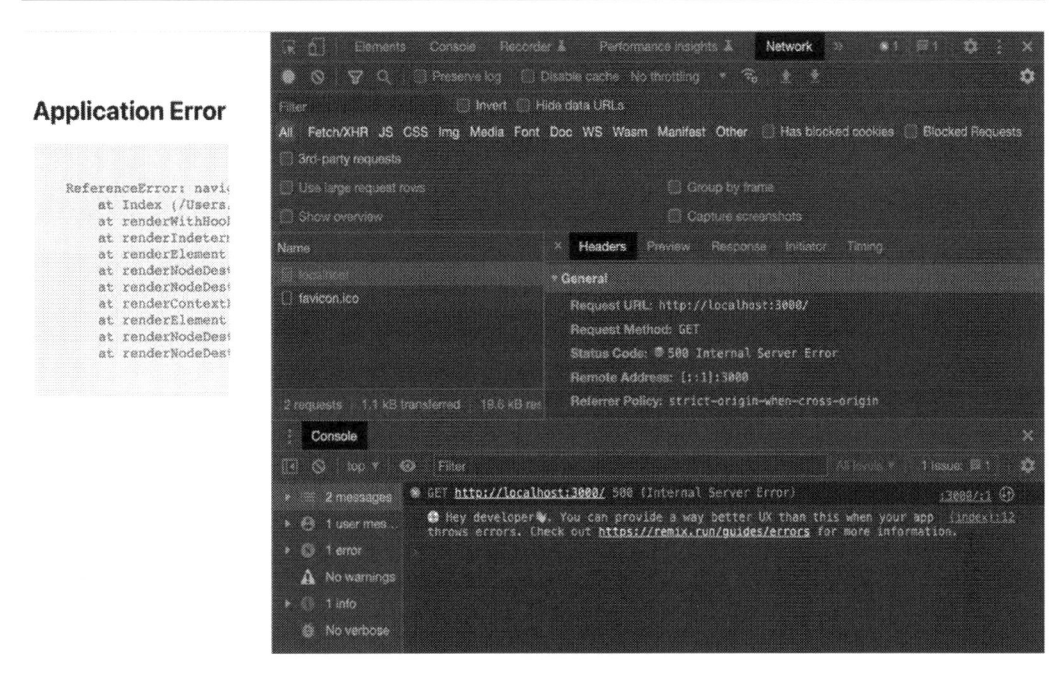

Figure 2.1 – Introducing the Network tab

The **Network** tab reveals that the document request failed. The **Network** tab's **Headers** tab displays the response and request headers. We can see that the server responded with status code 500. In the **Response** tab (not shown in *Figure 2.1*), we can further see that Remix returned an HTML document – the **Application Error** document we see on the screen.

What happened? The web server attempted to handle the GET request but threw a ReferenceError. The error was caught by Remix. Remix returned an error response document to the browser. Remix uses the status code 500 – the status code for internal server errors – to tell us and the browser that the response is an error response.

5. Turn it off and on again

If we can't identify the error thus far, it is a good idea to clean up any temporary files that might affect our local development server. Stop the development server if it is still running. Then run the following command to clean up all temporary build artifacts:

```
rm -rf build public/build .cache
```

This removes all temporary files and folders. Next, restart the development server by executing npm run dev in the terminal. This triggers a new build and results in a cleaned-up local environment. Does the error persist? In our case, it does, but we are able to verify that the error is not due to a broken build.

6. Google the issue

What would be your Google search query for this issue? Maybe see whether you can find the issue on Google. I would probably use one of the following searches:

- `Navigator undefined server-rendered React`
- `Server throws with navigator undefined`
- `Remix throws navigator not defined on the server`

The gotcha is that the `window` element and other browser globals do not exist in Node.js. Since we attempt to execute the React component on the server, it throws `ReferenceError` – not really a Remix issue but a common pitfall when rendering React code on the server. Case solved!

A quick fix for this type of error is to wrap references to browser APIs in `useEffect` calls:

```
import { useEffect, useState } from "react";

export default function Index() {
  const [userAgent, setUserAgent] = useState('the World');
  useEffect(() => {
    setUserAgent(navigator.userAgent);
  }, []);
  console.log(`Another hello to ${userAgent}!`);
  return (
    <h1>Hello to {userAgent}!</h1>
  );
}
```

`useEffect` only runs after the initial render. Since we only render once on the server, we know that `useEffect` is only executed on the client and never on the server. We can safely call browser APIs in `useEffect`.

Can you think of any disadvantages of this approach? Reload your application and have a look at the terminal. It logs `Another hello to the world!`. On the server, we do not have access to the `navigator` object and instead use the default value of the React state. We only re-render the appropriate greeting message on the client.

What if JavaScript fails to load or is disabled? What if the request is made by a web crawler that doesn't run JavaScript? On slow internet connections, the layout might flicker, and the user might first see the server value before it is updated once JavaScript is loaded. This is not a great user experience.

Remix provides utilities to work with user data right on the server – no need to use `useEffect` at all. Most of the time, we can avoid client-server state mismatches. For now, we can be pleased that we fixed the issue and learned how to investigate errors in Remix. We can summarize the described troubleshooting process as follows:

1. Find and read the error message in the terminal.
2. Locate the file that produces the error.
3. Understand whether it's a build time or runtime error.
4. Check the browser developer tools to get more context.
5. Remove all build artifacts and retry.
6. Google the issue.

Next, we will focus on *step 6*. Successful debugging takes practice and experience. Often, you just have to use Google. In the next section, we document where to find answers when working with Remix.

Looking for answers

Successful debugging takes practice. Once you encounter an issue once or twice, you will get faster at figuring out the root cause. Until then, it is good practice to search for a solution online. In this section, you will learn how to get help when working with Remix.

Follow the troubleshooting process as laid out in the last section. It is important that you gather as much information as possible. Once you start formulating your issue or question, you will find that a thorough investigation might already yield the answer. At least it will help identify the right keywords for your online search.

Most issues we encounter during development are not related to Remix. Most errors occur because of rendering React on the server, accidentally running server code on the client, or because of issues with node packages. In these cases, Stack Overflow, GitHub, and other places might have the answers we seek.

If that is not the case, then I can only encourage you to join the Remix Discord server (`https://discord.com/invite/xwx7mMzVkA`). The Remix community is very supportive.

Before asking a question, make sure to use Discord's search feature to see whether the question has already been asked and answered. This saves everyone time. By following the troubleshooting process, you should be able to provide plenty of context that can help the community debug your code. Providing code snippets (or, better, a code sandbox or public repository) will also greatly improve the likelihood that the community can assist you. The Remix community is amazing, and Discord is a great place to seek help.

If you have issues with Remix primitives or conventions, refer to the Remix documentation. The following page compiles a list of common pitfalls: `https://remix.run/docs/en/2/guides/gotchas`. These are issues that are harder to debug. Being aware of them ahead of time can save you costly debugging time.

In this section, you learned how to troubleshoot issues while working with Remix. You went through an example error and applied the proposed debugging process to uncover the root cause. You further learned more about how to search for answers and where to ask questions online.

Summary

In this chapter, we created our first Remix application. We used Remix's `create-remix` CLI script to bootstrap one Remix app with the basic template and one using Remix's Express.js template.

By following this chapter, you have learned how to build and run Remix applications locally using `npm run dev` and `npm run build`. More importantly, you understand where to find all available scripts (`package.json`) and additional information for running a specific template (`README.md`).

We reviewed Remix's file and folder structure. After reading this chapter, you know about the client and server entry points: `entry.client.tsx` and `entry.server.tsx`.

We also spent some time investigating the `root.tsx` file. The `root.tsx` file acts as the root of the route tree. Remix utilizes React to render the full HTML document, including the head, bundled scripts, links, and meta tags. This provides full control over what is rendered on the screen.

We changed the code of the `_index` route and rendered `Hello World!` to the screen. Next, we studied Remix's two environments: the client and the server. You learned that Remix runs in the browser and on a web server. Remix compiles the application code into a client and a server build. The web server exposes the client code as static files while calling the server bundle during runtime to handle incoming requests.

Remix uses adapters to run on different web servers and server runtimes. The adapter manages the communication between our Remix app and the underlying server code.

Finally, we practiced troubleshooting Remix applications by solving an example error. You learned how to investigate errors by looking both at the server's terminal and the **Console** tab in the browser. You also practiced searching for issues online, and you found out where to ask the Remix community for help.

In the next chapter, you will learn more about different templates, deployment targets, adapters, and Remix stacks. We will compare different server runtimes and deployment environments so you can pick the right one for your Remix apps. You will also be introduced to `Bee-Rich`, the demo application of this book. Get ready to build a Remix application start to finish following the chapters of this book!

Further reading

You don't need to use `create-remix` to bootstrap a new Remix project. You can also start from scratch by installing Remix's dependencies and setting up the file and folder structure yourself. If you are curious about this approach, follow the 5-minute tutorial from the Remix documentation: `https://remix.run/docs/en/2/start/quickstart`.

We introduced you to the Remix App Server. You can read more about the Remix's basic template here: `https://remix.run/docs/en/2/other-api/serve`.

As mentioned earlier in the chapter, refer to Remix's own troubleshooting guide to get help with common gotchas: `https://remix.run/docs/en/2/guides/gotchas`.

3
Deployment Targets, Adapters, and Stacks

During runtime, Remix runs on an underlying web server and handles incoming HTTP requests. Starting a new Remix project also means selecting a web server and JavaScript runtime. The Remix team and its community maintain starter templates and adapters for many popular deployment targets. In this chapter, we will review different deployment targets, templates, and Remix stacks.

We'll cover the following topics:

- Picking a deployment target
- Switching between adapters
- Using Remix Stacks
- Working with BeeRich

First, we will provide an overview of popular templates, deployment targets, JavaScript runtimes, and hosting environments. Next, will practice switching adapters and introduce you to Remix Stacks. At the end of this chapter, we will bootstrap a new Remix application using the custom template for this book.

After working through this chapter, you will know what to consider when picking a deployment target and template for a new Remix app. You will also learn more about different JavaScript runtimes and understand the main differences between long-running server, serverless, and edge environments. Additionally, you will gain practical experience switching between adapters and learn how to work with Remix Stacks.

Technical requirements

To complete this chapter, you will need a computer that can run Node.js. All popular operating systems should suffice. Please install both Node.js and npm on your machine. An editor such as VS Code is recommended.

You can download Node.js and npm here: `https://nodejs.org/en/download/`.

The code for this chapter can be found here: `https://github.com/PacktPublishing/Full-Stack-Web-Development-with-Remix/tree/main/03-deployment-targets-adapters-and-stacks`.

Picking a deployment target

One of Remix's most significant features is its flexibility. Remix supports many different web servers and runtime environments, including serverless and edge environments. Selecting a template also means choosing a JavaScript runtime, a hosting environment (server, serverless, edge), and potentially a hosting provider platform. To decide which template to pick for a project, we need to know the pros and cons of the different deployment targets to make an informed decision. In this section, we provide an overview of popular templates and adapters and review their differences.

In the previous chapter, we created a new Remix application using the `create-remix` CLI script. In the process, we had to specify a template or use Remix's basic template. The Remix team and community maintain adapters and templates for many different deployment targets. A template bootstraps a new Remix app with the required web server code. The web server code is not part of the Remix framework but is shipped with a Remix application to ease the development journey.

In the following, we provide an overview of popular deployment targets for Remix. *Table 3.1* lists templates that are maintained by the Remix team and community or by hosting provider companies. If a template is not set up for a specific hosting provider, then the **Hosting provider** column will show **Generic**.

All referenced templates are also listed in the Remix documentation: `https://remix.run/docs/en/dev/other-api/adapter`. Additionally, you can find all templates maintained by the Remix team on GitHub in the Remix repository: `https://github.com/remix-run/remix/tree/main/templates`.

Deployment target	Hosting provider	JavaScript runtime	Hosting environment
Architect (Arc)	AWS	Node.js	Serverless
Cloudflare Pages	Cloudflare	Workers runtime	Edge Isolate
Cloudflare Workers	Cloudflare	Workers runtime	Edge Isolate
Deno	Generic	Deno	Edge Isolate
Express.js	Generic	Node.js	Server
Fastify	Generic	Node.js	Server
Fastly Compute@Edge	Fastly	Wasmtime	Edge Isolate
Fly.io	Fly.io	Node.js	Distributed Server

Deployment target	Hosting provider	JavaScript runtime	Hosting environment
Netlify	Netlify	Node.js	Serverless
Remix App Server	Generic	Node.js	Server
Vercel	Vercel	Node.js	Serverless

Table 3.1 – Remix's deployment targets

As visible in the preceding table, many of the deployment targets are tied to specific hosting providers. The great thing about hosting service-specific adapters is the ease of deployment. You will find that you can get up and running with most of these services in a matter of minutes.

The advantage of generic adapters is the additional flexibility. For example, selecting the Express.js deployment target creates an Express.js server that can be hosted anywhere where Node.js server can run. This includes cloud computing platforms such as AWS, Azure, and Google Cloud Platform and popular hosting platforms such as Railway.app and Render.com.

Note that *Table 3.1* is incomplete, as the number of available deployment targets, templates, and adapters changes over time. The goal of this chapter is to help you effectively pick a deployment target by learning how to categorize and characterize them. First, let's see what is different between the various JavaScript runtimes.

Picking a JavaScript runtime

JavaScript can be executed in different runtime environments. In this section, we list popular JavaScript runtimes and discuss what to consider when selecting a runtime.

Some popular JavaScript runtime environments are as follows:

- Browser environments
- Node.js
- Deno
- Workers runtime
- Bun

The browser is JavaScript's most native environment. However, different browsers use different engines to execute JavaScript. Hence, they are technically different runtime environments. Luckily, they mostly adhere to the Open Web Platform and support the standard JavaScript APIs and runtime behavior. Since we are trying to pick a server-side deployment target, we are currently more interested in server-side runtimes.

The most prominent server-side runtime for JavaScript is Node.js. Node.js has a rich ecosystem of packages and libraries and is widely used and supported. However, there are also other server-side JavaScript runtimes, such as Bun, Deno, and Cloudflare's Workers runtime (workerd).

As visible in *Table 3.1*, some deployment targets use Deno or workerd under the hood. It is important to understand what this entails for your application development. If you are interested in starting a project with Deno or workerd, make sure to first familiarize yourself with the underlying runtime.

When comparing JavaScript runtimes, we must ensure they support the APIs and functionality we require for our application. For instance, workerd is an edge runtime that powers Cloudflare Workers. workerd does not support the execution of Node.js standard libraries. Consequently, you can use npm packages only if these packages do not use Node.js standard libraries. In contrast, most Node.js packages work in Deno as Deno aims to be Node.js compatible. You will also be able to use most Node.js standard libraries in Deno. However, this requires a special import syntax.

As a Remix developer, it is important to understand that some deployment targets are based on different JavaScript runtimes than Node.js. Each runtime comes with limitations and considerations. Next, we will investigate the differences between different hosting environments.

Picking a hosting environment

The way we host web applications has changed over time. Deploying can be as easy as pointing to a GitHub repository and branch or providing a Docker image. We rarely manage the underlying server infrastructure ourselves anymore. Instead, hosting providers and cloud platforms manage the infrastructure for us and provide the environment for our applications to run in.

Cloud platforms and hosting providers offer different hosting environments. These provide various advantages and disadvantages. As visible in *Table 3.1*, the different deployment targets each fit into one of the following three hosting environment categories:

- Server
- Serverless
- Edge

Let's see how the three different hosting environments differ. The following table provides an overview of the most important differences:

Trait	Server	Serverless	Edge
Long-running	Yes	No	No
Filesystem access	Yes (depends)	No	No
Isolated requests	No	Yes	Yes

Trait	Server	Serverless	Edge
Scale by default	No	Yes	Yes
Distributed by default	No	No	Yes

Table 3.2 – Traits of different hosting environments

Web servers are considered long-running environments. A web server is usually started once and only stops running in case of an upgrade, re-deployment, or when the service is sunset. Depending on the hosting provider, web servers have access to the filesystem. Long-running servers do not isolate individual requests. This means requests share global application states.

Serverless environments are fundamentally different from long-running servers. Serverless is a cloud computing model in which an application is treated as a function and orchestrated by the cloud platform provider. A serverless function is started specifically for an incoming request. After a designated timeout, the serverless function is terminated, and any application context, such as closures, cached application state, and global variables, is lost.

Serverless environments usually offer pay-per-use pricing. We are only charged for the time when our function is handling requests. Since the infrastructure provider can spawn multiple duplicate serverless functions in parallel, serverless is also inherently highly scalable.

It is important to note that serverless environments come with a very different set of requirements than web servers. Some things that are easily solved on long-running servers require more involvement on serverless. However, the solutions provided by serverless are designed to be scalable.

For instance, web servers create database connections during startup and share these connections across all incoming requests. Serverless functions must create a new database connection for every incoming request. Creating a new database connection can become a bottleneck for incoming requests and may lead to delays or timeouts. Additionally, database servers only support a limited number of open connections at a time. Opening a new connection per serverless function may exceed the maximum number of connections.

Serverless offers connection pooling as one way to counteract these issues. Connection pooling allows different functions to share connections across different instances. This is a common pattern with serverless. Things that work with long-running servers require more consideration with serverless. Serverless is designed to scale, but scaling also introduces complexity as a byproduct.

Scaling inevitably introduces complexity. Once you need to think about scaling long-running servers, you may run into many problems that serverless already solves for you. For instance, serverless environments implement load balancing out of the box.

Where serverless focus lies on scalability, edge computing focuses on providing geographic proximity. Most edge environments are serverless and share the same advantages, such as scalability and pay-per-use pricing. What makes edge environments special is their proximity to the end users. Edge functions are regionally distributed – for instance, on the servers of a CDN. The created proximity can significantly decrease response times.

Most server and serverless environments do not automatically distribute your application across different regions, at least not without additional configuration overhead and additional costs. Edge computing allows you to distribute your web application across the globe out of the box.

Edge environments come with their own limitations and considerations. In general, edge functions are the most limiting regarding their runtime capabilities. One limitation is that deploying on the edge requires a distributed database solution. Otherwise, response times will be delayed by the communication between the edge functions and your database server.

Different runtime environments also use different container technologies to deploy and run your code. Long-running servers can run directly on a physical or virtual machine. However, most cloud providers use lightweight container technologies to run your app. It's important to note that the container landscape is diverse. There are several different container technologies and standards, such as V8 isolates.

V8 is the JavaScript engine that powers Chrome and is also used by Node.js and Deno. V8 isolates are isolated V8 instances that reuse the same language runtime, avoiding the slow cold start of starting a new language runtime on an incoming request. Because they're lighter than most container technologies, V8 isolates are used in edge environments where computing is sparse in comparison to centralized cloud data centers.

When choosing a hosting provider and runtime, research the restrictions tied to their container technologies. These limitations could affect your app's size or the maximum running time before timing out.

There are many trade-offs to consider. Each environment comes with its own set of considerations. Next, we will connect the dots and conclude how to select the right deployment target for a given use case.

Making the final decision

In this section, we will conclude how to pick a deployment target based on what we learned about JavaScript runtimes and different hosting environments (server, serverless, edge).

In my experience, a long-running server environment provides a great amount of flexibility and introduces less complexity than its alternatives. That said, hosting providers such as Netlify and Vercel offer a great developer experience and complementary services for their serverless and edge offerings. If you are looking for a provider that can regionally distribute both your long-running web server and database, then maybe Fly.io could be a great fit.

Serverless provides many advantages but also introduces complexity. Edge computing may significantly improve response times but introduces further complexity. The additional complexity of serverless and edge environments is a byproduct of scale and regional distribution. Once you think about scale and regional distribution for your long-running web server, you will face similar challenges.

Personally, picking the right deployment target is more about avoiding unnecessary obstacles than anything else. The deployment target must fit the use case and fulfill the system requirements. Let's go over some examples.

If you want to utilize Node.js libraries or reuse Node.js code, you probably want to stick with a Node-based environment. The Express.js deployment target is an obvious choice. But what about serverless environments? If you use a conventional database without built-in solutions for serverless environments, then you will have to create a new database connection for every new incoming request. This might lead to longer response times or even timeouts. However, if you are already using a serverless-first database and are looking for scalability, then picking a serverless environment might be a great idea.

If you have one single database server in Oregon, then having your web app deployed all over the world won't bring you much benefit. Each instance of your app will have to request data from your database server in Oregon. In that case, you should pick a web server or serverless environment that is located as close as possible to your database.

If you want to build a blog you are likely looking for easy access to your blog posts. Blog posts are usually stored as files. Using a hosting provider and enviroment that lets you access the filesystem allows you to host your blog posts together with your code. Unless you run into issues with this approach (there are disadvantages to any approach), you might want to start with a simple web server architecture. In that case, you could pick the Express.js template. This will grant you access to the underlying filesystem with most hosting providers.

On the other hand, you might find that some serverless providers offer attractive free tiers and competitive pay-as-you-go pricing. Selecting the right runtime depends on your priorities and requirements. Picking a hosting environment without access to the filesystem doesn't mean that you won't be able to work with files. It just means you must store files somewhere else – such as in a file storage service. Therefore, it's more about making an informed decision to avoid obstacles down the road.

Finally, deciding on a deployment target also means deciding on a hosting provider. Each deployment provider comes with its own advantages and disadvantages. For instance, Fly.io hosts long-running Node.js servers but offers distribution to different regions. Fly.io might be a great alternative to serverless edge deployment. On the other hand, AWS and Cloudflare each provide rich ecosystems of services that can be used together with their serverless and edge offerings. For complex applications, hosting on AWS or Cloudflare might be the right call.

The line between long-running servers, serverless, and edge environments is blurry. Different providers further offer geographical distribution for both serverless and server environments that achieve edge-like proximity to users. Some may provide the best of both worlds.

Picking a deployment target heavily depends on your application's use case. Luckily, Remix is flexible enough to support a wide variety of different use cases. After all, Remix can run anywhere where JavaScript can be executed.

Fortunately, it is straightforward to swap the underlying server environment and adapter in your Remix project if needed. In the next section, we will practice how to do so.

Switching between adapters

We sometimes have to migrate from one template to another one. To do so, we must switch our Remix app's setup. In this chapter, we will walk through the process of switching templates and adapters.

The process of switching between templates and adapters can be summarized as follows:

1. Locate your Remix project and open it in an editor or file explorer.
2. Create a new Remix project using the new template and adapter.
3. Open the new Remix project side by side with your old project.
4. Rename the app folder in the new project to temp. Move the app folder from your old project to the new project.
5. Replace the code in app/entry.client.tsx with the code in temp/entry.client.tsx and integrate any custom code previously added to the file.
6. Replace the code in app/entry.server.tsx with the code in temp/entry.server.tsx and integrate any custom code previously added to the file.
7. For every Remix-specific file and folder in the root of your old project:

    A. Investigate whether you made any changes.

    B. Copy-paste any changes over to the new project.

    C. Resolve any conflicts (if any).

8. Follow the instructions in the new project's README.md file to run, build, and deploy the application.
9. Troubleshoot any remaining issues using the troubleshooting process from *Chapter 2, Creating a New Remix App*.

Let's practice the described process using the "Hello World!" Remix app that we created in *Chapter 2, Creating a New Remix App*. If you are looking for a challenge, see whether you can figure it out by yourself by following the nine steps listed before. Otherwise, let's walk through it together:

1. Open your "Hello World!" Remix app in an editor or file explorer. You can also find the code here: https://github.com/PacktPublishing/Full-Stack-Web-Development-with-Remix/tree/main/02-creating-a-new-remix-app/hello-world.

   In *Chapter 2*, we used the basic template, but this process works for other templates as well.

2. Run npm install and npm run dev to ensure that the project is running locally without any issues.

3. Now, create a new Remix project using the create-remix CLI script. Run the following command:

   ```
   npx create-remix@2 --template remix-run/remix/templates/cloudflare-workers
   ```

   To prove a point – that switching between adapters in Remix is easy – we'll pick a very different deployment. We will migrate from a long-running Node.js environment to a workerd-based edge environment (Cloudflare Workers). However, feel free to pick any other deployment target you are interested in.

4. Make sure to follow the prompts of create-remix to bootstrap the new Remix app.

5. After finishing the create-remix CLI script, we run npm install and npm run dev to ensure that the new project runs locally.

6. After asserting that both projects run without errors, we open the new Remix app in an editor or file explorer. It is easiest to have both editors/file explorers open side by side.

7. Let's rename the app folder in the new project to temp. Next, copy the app folder from your old "Hello World!" project to the new project. This allows us to inspect both temp and app side by side.

8. Run npm run dev in the new project. Remix will attempt to build and run the project using the "Hello World!" app folder:

   ```
   Could not resolve "@remix-run/node"
     app/entry.server.tsx:10:25:
       10 | import { Response } from "@remix-run/node";
   ```

   Snap! An error! Let's investigate the error message in the console.

   The error message states that the @remix-run/node package cannot be resolved. Also, notice that the errors originate from app/entry.server.tsx.

9. Compare the code in app/entry.server.tsx with the code in temp/entry.server.tsx.

   The Express.js template used in the "Hello World!" app uses Remix's node adapter (@remix-run/node), while the Cloudflare Worker template uses the @remix-run/cloudflare adapter.

   The Cloudflare Workers environment runs on workerd, which does not support Node.js libraries. To run on Node.js and workerd, Remix needs to set up two different entry point implementations and use different adapters.

10. Since we have no custom code in entry.server.tsx, replace the code in app/entry.server.tsx with the code in temp/entry.server.tsx.

11. Sure there is no other usage of @remix-run/node. Search for the package name in your editor's code search.

    You should find two matches: app/root.tsx and app/routes/_index.tsx.

12. Make sure to find and replace the imports with @remix-run/cloudflare.

    Remix exposes its server-side types and primitives through the different adapter packages. When switching adapters, we must find and replace all imports of the old adapter with the new one.

13. Next, compare and then replace the code in app/entry.client.tsx with the code in temp/entry.client.tsx as well. Different templates may use different versions of React or implement additional logic in the client entry file.

14. Run npm run dev again. It should now successfully build and run the new project!

15. Let's investigate the root folder of the old application. Are there any files that we did create or adapt? We should move all custom files and folders over to the new project.

16. Check the package.json file. We did not install any additional packages for our "Hello World!" app, but usually, we would now move any app dependencies over and install them in our new project.

    We should also compare the scripts of both package.json files. We have to make sure that any custom or adapted scripts are merged with the new scripts of our new project. In our case, there is nothing to do. We did not add any custom logic, which we would need to take over.

We did it! We moved from **Remix App Server** to **Cloudflare Workers** – a long-running server to an edge environment!

The two entry files in the app folder are bootstrapped by Remix and custom for each deployment target. Hence, we must make sure to update the code in these files. We also must merge our custom dependencies with the dependencies of the new project. This requires us to manually review the package.json files. Finally, we have to take over any other changes made to files and folders in the project.

In this section, we successfully moved from one adapter to another. In the next section, we will learn about Remix Stacks to bootstrap a production-ready Remix app.

Using Remix Stacks

In this section, you will learn about Remix Stacks. First, we will have a look at Remix's official stacks and how to use them. Next, you will learn how to use community templates.

Working with Remix official stacks

Remix also offers pre-configured templates ready for production. These templates are referred to as Remix Stacks. As of now, Remix provides three official stacks:

Stack	Deployment target	Comes with	Use case
Blues	Fly.io	PostgreSQL database	Large-scale applications and regional distribution
Indie	Express.js	SQLite database	Small-scale projects with dynamic data
Grunge	Architect (AWS Lambda)	DynamoDB database	Large-scale applications on AWS infrastructure

Table 3.3 – Official Remix stacks

Stacks are opinionated project starters. They are more complex than Remix's basic templates but also have more features. As visible in *Table 3.3*, the starters are built with different use cases in mind and utilize different deployment targets.

The **Blues stack** runs on Fly.io. From *Table 3.1*, you can infer that Fly.io hosts long-running servers. Fly.io offers regional distribution of long-running servers to achieve edge-like proximity. The Blues stack also ships with code to set up a PostgreSQL database. The stack is designed to scale and enable regional distribution out of the box.

The **Indie stack** uses the Express.js adapter and does not target a specific hosting provider. It ships with an SQLite database. The Indie stack is perfect for starting projects that work with smaller amounts of dynamic data. From *Table 3.2*, you can infer that this stack – depending on the hosting provider – can access the filesystem and will be able to share application states across different requests.

The **Grunge stack** serves similar use cases to the Blues stack but is set up using Architect, an AWS Lambda-based framework. From *Table 3.1*, you can derive that Architect runs on a serverless environment. AWS infrastructure is intended to support large-scale applications.

Let's try out one of the Remix Stacks Run the following command in the terminal:

```
npx create-remix@2 --template remix-run/indie-stack
```

We again use `create-remix` to bootstrap a new Remix app. This time, we refer to one of Remix's three official stack templates: the Indie stack. Feel free to select another stack based on your personal preferences.

Note that we point to a GitHub repository named `indie-stack` in the `@remix-run` GitHub organization.

Investigate the bootstrapped folder structure and refer to the `README.md` file to get an overview of all the technologies and packages in use. A few noteworthy things come with the Indie stack:

- A registration and login setup (`app/session.server.ts`).
- A convention for where to place your database logic (`app/models/`).
- A route for health checks (`app/routes/healthcheck.tsx`).

Remix Stacks implement styling, testing, authentication, and additional features out of the box. Where Remix's basic templates provide simple server and adapter setups, Remix Stacks are production-ready applications that ship with an opinionated setup. On top of that, Remix also supports the creation of custom templates. In the next section, we will learn how to use and create custom templates.

Working with custom templates

We can utilize community-developed templates or create our own to get up and running quickly with our preferred stack. Custom templates are also a great way to develop opinionated templates for an organization.

Any Remix project can be used as a template. The only limitation is that the template must be a valid Remix project with a `package.json` file in the root folder. The easiest way to access a template is via GitHub, but Remix can also access a template via a URL, a local path on your machine, a subfolder in a GitHub repository, or a local or remote tarball.

Let's try out the custom template from this book's GitHub repository. Run the `create-remix` command with the template flag in the terminal:

```
npx create-remix@2 --template PacktPublishing/Full-Stack-Web-
Development-with-Remix/03-deployment-targets-adapters-and-stacks/
bee-rich
```

Make sure to select **Yes** when prompted to install the dependencies. Also, select **Yes** when promoted to run the template's `remix.init` script.

After running the `init` script, you should see a short message in the terminal:

```
Running template's remix.init script...

Hey there! Great job practicing using a custom stack! You're doing
great!
```

This message originates from the `remix.init/index.js` script in the project's root folder. The script allows template authors to implement custom setup steps. You can also run the script again by calling `npx remix init` in the project root.

Conveniently, I just sneaked you into setting up the BeeRich application, which will be used as a demo application for the rest of this book. Next, we will kick off our development journey with BeeRich.

Working with BeeRich

Welcome to BeeRich! BeeRich is a dashboard-like application that mimics both personal and enterprise use cases. BeeRich is a personal finance management application that helps you stay on top of your bee – pardon me – bookkeeping. Well, at least that's the goal. There is nothing much there yet. In every chapter, we will add more code to this application. In this section, we will run BeeRich locally and review the folder structure.

We bootstrapped BeeRich in the preceding section using the `create-remix` script. BeeRich is nothing more than a simple skeleton application on top of Remix's Express.js template that we tried out in *Chapter 2, Creating a New Remix App*. You can also find the BeeRich Remix template in this book's GitHub repository: https://github.com/PacktPublishing/Full-Stack-Web-Development-with-Remix.

Let's run BeeRich locally. Open the terminal and navigate to the project's root folder. Then execute the following command in the terminal:

```
npm run dev
```

The application should now be running on port `3000`: http://localhost:3000/. Welcome to BeeRich!

The `npm run dev` command starts Remix's development server to build and watch the development environment. You can find a list of all available scripts in the `package.json` file. Also, review the `README.md` file in the root of the BeeRich project for additional information about BeeRich.

Tailwind CSS has been included so we can quickly add some styling without the need to leave our JavaScript modules. You can also find some styled reusable components in `app/components`. Visit the `/demo` route to inspect some of the reusable components (http://localhost:3000/demo).

Feel free to deviate from the lessons in this book and explore alternative solutions. If you get stuck, you can always reset your application and use the application in the current chapter's folder on GitHub as a baseline.

In the next chapter, we will add pages and routes to BeeRich.

Summary

In this chapter, you learned what to consider when selecting a deployment target for your Remix application. You learned more about different hosting providers, environments, and runtimes. You now understand that Remix runs on long-running servers, serverless environments, and edge runtimes. Each environment has advantages and disadvantages that you must consider when selecting a template and deployment target.

Remix's different deployment targets operate on different JavaScript runtimes, such as Node.js, workerd, and Deno. Different JavaScript runtimes support different web standards and either support or do not support Node.js standard libraries. When picking a template, you must consider what JavaScript runtime you want to work with.

This chapter introduces you to a nine-step process to migrate from one adapter to another. Switching out adapters enables you to try out different hosting providers and environments and to stay agile in case your requirements change over time.

Remix offers basic templates for different deployment targets that set up Remix's adapters. However, Remix also offers production-ready stacks. In this chapter, you practiced using the `create-remix` script to bootstrap a new Remix app using Remix's Indie Stack.

Next, we utilized a custom template to bootstrap the demo application, BeeRich, which we will use in the following chapters to practice our Remix skills. In the next chapter, we will learn about routing in Remix and add pages to BeeRich.

Further reading

You can find a list of available adapters in the Remix documentation: `https://remix.run/docs/en/2/other-api/adapter`.

The Remix documentation also provides more explanations about available templates here: `https://remix.run/docs/en/2/discussion/runtimes`.

The official announcement post for Remix stacks can be found here: `https://remix.run/blog/remix-stacks`.

Listen to Wes Bos and Scott Tolinski talk about the limitations of serverless on Syntax.fm: `https://syntax.fm/show/542/serverless-limitations`.

Learn more about the distinction between serverless computing and containers here: `https://www.cloudflare.com/learning/serverless/serverless-vs-containers/`.

You can find more information about V8 isolates here: `https://developers.cloudflare.com/workers/learning/how-workers-works/#isolates`.

4
Routing in Remix

> *"Routing is possibly the most important concept to understand in Remix."*
>
> – Remix documentation

Michael Jackson and Ryan Florence spent years building React Router. It is not a surprise that routing plays an integral role in Remix. One core idea that Michael and Ryan brought over from React Router to Remix is nested routing. Nested routing is a powerful feature that enables the composition of route components.

In this chapter, you will learn about routing in Remix. We'll cover the following topics:

- Working with Remix's route module API
- Composing pages from nested routes
- Using route parameters for dynamic routing
- Sharing layouts
- Handling navigations in Remix

In this chapter, we will dive into nested routing and cover Remix's route convention. We will start by creating standalone pages and reviewing Remix's route module exports. Next, we will review nested, index, dynamic, and (pathless) layout routes. Finally, we will learn how to transition between routes and learn about the global navigation object.

By the end of this chapter, you will understand the core principles behind Remix's routing solution. You will have practiced creating new route modules and know which exports Remix supports. You will understand the advantages of nested routing and layout routes. You will also practice how to work with route parameters. Finally, you will know how to work with Remix's global navigation object.

In this chapter, we will add a login and a signup page to the BeeRich application. We will further create a dashboard route with nested expenses and income child routes. Then, we will create a shared layout for the index, login, and signup pages. Finally, we will animate page transitions using the global navigation object. Let's jump right into it and create our first routes in Remix.

Technical requirements

In *Chapter 3*, *Deployment Targets, Adapters, and Stacks*, we set up the demo application for this book. If you haven't already, make sure to follow the instructions of *Chapter 3*, as we will continue working with BeeRich in this chapter.

You can find the solution code and additional information to this chapter on GitHub: `https://github.com/PacktPublishing/Full-Stack-Web-Development-with-Remix/tree/main/04-routing-in-remix`.

Working with Remix's route module API

Remix takes on the responsibilities of a compiler, a runtime, and a router. In Remix, you create routes (route modules) as part of a hierarchy. Among other things, Remix's router determines which route modules to match and render on a request.

This section will walk you through the creation of route modules in Remix. You will learn how to create standalone pages and understand how routes tie back to the `root.tsx` file. You will further understand how index routes fit into the picture (or, I should say, on a screen). Finally, the section will introduce you to the different available exports that route modules can expose.

Route file-naming conventions

Before we get started, note that Remix switched to a new route file-naming convention with Remix v2. This book follows that convention.

If you are new to Remix, then this chapter will get you started with Remix's latest convention. If you have prior experience with Remix's v1 filesystem route convention, you can refer to this guide to learn what has changed: `https://remix.run/docs/en/1.19.3/file-conventions/route-files-v2`.

Working with file-based routing

We start by inspecting the current route structure of BeeRich. We will continue with the BeeRich code from the previous chapter. Alternatively, you can find the start code for this chapter here: `https://github.com/PacktPublishing/Full-Stack-Web-Development-with-Remix/tree/main/03-deployment-targets-adapters-and-stacks/bee-rich`.

Let's review the current route hierarchy:

1. Run the following command in a terminal at the root of your Remix project:

    ```
    npx remix routes
    ```

This command prints the current routes hierarchy to the terminal:

```
<Routes>
  <Route file="root.tsx">
    <Route index file="routes/_index.tsx" />
    <Route path="demo" file="routes/demo.tsx" />
  </Route>
</Routes>
```

2. Next, open the BeeRich project in your editor and inspect the `app/routes` folder. We can see that there are currently two files in the folder:

- `demo.tsx`
- `_index.tsx`

You will find that this matches the hierarchy displayed by the `remix route` command. The hierarchy can be interpreted as a tree. Everything starts at the root (`root.tsx`). Nested, we have two child routes, each pointing to a file in the `routes` folder. Since the two route modules themselves have no children, they are leaves.

Note that one route is flagged as `index`, while the demo route has a `path` property, which matches its filename. Each route segment in the routes hierarchy can have one index file. The index file is the default child route for a parent route and its URL path segment. The root of the `routes` folder maps to the `/path`. The `_index.tsx` file on the root level of the `routes` folder acts as the default route module for that path segment (`/`).

3. Let's run our application locally by executing `npm run dev` in a terminal.
4. Open the application in your browser by navigating to `http://localhost:3000/`. This routes us to the `/path` of the application. Welcome (again) to BeeRich!
5. Back in your editor, open the `app/routes/_index.tsx` file. The file contains the following code:

```
import { H1 } from '~/components/headings';

export default function Component() {
  return (
    <main>
      <H1>Welcome to BeeRich!</H1>
    </main>
  );
}
```

The route defines a React component, which is exported as the default export of the module.

Compare the JSX code to the content of the current page in your browser window. It matches! The `_index.tsx` route module maps to the `/` path of the application. It is the default child route of the `routes` foler and renders when we visit the homepage of BeeRich. We will later see that this pattern holds true for every nested index file inside the routes hierarchy.

6. Now, let's visit the `/demo` page. Add `demo` to the URL in the address bar of your browser. The demo page showcases available reusable components that we can use to build our BeeRich application.
7. Open the `app/routes/demo.tsx` file. Note that we again export a React component as the default export of the module.

There is some magic at play here. We didn't need to specify the routes hierarchy to Remix explicitly through code. No configuration file maps components to pathnames. This is the power of **file-based routing**. It reduces configuration overhead. Remix compiles your code during build time and parses the `routes` folder's hierarchy. It creates an **asset manifest** that includes the route hierarchy of the application.

When visiting a page, Remix knows which route components to render. Exporting the route component as the default export is a convention so that Remix can find your code.

Let's dive into the conventions of Remix's file-based routing and create some standalone pages.

Creating route modules

In *Chapter 8*, *Session Management*, we will add a signup and login authentication flow to BeeRich. In this chapter, we will set up the general route structure to do so:

1. Create a new file in the `routes` folder and name it `login.tsx`.
2. Next, use the address bar of your browser to navigate to the newly created page (`http://localhost:3000/login`).

    We will see the following error pop up on the screen:

    > Error: Element type is invalid: expected a string (for built-in components) or a class/function (for composite components) but got: object. **You likely forgot to export your component from the file it's defined in, or you might have mixed up default and named imports.**

    Remix communicates that we did not adhere to its convention. When creating a route, we must define it as either a **resource route** (more on this later) or a **UI route**. By using the browser to request the page (a GET request for an HTML document), Remix looked for a default export of a React component. However, we did not specify a default export, or even a React component for that matter.

> **Important note**
>
> A UI route must export a React component as its default export. This is part of the conventions of Remix's file-based routing.

3. To remove the error from the screen, switch to your editor and add a React component to the newly created `login.tsx` file. The following code should suffice for now:

   ```
   import { H1 } from '~/components/headings';

   export default function Component() {
     return <H1>Login!</H1>;
   }
   ```

   Note that we use `H1`, a reusable component from the `app/components` folder, to avoid rewriting a bunch of custom styling.

   Also, note that the import path starts with a tilde symbol (~). This is a neat TypeScript feature. We map the `app` folder to ~ in our `tsconfig.json` path configuration. This allows us to use the tilde symbol as a shorthand to target any file or folder in the `app` folder.

4. Refresh the browser window. The `/login` page should now render correctly. Awesome! You just created your first standalone page with Remix!

5. Next, create a `signup.tsx` file in the `routes` folder. Then, copy and paste the code from the login page and adapt the code to better fit the signup page.

6. Use the address bar of your browser to navigate to the newly created page (`http://localhost:3000/signup`).

7. Let's run the `remix routes` command again to see how the routes hierarchy grew. Execute the following command in your terminal:

   ```
   npx remix routes
   ```

   This yields the following route hierarchy:

   ```
   <Routes>
     <Route file="root.tsx">
       <Route index file="routes/_index.tsx" />
       <Route path="signup" file="routes/signup.tsx" />
       <Route path="login" file="routes/login.tsx" />
       <Route path="demo" file="routes/demo.tsx" />
     </Route>
   </Routes>
   ```

As expected, the routes hierarchy grew by two leave routes. Each leaf route represents a page in the application. Our application now handles the following four pathnames:

- `/`
- `/demo`
- `/login`
- `/signup`

So far, all our route modules in the `routes` folder are document/UI routes that render React components as part of the route hierarchy to the page. In the following section, we will provide a short overview of available route module exports and discuss the differences between UI and resource routes.

Available route module exports

In Remix, we distinguish between resource routes and UI routes. Each UI route must export a React component as the default export. Resource routes do not export a React component as the default export. Instead, resource routes must export an `action` and/or a `loader` function. Among other things, resource routes can expose API endpoints, handle Webhooks, or create assets on the fly. We will create our first resource route later in this chapter.

Remix inspects the exported functions of a route module to determine whether it is a UI or a resource route. While resource routes only support exporting an `action` or a `loader` function, UI routes can export the following named exports:

- `action`
- `ErrorBoundary`
- `handle`
- `headers`
- `links`
- `loader`
- `meta`
- `shouldRevalidate`

We will learn more about the role of these exports in the following chapters. For now, let's focus on how Remix uses the route module exports. Remix compiles the route hierarchy during build time.

In your file explorer, navigate to `public/build/` and open the `manifest-*.js` file. The manifest file is created after building the application (`npm run build` or `npm run dev`) and includes a routes section. The routes section contains an entry for every route module in the app. The entry for the `demo.tsx` route looks as follows:

```
'routes/demo': {
    id: 'routes/demo',
    parentId: 'root',
    path: 'demo',
    module: '/build/routes/demo-EKLEFBX2.js',
    imports: ['/build/_shared/chunk-AATHADRZ.js'],
    hasAction: false,
```

```
    hasLoader: false,
    hasErrorBoundary: false,
  },
```

As shown in the code, Remix keeps track of the exported functions via Boolean flags. The Boolean flags are set to `false`, since our demo route does not export `action`, `loader`, or `ErrorBoundary`.

Remix's route module exports are part of the file-based route convention. Remix compiles the content of the route folder and generates a manifest file. This is how Remix lets us avoid a route hierarchy configuration in code and instead promotes a convention-based route hierarchy.

In this section, we created two new route modules and learned about the supported named exports of route modules in Remix. We also used the `remix routes` command to visualize our routes hierarchy. In the following section, we will dive into nested routing.

Composing pages from nested routes

BeeRich is a personal bookkeeping application. Users should be able to view their expenses and sources of income. In this section, we will create a hierarchy of nested routes to compose the dashboard pages of BeeRich.

So far, we have seen `Outlet` being used in the `root.tsx` file. The `Outlet` component declares the location of the child route inside the markup of the parent route. The `Outlet` component in `root.tsx` is rendered inside the HTML `body`. Hence, all child routes are wrapped inside the body element. This is the power of nested routing. With nested routing, you can compose pages out of several route modules.

Let's use nested routing and the `Outlet` component to construct our dashboard. The two routes, `/dashboard/expenses` and `/dashboard/income`, will serve as our overview pages:

1. First, add two files inside the `routes` folder:

    - `dashboard.expenses.tsx`
    - `dashboard.income.tsx`

    Note that we use dot delimiters (`.`) to separate path segments (`/`) in the URL.

2. Add a simple route component to both files. Review `login.tsx` for reference. In both files, export the component as the default export.

3. Then, run the application (`npm run dev`), and review the changes in a browser window.

    The goal is to list all expenses and sources of income (invoices), respectively. For now, we will mock the data and focus on setting up the route hierarchy.

4. Add the following code to the `dashboard.expenses.tsx` file:

```
import { H1 } from '~/components/headings';

export default function Component() {
  return (
    <div className="w-full">
      <H1>Your expenses</H1>
      <div className="mt-10 w-full flex flex-col-reverse
        lg:flex-row">
        <section className="lg:p-8 w-full lg:max-w-2xl">
          <h2 className="sr-only">All expenses</h2>
          <ul className="flex flex-col">
            <li>
              <p className="text-xl font-semibold">Food</p>
              <p>$100</p>
            </li>
            <li>
              <p className="text-xl font-semibold">Transport</p>
              <p>$100</p>
            </li>
            <li>
              <p className="text-xl font-semibold">Entertainment
                </p>
              <p>$100</p>
            </li>
          </ul>
        </section>
      </div>
    </div>
  );
}
```

The provided code renders a hardcoded list of expenses to the page.

You can also find the final code for this chapter on GitHub: `https://github.com/PacktPublishing/Full-Stack-Web-Development-with-Remix/tree/main/04-routing-in-remix/bee-rich/solution`.

5. Similarly, we want to render a list of all sources of income on the `/dashboard/income` page. Copy the code from the `dashboard.expenses.tsx` file, and adapt it to render hardcoded invoices instead of expenses in `dashboard.income.tsx`.

As shown in *Figure 4.1*, both pages now render a list of items. In the future, users should also be able to edit an expense or invoice. For that, we will now create a nested details view.

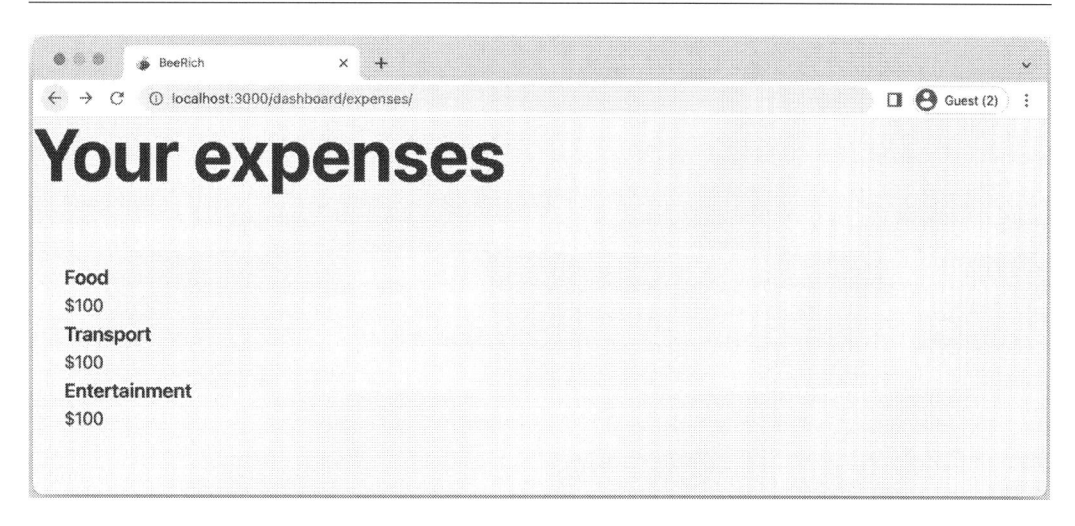

Figure 4.1 – A screenshot of the expenses overview page

6. So far, we have navigated between pages by changing the URL in the address bar of the browser. Now, it's time to add anchor tags. A user should be able to click on a list item in the expenses overview to view the details view of the expense. Let's wrap the content of the hardcoded list items with anchor tags. The first list item might look as follows:

   ```
   <li>
     <a href="/dashboard/expenses/1">
       <p className="text-xl font-semibold">Food</p>
       <p>$100</p>
     </a>
   </li>
   ```

   Make sure to wrap each item with an anchor tag.

   Each list item now links to a unique URL that includes the mock identifier of the expense. In the following section, we will learn more about dynamic routes with parameters. For now, let's work with made-up mock identifiers to focus on the route structure.

7. In your browser window, click on one of the list items. A click on an item should navigate you to a **404 Not Found** page. That's expected, considering we did not create the associated route module yet.

8. Let's add a hardcoded details page for the expense with the identifier 1. Create a `dashboard.expenses.1.tsx` file.

9. Add the following code to `dashboard.expenses.1.tsx`:

   ```
   import { H2 } from '~/components/headings';

   export default function Component() {
   ```

```
    return (
      <div className="w-full h-full p-8">
        <H2>Food</H2>
        <p>$100</p>
      </div>
    );
}
```

The newly created details route is dedicated to the expense with the identifier 1. By clicking on a list item in the expenses overview, we should be redirected to the details view of the list item.

10. Let's test our implementation. Use the address bar to navigate back to the `/dashboard/expenses/` page. Then, click on the list item with the identifier 1.

    Snap! Something is wrong! We can see that the URL changes as expected. A click on the list item updates the pathname of the URL to `/dashboard/expenses/1`. However, the content of the page does not update. We still see the content of the expenses overview page. What's wrong?

    We created a nested `dashboard.expenses.1.tsx` file within the `/expenses` path. But why is the content of the file not appearing on the page? Remix only seems to render the `dashboard.expenses.tsx` file.

    The issue is that `dashboard.expenses.tsx` and `dashboard.expenses.1.tsx` both match the same path (`/dashboard/expenses/`). By doing so, we promoted the `dashboard.expenses.tsx` file to be a parent layout route module (such as `root.tsx`). If we want to display either the content of the `dashboard.expenses.tsx` file or the content of the `dashboard.expenses.1.tsx` file, then we need to make `dashboard.expenses.tsx` a sibling instead of a parent route.

    You learned earlier that index routes are used as the default child routes of a URL path segment. Let's try to fix the issue by adding an index route.

11. Rename the `dashboard.expenses.tsx` file to `dashboard.expenses._index.tsx`.

    By doing so, we declare the two route modules in the expenses path as siblings. Sibling route modules always match different pathnames.

12. In your browser window, navigate back to the `/dashboard/expenses/` page. Now, click on the list item to navigate to `/dashboard/expenses/1`.

    The UI now updates as expected between the two pages. By declaring the two route modules as siblings, we either show the overview or the details page content.

Remix's route hierarchy distinguishes parent and sibling routes of a specific URL path. `dashboard.expenses.tsx` is a **parent layout route** (or parent route for short) for the `/expenses` path.

A parent route utilizes the `Outlet` component to declare where its child components should be rendered alongside its own layout. `root.tsx` is the top-level parent route.

Let's try it out:

1. Undo your changes. Rename the `dashboard.expenses._index.tsx` file back to `dashboard.expenses.tsx`.

2. Now, import the `Outlet` component from Remix, and add it below the **All expenses** section:

   ```tsx
   import { Outlet } from '@remix-run/react';

   import { H1 } from '~/components/headings';

   export default function Component() {
     return (
       <div>
         <H1>Your expenses</H1>
         <div>
           <section>
             <h2>All expenses</h2>
             <ul>
               <li>
                 <a href="/dashboard/expenses/1">
                   <p>Food</p>
                   <p>$100</p>
                 </a>
               </li>
             </ul>
           </section>
           <Outlet />
         </div>
       </div>
     );
   }
   ```

   Note that we redacted the `className` attributes and the last two list items from this example for easier readability. You can find the complete code on GitHub.

3. Refresh your browser window. You should now see the expenses overview and the details view side by side when visiting `/dashboard/expenses/1`.

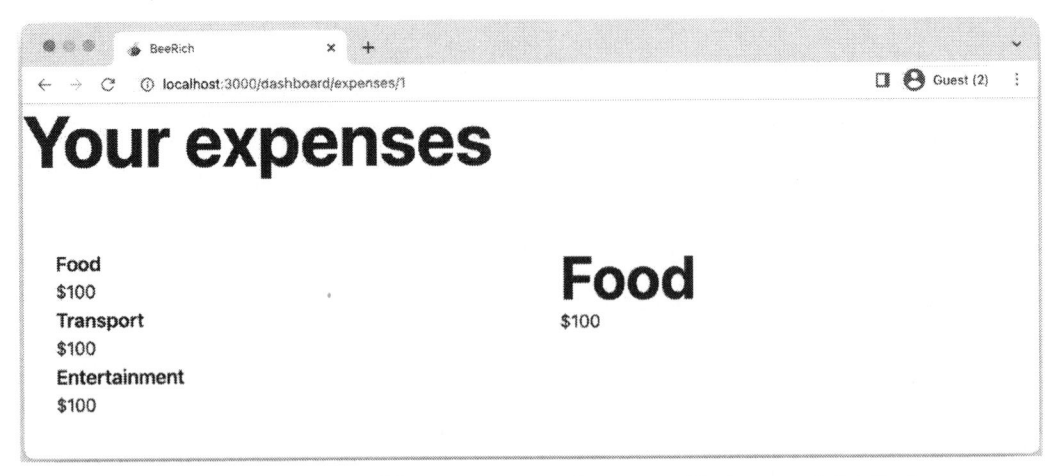

Figure 4.2 – A screenshot of the expenses overview page with the nested details view

Awesome! We created our first layout route to compose a page from different route modules. By using nested routing, we map different segments of the URL to different route modules. This creates a hierarchically nested structure. Parent routes utilize the `Outlet` component to declare where the child route should be rendered on the page.

Note that the `/dashboard` path is not accompanied by a `dashboard.tsx` file. This should tell us that layout route modules are optional. We can use layout routes to share a common layout across all child routes or create complex pages that are made up of different route modules. However, if they're not needed, they can be omitted.

For BeeRich, we want to use a parent layout route instead of an index route to render the overview page. With this page architecture, a user can see all expense-related information on one page.

To practice working with parent layout routes, make sure to update the income pages and add the `Outlet` component to the `dashboard.income.tsx` file.

In this section, you learned how you can compose a page out of different route modules. Remix maps segments of the URL to different route modules in the routes hierarchy. With parent layout routes, we can nest and render child routes inside parent routes. Each page is then made up of code from different nested route modules. Next, we will refactor the hardcoded parameter routes and utilize parameterized path segments to create dynamic expense details pages.

Using route parameters for dynamic routing

URLs often include parameters such as identifiers to specify associated resources. This allows the application to retrieve the right data for the request. In this section, you will learn how to work with URL parameters in Remix.

So far, we have created a route module for a hardcoded expenses details page (`/dashboard.expenses.1.tsx`). The number `1` in the URL refers to the expense with the expense identifier `1`. However, the goal is to create a dynamic route module capable of handling variable identifiers. Luckily, Remix provides a convention for how to define a parameterized route segment.

Parameterized route segments

In Remix, dynamic segments of the URL are referred to as parameterized segments. We use the `$` symbol to declare a route parameter. This turns the URL segment into a parameter that we can access and use to fetch data.

Let's see how we can use a parameterized segment in BeeRich for the expenses details route:

1. Rename `dashboard.expenses.1.tsx` to `dashboard.expenses.$id.tsx`.

   The $ symbol is part of Remix's routing convention and declares a parameter for a dynamic route segment.

2. Next, update the code inside the file and add the following mock data:

   ```
   const data = [
     {
       id: 1,
       title: 'Food',
       amount: 100,
     },
     {
       id: 2,
       title: 'Transport',
       amount: 100,
     },
     {
       id: 3,
       title: 'Entertainment',
       amount: 100,
     },
   ];
   ```

   The mock data acts as our data source for now. We will add a real database in *Chapter 5*, *Fetching and Mutating Data*.

3. After that, add a `loader` function with the following code:

   ```
   import type { LoaderFunctionArgs } from '@remix-run/node';
   import { json } from '@remix-run/node';

   export function loader({ params }: LoaderFunctionArgs) {
     const { id } = params;
     const expense = data.find((expense) => expense.id === Number(id));
     if (!expense) throw new Response('Not found', { status: 404 });
     return json(expense);
   }
   ```

   A `loader` function runs server-side before its route component is rendered. It is the perfect place to fetch data (on the server) dynamically based on route parameters.

   Remix exposes the `LoaderFunctionArgs` type to type the `loader` function's arguments. As visible in the code, Remix provides a `params` argument that can be used to access the route parameters of the current URL.

   Using a parameterized route, we can now utilize the `params` argument to access the dynamic values of our URL. We access the `id` parameter from the parameter argument and use it to find the right expense from our mock data.

   We then return the expense object (using the `json` helper function provided by Remix). We will learn more about server-side data fetching and Remix's server-side conventions and primitives in *Chapter 5, Fetching and Mutating Data*.

4. In the file's route component, we can access the loader response data with the `useLoaderData` hook. Update the existing component code as follows:

   ```
   import { useLoaderData } from '@remix-run/react';

   export default function Component {
     const expense = useLoaderData<typeof loader>();
     return (
       <div className="w-full h-full p-8">
         <H2>{expense.title}</H2>
         <p>${expense.amount}</p>
       </div>
     );
   }
   ```

   Remix's `useLoaderData` hook provides access to the route module's loader data. In our case, we returned an expense object that we can now access in our React application.

We pass `typeof loader` as the generic type variable to `userLoaderData` to infer the type of the loader data, based on the `loader` function's return value. These type hints are great for autocompletion.

With that, we have created a dynamic route that renders its content based on the URL!

5. Make sure to test the implementation. Use the anchor tags of the expenses list to navigate between the different expenses details routes.

   As visible in the code, the `loader` function throws a **404 Not Found** `Response` if no expense identifier matches the route parameter. If you see an error, double-check that the identifier exists in the mock expenses array. And yes, you can throw `Response` objects with Remix – something we will explore in the next section.

Once you have tested your implementation, create a similar experience for the income page. This will help you practice what you have learned so far.

If you haven't already, wrap each list element in the `dashboard.income.tsx` file with an anchor element. Then, create the `dashboard.income.$id.tsx` file and implement the `loader` function. In case you get stuck, review the implementation of the expenses details route and apply it to `dashboard.income.$id.tsx`. You can also refer to the troubleshooting process from *Chapter 2, Creating a New Remix App*. Finally, you can find the final solution for this chapter here: https://github.com/PacktPublishing/Full-Stack-Web-Development-with-Remix/tree/main/04-routing-in-remix/bee-rich.

In this section, you learned how to work with dynamic route segments and how to declare route parameters. You also got a short introduction to Remix's `loader` function and the `useLoaderData` hook. In the following section, we will utilize shared layouts to improve our application's look and feel.

Sharing layouts

Nested routing enables us to compose a page from a nested route hierarchy. In this section, we will utilize parent routes to reuse layouts between nested child routes. We will also learn how to share code between routes without creating new segments in the URL, with pathless layout routes.

Using parent layout routes

Let's improve the look and feel of the BeeRich dashboard. Ideally, a user should be able to quickly switch between the income and expenses overview pages. It's time to add a navigation bar.

We already utilized parent layout routes for the `dashboard/expenses` and `dashboard/income` pages. By rendering the list of expenses and income in a parent route (`dashboard.expenses.tsx` and `dashboard.income.tsx`, respectively), we nested the content of the child routes on the same page.

Now, we will take advantage of nested routing again to add a shared navigation bar to all dashboard pages. Follow these steps:

1. Create a `dashboard.tsx` file inside the `routes` folder.

    Since the `dashboard.tsx` route module matches the `dashboard` path segment, it acts as the parent route for the segment's nested route modules.

2. Add the following code to `dashboard.tsx`:

    ```
    import { Outlet } from '@remix-run/react';

    import { Container } from '~/components/containers';

    export default function Component() {
      return (
        <>
          <header>
            <Container className="p-4 mb-10">
              <nav>
                <ul className="w-full flex flex--row gap-5 font-bold
                  text-lg lg:text-2xl">
                  <li>
                    <a href="/">BeeRich</a>
                  </li>
                  <li className="ml-auto">
                    <a href="/404">Log out</a>
                  </li>
                </ul>
                <ul className="mt-10 w-full flex flex-row gap-5">
                  <li className="ml-auto">
                    <a href="/dashboard/income">Income</a>
                  </li>
                  <li className="mr-auto">
                    <a href="/dashboard/expenses">Expenses</a>
                  </li>
                </ul>
              </nav>
            </Container>
          </header>
          <main className="p-4 w-full flex justify-center items-
            center">
            <Outlet />
          </main>
        </>
      );
    }
    ```

The code adds a navigation bar inside an HTML `header` element and renders Remix's `Outlet` component inside a `main` element.

3. Run the app (`npm run dev`), and visit `/dashboard/expenses` in your browser window to review the changes.

   As visible in *Figure 4.3*, by adding a parent route module, we wrap every child route of `dashboard` with the markup rendered inside `dashboard.tsx`. Layout routes provide a great way to wrap all child routes in a common layout.

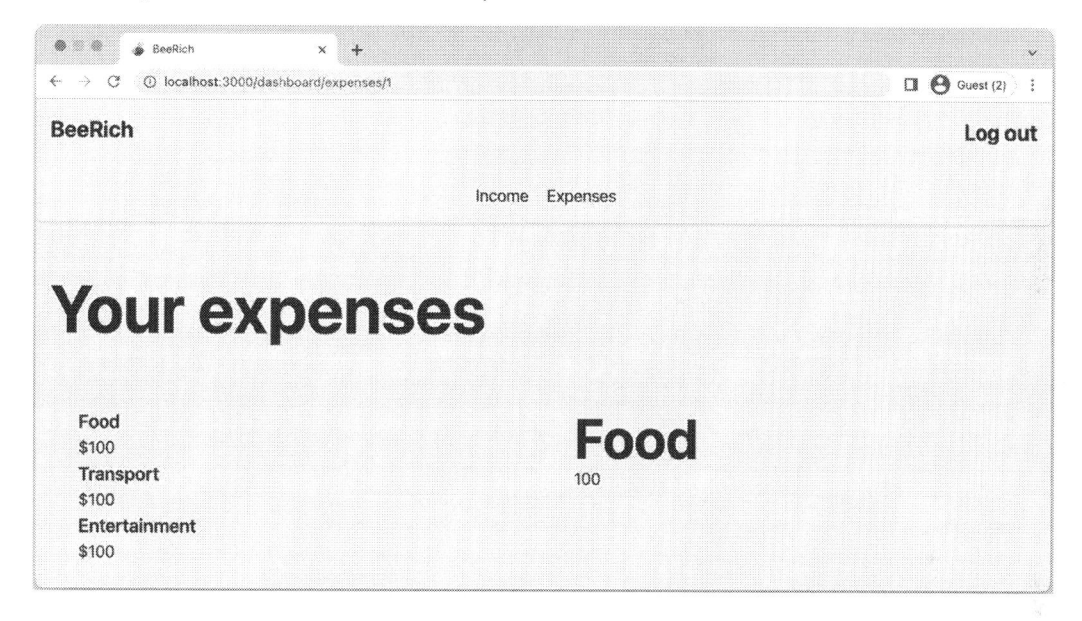

Figure 4.3 – A screenshot of the expenses page with a shared dashboard layout

Let's also add a navigation bar to our login, signup, and home (`_index.tsx`) pages. We could again use a parent layout route to share a common layout. However, this would add a new route segment to the path. It turns out that adding a parent route is not what we want. A parent route would alter the URL, but the home page should be located at the `/` path. Likewise, we want the login page to be located at `/login` and signup at `/signup`. Instead, let's see how we can make a layout route pathless.

Using pathless layout routes

Luckily, Remix has a way of declaring **pathless layout routes**, or pathless routes for short. Like how the $ symbol declares a parameterized route module, using an underscore prefix (_) declares a pathless layout route. Pathless routes behave just like parent layout routes but do not add segments to the URL path.

Let's add a pathless layout route to share a layout between the login, signup, and home pages:

1. Create a new `_layout.tsx` file in the `routes` folder.

   The underscore tells Remix to treat the route module as pathless. The route module's name will not be added to the URL. You already know the underscore prefix from index routes, which serves a similar purpose.

   Note that the chosen name, `layout`, is not part of the convention – you can name the route module as you like.

2. Next, add the following code to the `routes/_layout.tsx` file:

   ```
   import { Outlet } from '@remix-run/react';

   export default function Component() {
     return (
       <>
         <header className="mb-4 lg:mb-10">
           <nav className="p-4">
             <ul className="w-full flex flex-row gap-5 text-lg
               lg:text-2xl font-bold">
               <li>
                 <a href="/">Home</a>
               </li>
               <li className="ml-auto">
                 <a href="/login">Log in</a>
               </li>
               <li>
                 <a href="/signup">Sign up</a>
               </li>
             </ul>
           </nav>
         </header>
         <main className="p-4 w-full flex justify-center items-
           center">
           <Outlet />
         </main>
       </>
     );
   }
   ```

   The code adds a navigation bar and renders `Outlet` in a styled `main` element.

3. Rename the `_index.tsx`, `login.tsx`, and `signup.tsx` route modules `_layout._index.tsx`, `_layout.login.tsx`, and `_layout.signup.tsx`, respectively.

4. Remove the `main` HTML tag from the `_index.tsx` JSX code, as it is now already rendered by the `__layout.tsx` module. That is the power of composition and nested routing. We can reduce code duplication and reuse layouts.

5. As always, make sure to test your changes before moving on. Run the application, and visit the `/`, `/login`, and `/signup` pages by trying out the new navigation bar.

In this section, you learned how to utilize layout routes to add common structure and styling to nested child routes. You were also introduced to pathless layout routes to share a layout without adding route segments to the URL path. In the following section, we will learn more about page navigations in Remix.

Handling navigations in Remix

So far, we have used anchor tags to navigate between pages. You might have noticed that every navigation – using an anchor tag – triggers a full-page reload. This is the browser's default behavior when navigating between pages. However, Remix also offers primitives for client-side navigations.

In this section, we will introduce you to Remix's link components and Remix's global navigation object. We will practice utilizing the navigation object to indicate page loads and learn more about server-side redirects with Remix.

Navigating with Remix's link components

By default, a page navigation triggers a document request to the web server of the resource. The web server forwards the request to Remix (our HTTP request handler). Remix then renders a new document on the server to fulfill the request and responds with the rendered HTML document (or any other HTTP response).

When utilizing Remix's link components, Remix prevents the browser's default behavior from making full-page requests. Instead, Remix executes fetch requests using the web's Fetch API to fetch the required data for the requested URL. We avoid a full-page reload and instead execute a client-side navigation. Let's replace the anchor tags in BeeRich with Remix's links components – `Link` and `NavLink`. You can find styled example implementations for both link components in `/app/components/links.tsx`. For more information about the two components, visit the React Router documentation: `https://reactrouter.com/en/6.15.0/components/nav-link`:

1. Fiirst, replace the anchor tags in `routes/_layout.tsx` with. Update the code as follows:

```
import { Outlet } from '@remix-run/react';
import { NavLink } from '~/components/links';

export default function Component() {
  return (
    <>
      <header className="mb-4 lg:mb--10">
```

```
              <nav className="p-4">
                <ul className="w-full flex flex-row gap-5 text-lg
                  lg:text-2xl font-bold">
                  <li>
                    <NavLink to="/">Home</NavLink>
                  </li>
                  <li className="ml-auto">
                    <NavLink to="/login">Log in</NavLink>
                  </li>
                  <li>
                    <NavLink to="/signup">Sign up</NavLink>
                  </li>
                </ul>
              </nav>
            </header>
            <main className="p-4 w-full flex justify-center items-
              center">
              <Outlet />
            </main>
          </>
       );
  }
```

Instead of using Remix's NavLink component directly, we use a styled wrapper component.

2. Next, run the application (`npm run dev`) and open it in a browser window. Navigate to the home page of the app. The navigation bar should now show three decently styled links.

3. On the home page, click on either the **Log in** or **Sign up** link. You should see that the favicon in the tab of the browser window no longer indicates a full-page reload. Instead, Remix now fetches the required data and assets using JavaScript's Fetch API, performing a client-side navigation. With these changes, our Remix app feels much more like an SPA.

4. Now, let's refactor the code of the `dashboard.tsx` parent route. Import the `Container` and `NavLink` components from the `components` folder, import `Link` from Remix, and apply the following changes:

```
import { Link as RemixLink, Outlet } from '@remix-run/react';

import { Container } from '~/components/containers';
import { NavLink } from '~/components/links';

export default function Component() {
  return (
    <>
      <header>
        <Container className="p-4 mb-10">
          <nav>
```

```
              <ul className="w-full flex flex-row gap-5 font-bold
                text-lg lg:text-2xl">
                <li>
                  < RemixLink to="/">BeeRich</RemixLink>
                </li>
                <li className="ml-auto">
                  <RemixLink to="/404">Log out</RemixLink>
                </li>
              </ul>
              <ul className="mt-10 w-full flex flex-row gap-5">
                <li className="ml-auto">
                  <NavLink to="/dashboard/income">Income</NavLink>
                </li>
                <li className="mr-auto">
                  <NavLink to="/dashboard/expenses">Expenses</
                    NavLink>
                </li>
              </ul>
            </nav>
          </Container>
        </header>
        <main className="p-4 w-full flex justify-center items-
          center">
          <Outlet />
        </main>
      </>
  );
}
```

We renamed Remix's `Link` components `RemixLink` to highlight that we are not using our own `Link` wrapper component. We also utilize another wrapper component – `Container` – to reuse some additional styling.

5. Next, refactor the `dashboard.expenses.tsx` route module:

```
import { Outlet } from '@remix-run/react';

import { H1 } from '~/components/headings';
import { ListLinkItem } from '~/components/links';

export default function Component() {
  return (
    <div className="w-full">
      <H1>Your expenses</H1>
      <div className="mt-10 w-full flex flex-col-reverse
        lg:flex-row">
        <section className="lg:p-8 w-full lg:max-w-2xl">
```

```
          <h2 className="sr-only">All expenses</h2>
          <ul className="flex flex-col">
            <ListLinkItem to="/dashboard/expenses/1">
              <p className="text-xl font-semibold">Food</p>
              <p>$100</p>
            </ListLinkItem>
            <ListLinkItem to="/dashboard/expenses/2">
              <p className="text-xl font-semibold">Transport</p>
              <p>$100</p>
            </ListLinkItem>
            <ListLinkItem to="/dashboard/expenses/3">
              <p className="text-xl font-semibold">Entertainment
                </p>
              <p>$100</p>
            </ListLinkItem>
          </ul>
        </section>
        <Outlet />
      </div>
    </div>
  );
}
```

We use the reusable `ListLinkItem` component from the `components` folder to add custom styling to the expenses list. Under the hood, the component renders Remix's `NavLink` component.

6. Also, replace the anchor tags in `dashboard.income.tsx` with the `ListLinkItem` component. Use the `dashboard.expenses.tsx` file for reference.

7. Run the application locally, and visit a browser window. Test the links on the expenses and income overview pages. Note how Remix no longer executes full-page reloads to navigate between the pages.

Opting for Remix's link components avoids page reloads. With full-page reloads, we must re-fetch all data on every navigation. When using Remix's link components, Remix only fetches the data required for newly added route modules. However, we can also see that Remix works just fine when using anchor tags. Remix enhances the experience with JavaScript where possible but can fall back to a browser's default behavior if necessary.

Sometimes, when we attempt to enhance the experience with JavaScript, we might accidentally degrade the experience instead. By default, a browser replaces the tab's favicon with a loading indicator during page load. Without a full-page reload, we lose any indication that a page transition is happening. This is especially frustrating for users with slower internet connections. In the following section, we will utilize Remix's global transition object to re-add page loading indicators.

Indicating page transitions

You might ask yourself why we would need page load indicators. Navigations are so fast on `localhost` that you barely notice them. However, they can feel brutally long on **slow 3G** connections. Let's prove that page transitions are necessary:

1. Run BeeRich by executing `npm run dev` in the project's `root` folder.
2. Open the application in your browser by visiting `http://localhost:3000`.
3. Open the developer tools of your browser, and navigate to the **Network** tab.
4. Search for the throttling functionality, and select **Slow 3G** from the provided dropdown.
5. Also, check the **Disable cache** checkbox to simulate a user's first visit.

   All popular browsers offer similar settings. Search on Google if you can't find the described throttle and cache functionalities.

6. Make sure to reload the browser window to reset the browser cache.
7. Finally, navigate between the different pages of your app.

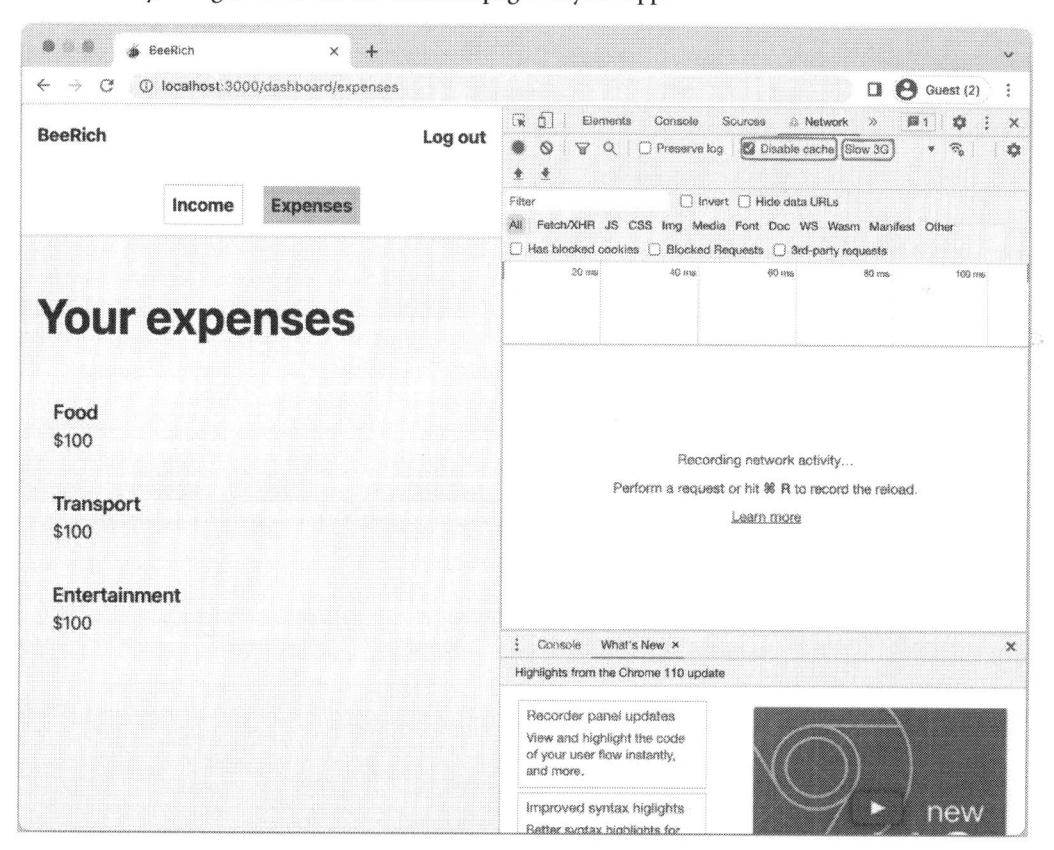

Figure 4.4 – A screenshot of the Network tab of the Chrome DevTools

How is the experience? Using a slow internet connection shows how important loading indicators are. By removing the browser's default behavior (the loading spinner on the browser window tab), we robbed the user of a clear loading indication. We degraded the user experience. Luckily, Remix provides a global navigation object, which we can use to re-add loading indicators with JavaScript.

First, let's add a loading indicator to the expense and income detail views:

1. Open the `/routes/dashboard.expenses.tsx` file, and import the `useNavigation` hook from Remix:

    ```
    import { Outlet, useNavigation } from '@remix-run/react';
    ```

2. Call the hook inside the route component to access the global navigation object:

    ```
    const navigation = useNavigation();
    console.log(navigation.state);
    ```

    The global navigation object provides information about the current navigation state. The `navigation.state` property can have one of the following three values:

    - `idle`
    - `loading`
    - `submitting`

3. Let's see for ourselves! Open a browser window, and navigate to the `expenses` page.

4. Open the **Console** tab in the browser's developer tools.

5. Click on the different expenses in the expenses list.

    `navigation.state` is set to `idle` if there is no page navigation. On `GET` requests, `navigation.state` is set to `loading`. On form submissions, the state is set to `submitting` and then `loading` (as every submission also involves a page navigation).

    With Remix, we can easily display pending UIs by checking the `navigation.state` value.

6. Let's add a simple CSS animation to `dashboard.expenses.tsx`. First, import `clsx` to manage the Tailwind CSS classes:

    ```
    import clsx from 'clsx';
    ```

7. Then, wrap the existing `Outlet` component by a styled section:

    ```
    <section className={clsx('lg:p-8 w-full', navigation.state ===
    'loading' && 'motion-safe:animate-pulse')}>
      <Outlet />
    </section>
    ```

    We will check whether the navigation object is currently in the `loading` state and conditionally render Tailwind's built-in pulse animation.

8. Ensure that your browser window is still throttling the network bandwidth. Click on the expense items in the expenses overview list, and note that the details view pulses when page navigations are in progress.
9. Add the same animation to `dashboard.income.tsx` to practice working with Remix's navigation object.

Let's also add a global progress bar to the application:

1. Open the `root.tsx` file in your editor.
2. Import `PageTransitionProgressBar` from the `components` folder:

   ```
   import { PageTransitionProgressBar } from './components/
   progress';
   ```

3. Then, render the `PageTransitionProgressBar` component inside the root component. This ensures that the component is rendered across all routes and pages of our application. We place the component inside the body above the `Outlet` component:

   ```
   <body className="bg-background dark:bg-darkBackground text-lg
   text-text dark:text-darkText">
     <PageTransitionProgressBar />
     <Outlet />
     <ScrollRestoration />
     <Scripts />
     <LiveReload />
   </body>
   ```

   The `PageTransitionProgressBar` component uses the navigation object and tracks a CSS animation across the `idle`, `loading`, and `submitting` states.

4. Open the `components/progress` file in your editor, and review the implementation of the `PageTransitionProgressBar` component.

In this section, you learned how to utilize the navigation object and the `useNavigation` hook to indicate loading states to a user. Now, we will wrap up the chapter by introducing server-side redirects.

Redirecting a user from the server

Sometimes, the right place to trigger a navigation is on the server. In Remix, `loader` functions are a great place to check whether the requested resources exist and whether the user can access it. In this section, you will learn more about server-side redirects in Remix.

Review the `dashboard.expenses.$id.tsx` route file:

```
export function loader({ params }: LoaderFunctionArgs) {
  const { id } = params;
```

```
  const expense = data.find((expense) => expense.id === Number(id));
  if (!expense) throw new Response('Not found', { status: 404 });
  return json(expense);
}
```

In the `loader` function, we access the route parameter to find the matching expense in the mock data. If we cannot find an expense that matches the `id` parameter, we throw a **404 Not found** Response. Throwing responses is a great way to stop the execution early and return an error response. We will learn more about how to handle thrown `Response` objects in *Chapter 7, Error Handling in Remix*.

For now, let's focus on Remix's `request/response` flow. It's important to understand that Remix operates both a frontend and a backend, following the client/server model of the web. Our frontend app runs in the browser and makes requests to the web server (backend). The backend application handles incoming HTTP requests and answers with HTTP responses.

The great thing about Remix's request/response model is that instead of being custom, it follows the web's Fetch API standard. In `loader` functions, we return `Response` objects, following the Fetch API's `Response` specification: https://developer.mozilla.org/en-US/docs/Web/API/Response.

On top of that, Remix provides primitives to create `Response` objects. Instead of creating `Response` objects ourselves, we can also use the following three helper functions:

- defer
- json
- redirect

We have already used the `json` helper in our `loader` function. The helper returns a `Response` object, with the `Content-Type` HTTP header to `application/json`. The `redirect` helper creates `Response` with a `302` status code. `defer` is an advanced helper for streaming responses. We will practice working with defer in *Chapter 13, Deferring Loader Data*.

Let's use `redirect` to fix a bug in our app. Have you noticed what happens if you directly navigate to `http://localhost:300/dashboard`? We render an empty dashboard.

Can you think of a reason for that behavior? The `/dashboard` path segment currently has no default child (a nested index route module). Conclusively, the `/dashboard` path matches with neither of the child routes when visiting the `/dashboard` path. When visiting `http://localhost:300/dashboard`, `Outlet` in `dashboard.tsx` returns `null`, and our dashboard remains empty.

Sometimes, not having a default child route is not an issue. On the `/dashboard/expenses` and `/dashboard/income` overview pages, the `Outlet` also returns `null` when no identifier is added to the URL. Displaying an overview list without rendering a details view seems fine.

For `/dashboard`, we should think of a better solution than rendering an empty dashboard. For instance, we could create a `dashboard._index.tsx` file and export a route component that renders a simple welcome message. Or we redirect the user to another page!

Create a `dashboard._index.tsx` file in the `routes` folder, and add the following code:

```
import { redirect } from '@remix-run/node';

export function loader() {
  return redirect('/dashboard/expenses');
}
```

With these simple four lines of code, we create our first resource route. A resource route does not export a route component (otherwise, it would be a UI route). Instead, a resource route exports a `loader` function and/or `action` function.

Here, we use a `loader` function to immediately redirect the user to the expenses overview page. If a user enters `http://localhost:3000/dashboard` into the address bar, then the `loader` function returns a `Response` with the `30x` status code – a redirect.

Try it out by navigating to `http://localhost:3000/dashboard`. In your terminal, the server logs should look as follows:

```
GET /dashboard 302 - - 2.918 ms
GET /dashboard/expenses 200 - - 8.031 ms
```

On navigation to `/dashboard`, we redirect (the `302` status code) to the `/dashboard/expenses` route, which is then served (the `200` status code).

Note that `redirect` is just a helper function to create a redirect `Response` object. It is nothing more than a simple wrapper for convenience:

```
return new Response(null, {
  status: 302,
  headers: {
    Location: '/dashboard/expenses',
  },
});
```

Remix provides full access to the web platform. You can create and return `Response` objects with varying status codes, instance properties, caching headers, and much more. All you need to do is follow the MDN Web Docs (`https://developer.mozilla.org/en-US/docs/Web/API/Response`). Later in this book, we will implement real-time functionality, add caching headers, and elegantly handle authentication errors, all by using the web platform's `Response` API.

In this section, you learned about server-side redirects. You now understand that Remix executes `loader` functions on the server and that `loader` functions must return a `Response` object (or something that Remix can parse into a `Response` object). You also practiced redirecting a user from a resource route to a UI route. Now, let's reflect on what you learned in this chapter.

Summary

Remix provides a convention-based file-based router. Arguably the most powerful feature of Remix's router is nested routing. In Remix, you create routes (route modules) as part of a hierarchy. Remix's router maps the pathname of the URL to a set of matching route modules. Route modules make up the pages of your Remix application.

In this chapter, you created your first routes in Remix. We started off by creating two standalone pages. You learned about the special role of index routes as the default children of their parent routes. You were also introduced to the exports available in Remix's route modules.

Next, we created a nested route hierarchy for our dashboard. We used parent layout routes and the `Outlet` component to reuse styling and content across different child routes.

We also used a `loader` function and a route parameter to create routes for our income and expenses details views. You learned how to declare parameterized route modules using the `$` syntax. You also used Remix's `userLoaderData` hook to access JSON data returned from a `loader` function.

Thereafter, we used pathless layout routes to share layouts across different child routes without adding a path segment to a URL. You created a pathless route that wraps the login, signup, and home pages of BeeRich.

You also learned about navigations and transitions in Remix. We replaced the HTML anchor tags with Remix's `Link` and `NavLink` components. Now, you understand the benefits of avoiding full-page reloads and know that Remix fetches required scripts and data on each page request.

You further learned about the `useNavigation` hook and Remix's navigation object. You practiced adding loading indicators to a page by using the state property of the navigation object. Finally, you learned more about the `Request/Response` model in Remix and how to redirect a user from the server.

In the following chapter, you will learn about data loading and mutations in Remix. We will use Remix's `action` and `loader` functions to implement the UI necessary to manage our expenses and income data in BeeRich.

Further reading

In this chapter, you learned about the key concepts of Remix's routing solution. You can find more concepts, such as optional route modules, in Remix's route documentation: `https://remix.run/docs/en/2/file-conventions/routes`.

Read about Remix's `Link` and `NavLink` components in the Remix documentation:

- `https://remix.run/docs/en/2/components/link`
- `https://remix.run/docs/en/2/components/nav-link`

You can read more about the `Request/Response` model of the Fetch API here: `https://developer.mozilla.org/en-US/docs/Web/API/Fetch_API`.

Part 2 – Working with Remix and the Web Platform

In this part, you will gain hands-on experience with Remix's primitives, conventions, and levers and build a full stack web application from start to finish. You will gain a deep understanding of Remix's request-response flow, progressive enhancement, and how to build robust user experiences with error and session management in mind. Finally, you will practice working with web assets and file uploads in Remix.

This part has the following chapters:

- *Chapter 5, Fetching and Mutating Data*
- *Chapter 6, Enhancing the User Experience*
- *Chapter 7, Error Handling in Remix*
- *Chapter 8, Session Management*
- *Chapter 9, Assets and Metadata Handling*
- *Chapter 10, Working with File Uploads*

5
Fetching and Mutating Data

Handling dynamic data is crucial in today's web development landscape. Most modern apps interact with data from various sources. The way an app manages loading states, errors, and data updates plays a big role in user experience. Fortunately, Remix offers a comprehensive solution for both retrieving and updating data.

This chapter covers the following topics:

- Fetching data
- Mutating data

In this chapter, we will implement data reads and writes in BeeRich. First, we will practice data loading. Then, we will learn about data mutations in Remix and implement an expense creation form.

By the end of this chapter, you will know how to fetch and mutate data in Remix. You will also understand how Remix executes `loader` and `action` functions and how Remix revalidates loader data after mutations. Finally, you will have practiced building applications with progressive enhancement in mind, which we will build upon in *Chapter 6, Progressively Enhancing the User Experience*.

Technical requirements

You can find the setup instructions for this chapter here: `https://github.com/PacktPublishing/Full-Stack-Web-Development-with-Remix/blob/main/05-fetching-and-mutating-data/bee-rich/README.md`.

Note that the code in the `start` folder of this chapter is different from our final solution from *Chapter 4, Routing in Remix*. Read the instructions in the `README.md` file of this chapter's folder on GitHub before you continue.

Fetching data

Before diving into this chapter, make sure you've followed the steps in the technical requirements section. Once you've completed the setup guide, let's briefly revisit the key steps to prevent any issues:

1. Run `npm i` to install all dependencies.

2. If you are missing a `.env` file in your project's root, create a new `.env` file and add the following line to it:

   ```
   DATABASE_URL="file:./dev.db"
   ```

   Prisma – our database toolkit of choice – uses the `DATABASE_URL` environment variable to connect to our database.

3. Next, run `npm run build` to generate the Prisma client for our data schema. Prisma reads our Prisma schema from the `prisma/schema.prisma` file and generates types and functions for us to work with.

4. Run `npm run update:db` to create or update the SQLite database. We use SQLite with Prisma to persist our development data.

5. Finally, run `npm run seed` to seed our local database with mock data. You can find the mock script in `prisma/seed.tsx`.

Our datatabase is set up, and we can now use Prisma to query the database. Next, let's add the code to fetch data from the database to BeeRich.

Fetching data at the route level

Let's use Remix's `loader` functions and route-level data fetching to query the database for expense data:

1. Open the `app/routes/dashboard.expenses.tsx` file in your editor.

2. Add a `loader` function to the route module:

   ```
   export async function loader() {
     return {};
   }
   ```

   `loader` functions are Remix's HTTP **GET** request handlers and work with request and response objects that follow the Fetch API's Request-Response interface. Remix's `loader` functions are executed only on the server and must return a `Response` object (https://developer.mozilla.org/en-US/docs/Web/API/Response).

   For now, we return an empty JavaScript object. Remix serializes the object for us (`JSON.stringify`) and creates a `Response` object with `Content-Type application/json`.

3. Next, import our new database client:

    ```
    import { db } from '~/modules/db.server';
    ```

> **Important note**
>
> You can find more information about our Prisma client setup in the `README.md` file here: `https://github.com/PacktPublishing/Full-Stack-Web-Development-with-Remix/blob/main/05-fetching-and-mutating-data/bee-rich/README.md`.

4. Use the database client to query for all expenses and return the results array from the `loader` function:

    ```
    import { db } from '~/modules/db.server';

    export async function loader() {
      const expenses = await db.expense.findMany({});
      return expenses;
    }
    ```

5. Import the `json` helper function from Remix and pass the expenses array to it:

    ```
    import { json } from '@remix-run/node';
    import { db } from '~/modules/db.server';

    export async function loader() {
      const expenses = await db.expense.findMany({});
      return json(expenses);
    }
    ```

    The `json` helper function returns a `Response` object with `Content-Type application/json`. Using the helper function allows us to provide an `init` object as the second argument to add HTTP headers, a status text, and a status code to the response.

    This step is optional as we don't return any HTTP headers or cookies with the `Response` object just yet. We'll cover this in more detail later in this book.

6. Update the database query to order the data by date:

    ```
    const expenses = await db.expense.findMany({
      orderBy: {
        createdAt: 'desc',
      },
    });
    ```

Note that we have complete control over what to query based on our frontend needs. Rather than sorting the expenses array on the client side, we can modify the database query in the `loader` function. Performing as much logic as we can on the server minimizes the need for client-side state management. This is a best practice we should keep in mind.

> **Move as much logic as possible to the server**
>
> We should try to move as much code as possible to the server-side `action` and `loader` functions.
>
> Moving code to the server ensures that less code is shipped to the client. It also increases the amount of logic that works before JavaScript has fully loaded on the client. Finally, we make sure we decrease the complexity of our client-side application by moving the code to our fast and powerful server and database runtimes.

7. Thereafter, add `console.log` to the `loader` function so that we can track its execution on the terminal.
8. Run the app (`npm run dev`) and open BeeRich in a browser window.
9. Finally, navigate between different pages and check the server terminal for your `console.log` message. Take note when the `loader` function is executed. Since `loader` functions only run on the server, you will find the log statements in the terminal and not the browser console.

Great! Whenever the `dashboard/expenses` path is added to the URL, Remix calls the `dashboard.expenses.tsx` route module's `loader` function.

Next, we need to figure out how to access the data in React. Luckily, this is as easy as it gets in Remix.

1. Again, open the `dashboard.expenses.tsx` route module in your editor.
2. Import the `useLoaderData` hook from `@remix-run/react`.
3. Next, call the hook in the route module component:

   ```
   const expenses = useLoaderData();
   ```

   We use the `useLoaderData` hook to access the loader data **of the same route module**. It's as easy as that; no prop drilling or other shenanigans are required.

   Remix executes `loader` functions first and then renders the React application on the server. In our React component, we access the fetched data without having to manage loading states. This allows us to eliminate a big chunk of boilerplate code that many React apps suffer from.

4. So far, the `expenses` variable in our route component is typed as `any`. This isn't ideal. Luckily, we are using TypeScript for both our frontend and backend code. We are further co-locating client and server code in the same `app` folder. This allows us to do powerful things, such as inferring the type of the loader data when calling `useLoaderData`.

Pass the type of the `loader` function to the generic slot of `useLoaderData`:

```
const expenses = useLoaderData<typeof loader>();
```

Now, inspect the type of `expenses` (that is, by hovering over the variable name in your editor). The variable is now typed as an expense object array that is wrapped by `JsonifyObject<{...}>`.

Remix co-locates your client and server code in the same file. This allows us to infer the types of fetched data across the network (from server to client). However, since we work with `Response` objects in `loader` functions, the returned data is serialized as JSON. This changes the shape of the data. For instance, JSON cannot manage `Date` objects but serializes them to `string`.

`JsonifyObject` is a helper type from Remix that ensures that the expense object is correctly typed after being serialized to JSON. We will return to that later; for now, we are happy that we can easily access the `loader` data and have it fully typed.

5. Let's use the expense array to replace the hardcoded expense list. Loop over the expense data to render the list of expenses:

```
<ul className="flex flex-col">
  {expenses.map((expense) => (
    <ListLinkItem key={expense.id} to={`/dashboard/expenses/${expense.id}`}>
      <p>
        <i>{new Date(expense.createdAt).toLocaleDateString('en-US')}</i>
      </p>
      <p className="text-xl font-semibold">{expense.title}</p>
      <p>
        <b>
          {Intl.NumberFormat('en-US', { style: 'currency', currency: expense.currencyCode }).format(
            expense.amount,
          )}
        </b>
      </p>
    </ListLinkItem>
  ))}
</ul>
```

Notice that the `createdAt` property is of the `string` type. We turn it into a `Date` object by calling `new Date(expense.createdAt)`. In the `loader` function, the expenses array carries `createdAt` properties of the `Date` type. On the client, we need to deserialize the data as it was parsed to JSON.

6. Finally, run the application and visit the expense overview page. You should be able to view a list of expenses from the seed data.

   Amazing! We utilize a server-side `loader` function to fetch data, and then we access the data in React to render our page. Remix's `loader` function allows us to co-locate server-side data loading and data rendering in the same file.

Note that data fetching in Remix happens in `loader` functions at the route level. Route-level data fetching offers many advantages by giving up some of the flexibility of fetching from components.

Component-based data loading is susceptible to blocking requests, which may lead to fetch waterfalls. A component that fetches data often defers rendering its child components until the data is loaded. This blocks the children from kicking off their own fetch requests, effectively creating a waterfall of fetch requests.

Imagine a component that renders the layout of the page. First, it fetches the user object and displays a big loading spinner until the user data has been fetched. After the user data has been fetched, the page is rendered. Nested components now fetch their own data. The user fetch request blocked these requests. This behavior may repeat itself several times in nested subtrees of an app.

> **Remix promotes route-level data fetching**
> In Remix, we aim to fetch data in route modules instead of components. By avoiding granular data fetching at the component level, we aim to optimize data loading and prevent fetch waterfalls. We should remember this as a best practice.

Note that route-level data fetching does not imply that you can only access the data at the route level. You can use the `useLoaderData`, `useRouteLoaderData`, and `useMatches` hooks in any custom hook or component of your application to access loader data.

The `useRouteLoaderData` and `useMatches` hooks are used to access data from any currently active route – compared to `useLoaderData`, which returns the data of the route module that the hook is called in. Refer to the Remix documentation for more information: `https://remix.run/docs/en/2/hooks/use-route-loader-data`.

As always, make sure to implement the same functionality for the income routes. This ensures you revisit the concepts introduced in this section before moving on.

Next, let's have a look at how we can fetch data based on dynamic route parameters.

Fetching dynamic data in parameterized routes

Now that we've updated the expenses overview page, you might have noticed that this broke our hardcoded expense details route. Let's fix that.

You may remember from *Chapter 4, Routing in Remix*, that we designed the expense details page as a nested route that renders within the expenses overview page. It is also a parameterized route that uses a dynamic route parameter.

Let's update the code so that it queries the requested expense from the database based on the route parameter:

1. Open the `/app/routes/dashboard.expenses.$id.tsx` file in your editor. We're already using a `loader` function to render our mock data.
2. Delete the mock data array from the file.
3. Next, update the `loader` function to query the database and find a unique expense object with the `id` parameter that we access from the URL:

    ```
    import { db } from '~/modules/db.server';

    export async function loader({ params }: LoaderFunctionArgs) {
      const { id } = params;
      const expense = await db.expense.findUnique({ where: { id } });
      if (!expense) throw new Response('Not found', { status: 404 });
      return json(expense);
    }
    ```

    We now call our database to dynamically query for the correct expense.

    Note that we still throw a `404 Response` if we cannot find an expense that matches the `id` parameter. This is a great way to stop further executions and show the user that something went wrong.

4. Run BeeRich by executing `npm run dev` in a terminal.
5. Open a browser window and navigate to `http://localhost:3000/dashboard/expenses/`.
6. Click on one of the listed expenses.

    Notice that the URL changes to include the `id` parameter of the expense. Remix executes a client-side navigation (when JS is available) to update the URL.

Remix executes a `loader` function when we navigate to the associated route segment. On every page navigation, Remix fetches the loader data of each new route module that matches the newly requested page. If we navigate to `/login`, then the `loader` functions of all **newly matching routes** are executed. This may include the following route modules (from root to leaf):

- `root.tsx`
- `routes/_layout.tsx`
- `routes/_layout.login.tsx`

If we further navigate from `/login` to `/signup`, then only the `_layout.signup.tsx` route module's `loader` function is executed as it's the only route segment that wasn't already active before.

Let's visualize what's going on by reviewing the **Network** tab in the developer tools of the browser window:

1. Open the developer tools in the browser window that runs your app.
2. Open the **Network** tab of the developer tools.
3. Filter by `Fetch/XHR` network requests. This is optional but helps you find all fetch requests made to the `loader` functions.
4. Now, change the URL in the URL bar to `http://localhost:3000/dashboard/expenses/` and reload the browser window.
5. You should see no fetch requests in the **Network** tab yet.

    This is because Remix initially server renders your application. Your `dashboard.expenses.tsx` route module's `loader` function is executed, and the data is used to render the HTML on the server.

6. Next, click on any of the expenses in the expenses list.

    Remix is now running client-side. After hydration, the client-side Remix app takes over the routing of our application. This allows us to avoid full-page requests, which would require more network bandwidth and increase response times.

    Since we are using Remix's `Link` component, Remix can intercept page transitions. Remix prevents the browser's default behavior (full-page reload) if JavaScript is loaded. Instead, it emulates the behavior by making fetch requests to our `loader` functions to fetch the required data.

7. Inspect the request in the **Network** tab. The navigation to `/dashboard/expenses/$id` invokes a fetch request to the `dashboard.expenses.$id.tsx` route module's `loader` function, as shown in *Figure 5.1*:

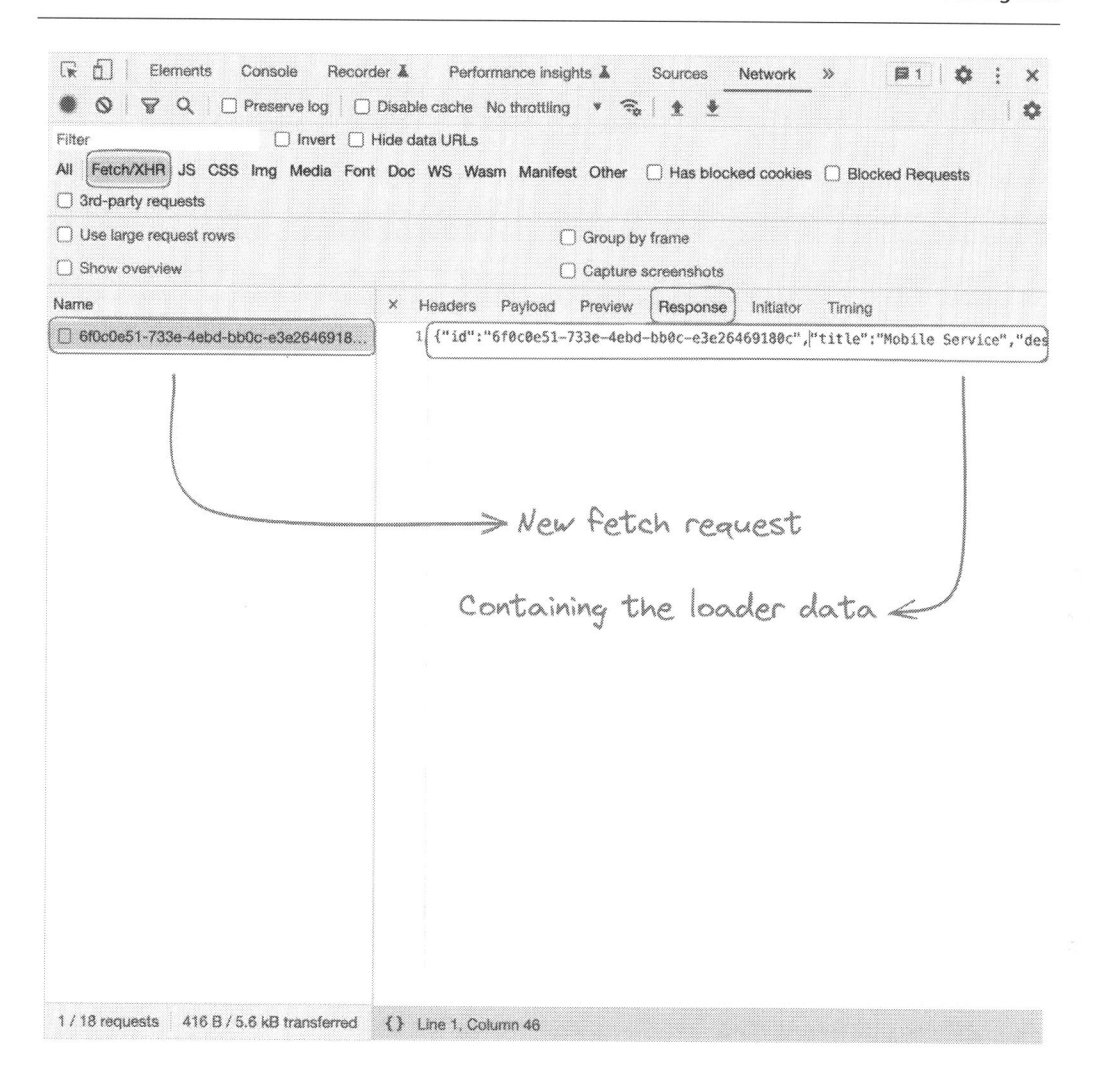

Figure 5.1 – Screenshot of the fetched loader data after a route transition

As visible in *Figure 5.1*, Remix executes a fetch request to the `loader` function, which then returns the expense object as JSON.

8. Click on another expense. Notice that Remix repeats the behavior for each navigation to an expense details route. Every time we click on a new expense, the URL changes, and the `loader` function of the details page is called again with the next `$id` route parameter.

Notice that Remix never re-fetches the expenses array for the overview page. That is because we remain on the `dashboard.expenses.tsx` route segment. **Remix only loads data for newly matching route segments.**

Great! We are now able to fetch dynamic data with parameterized routes. Note that Remix only fetches data for newly matching route segments. This avoids unnecessary requests. We also learned that Remix fetches from `loader` functions during server-side rendering and client-side navigations. Remix handles data loading on a per-route level on both sides of the network.

> **Remix is both a frontend and a backend framework**
> Remix calls `loader` functions on the initial request on the server before rendering React server-side. On the client, Remix fetches loader data on client-side navigations with AJAX requests (fetch requests).

Revisit the concepts introduced in this section by updating the `dashboard.income.$id.tsx` route module so that it matches `dashboard.expenses.$id.tsx`. Make sure you test your implementation before moving on. Inspect which `loader` functions are executed when switching between the `/income` and `/expenses` routes by using the **Network** tab.

Next, let's see how `loader` functions are called in parallel. For this, we need to adapt our application logic a bit.

Loading data in parallel

As visible in *Figure 5.2*, the expense overview page has two sections – the list of all expenses (`dashboard.expenses.tsx`) and the details view of the currently selected expense (`dashboard.expenses.$id.tsx`). The details view is empty when navigating to `/dashboard/expenses` since the nested `$id` route module does not appear on the screen:

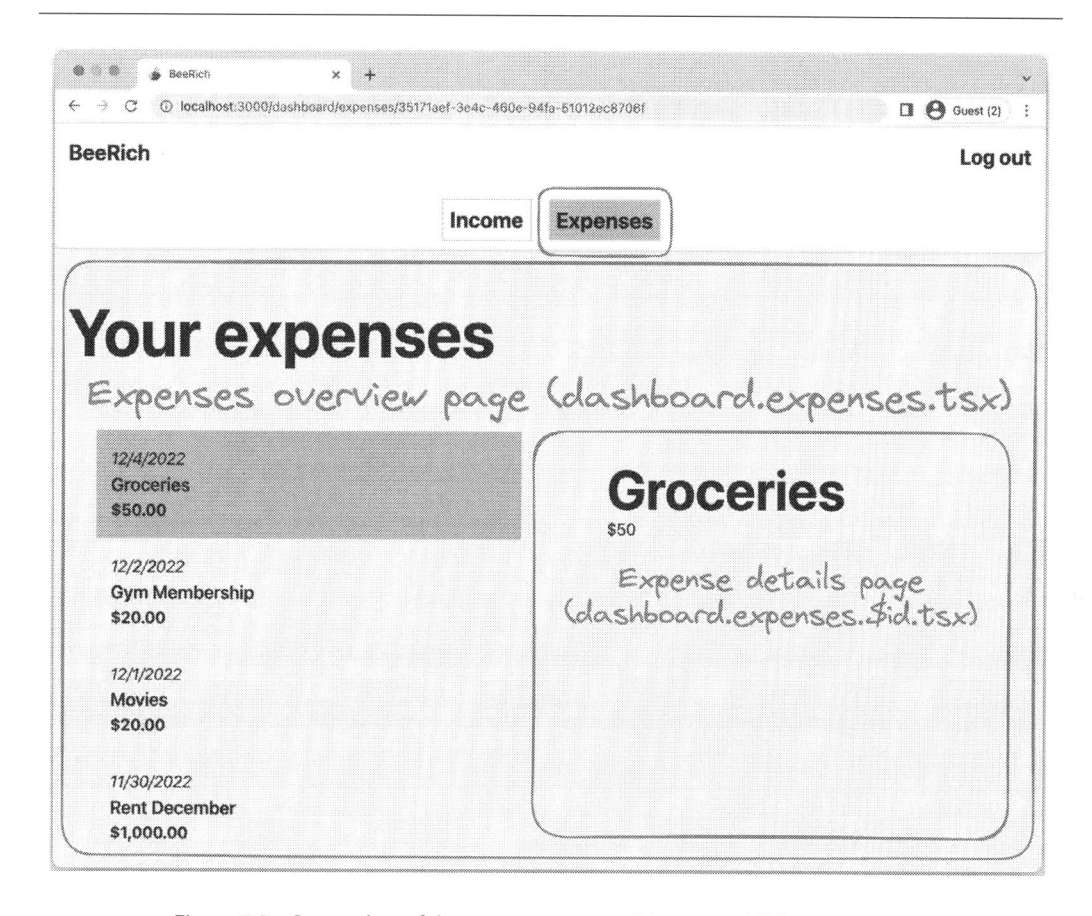

Figure 5.2 – Screenshot of the expenses route with a nested $id route module

Let's update the **Expenses** navigation link on the dashboard's navigation bar (highlighted in *Figure 5.2*). Currently, the **Expenses** link points to /dashboard/expenses. We will update this link so that it points to the most recently created expense instead:

1. Open the dashboard.tsx route module in your editor.
2. Add the following loader function to the route module:

    ```
    import { json } from '@remix-run/node';
    import { db } from '~/modules/db.server';

    export async function loader() {
      const firstExpense = await db.expense.findFirst({
        orderBy: { createdAt: 'desc' },
      });
      return json({ firstExpense });
    }
    ```

The `loader` function queries the database for the most recently created expense. It then returns the queried `firstExpense`.

Note that `firstExpense` can also be `null` if the database has no expense entries.

3. Next, access the `firstExpense` object using the `useLoaderData` hook:

   ```
   const { firstExpense } = useLoaderData<typeof loader>();
   ```

   We type the `useLoaderData` hook with the type of the `loader` function. `firstExpense` is now correctly typed as the serialized version of an expense object or `null`.

4. Use `firstExpense` to update the `to` property of the **Expenses** `NavLink`. Since `firstExpense` can be `null`, we must ensure we make this change conditionally:

   ```
   <li className="mr-auto">
     <NavLink
       to={firstExpense ? `/dashboard/expenses/${firstExpense.id}`
   : '/dashboard/expenses'}
     >
       Expenses
     </NavLink>
   </li>
   ```

   Great! The **Expenses** `NavLink` component now navigates the user to the most recently created expense.

5. Run BeeRich by executing `npm run dev` and open the expenses overview page in a browser window: `http://localhost:3000/dashboard/expenses`.

   Notice that the **Expenses** `NavLink` component lost its active styling. This is because the link now points to a nested route, which does not trigger the `isActive` condition on Remix's `NavLink` component. Luckily, our custom `NavLink` component offers a `styleAsActive` prop, which can be used to apply the active styling whenever we want.

6. Import the `useLocation` hook from `@remix-run/react`.

7. Next, call the hook in the route module component:

   ```
   const location = useLocation();
   ```

   Remix's `useLocation` hook lets us access a global location object with information about the current URL.

8. Add the `styleAsActive` prop to the **Expenses** `NavLink`. Set the property to `true` whenever the user is on an `/expenses` route:

   ```
   <NavLink
     to={firstExpense ? `/dashboard/expenses/${firstExpense.id}` :
   '/dashboard/expenses'}
     styleAsActive={location.pathname.startsWith('/dashboard/
   expenses')}
   >
   ```

```
      Expenses
    </NavLink>
```

With that, we've restored the active styling on the `/dashboard/expenses` route.

With these changes in place, let's learn about parallel data fetching.

9. Visit the `/dashboard/income` page in a browser window and clear the **Network** tab.

10. Now, navigate to the details page of the most recently created expense by clicking on the **Expenses** navigation menu link.

11. As visible in *Figure 5.3*, you should now see two fetch requests in the **Network** tab. The requests are made to the two `loader` functions:

    - `dashboard.expenses.tsx`
    - `dashboard.expenses.$id.tsx`

The `loader` function in `dashboard.tsx` is not executed as the route module was already active on the page before the navigation:

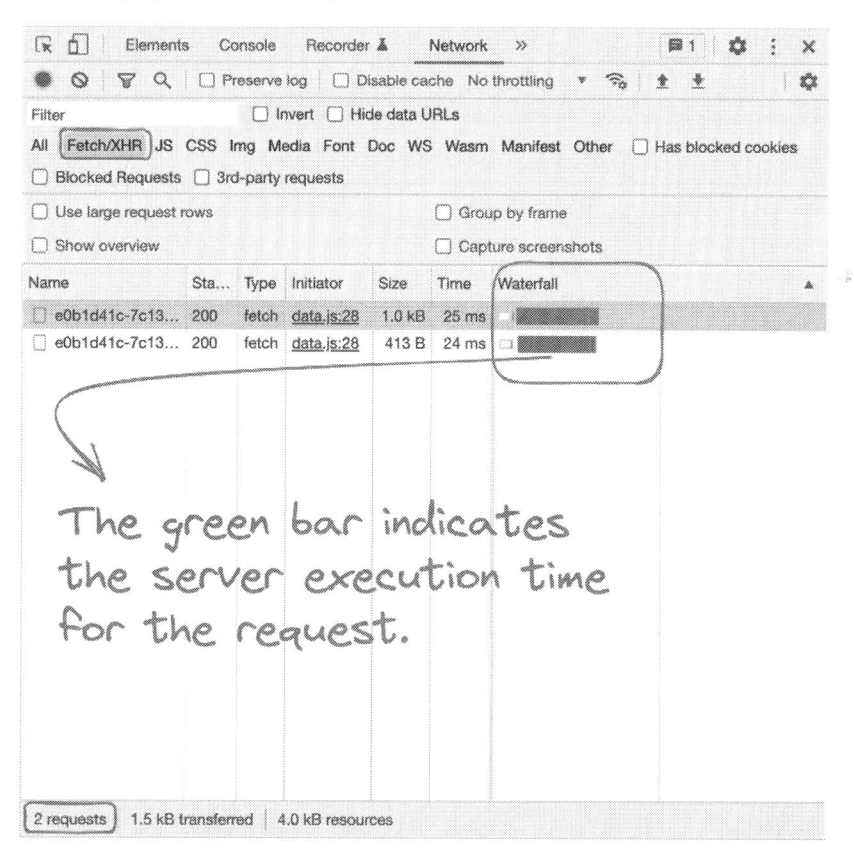

Figure 5.3 – Inspecting the fetch request waterfall

As visible in *Figure 5.3*, we can inspect the waterfall of the fetch requests in the **Network** tab. The green bar indicates the server execution time for the request. Note that both fetch requests are executed in parallel. This flattens the request waterfall and improves the response time.

You might have noticed that we query the database again in the `loader` function in `dashboard.expenses.$id.tsx`. You might have asked yourself why we are not reusing the loader data from `dashboard.expenses.tsx` as we already fetch all expenses from the database. This is a trade-off for the parallel execution of `loader` functions. Several loaders cannot depend on each other's data as they are all executed in parallel.

Let's summarize our observations:

- On initial request, Remix renders our app on the server.
- All active `loader` functions are executed in parallel and passed to the React app during server-side rendering.
- With loaders, we fetch application data on a per-route level.
- Remix emulates the browser's default behavior with JavaScript. All subsequent page navigations execute client-side if JavaScript has loaded.
- Remix uses fetch requests to load all required loader data on navigation.
- The `loader` functions of all newly matching route segments are executed in parallel.
- Already active `loader` functions are not executed again.

Practice what you've learned in this section by implementing the same functionality on the `/income` routes. Query for the most recently created invoice in the `dashboard.tsx` route module's `loader` function. Then, update the **Income** `NavLink` component. Finally, use the `useLocation` hook to add the `styleAsActive` prop.

Next, let's see whether we can optimize the code a bit:

1. Open the `app/routes/dashboard.tsx` file in your editor.
2. After adding the invoice query to the `loader` function, the function may look like this:

```
export async function loader() {
  const firstExpense = await db.expense.findFirst({
    orderBy: { createdAt: 'desc' },
  });
  const firstInvoice = await db.invoice.findFirst({
    orderBy: { createdAt: 'desc' },
  });
  return json({ firstExpense, firstInvoice });
}
```

This naïve implementation awaits the invoice query after executing the expense query. Whenever independent queries are executed in a `loader` function, we have the opportunity to execute the queries in parallel to reduce the response time.

3. Refactor the code so that it executes the two queries in parallel:

```
export async function loader() {
  const expenseQuery = db.expense.findFirst({
    orderBy: { createdAt: 'desc' },
  });
  const invoiceQuery = db.invoice.findFirst({
    orderBy: { createdAt: 'desc' },
  });

  const [firstExpense, firstInvoice] = await Promise.all([expenseQuery, invoiceQuery]);
  return json({ firstExpense, firstInvoice });
}
```

Instead of awaiting both queries after each other, we can pass both query promises to `Promise.all` to execute them in parallel.

In this section, we went over data fetching in Remix. You learned how to use and type the `useLoaderData` hook and how to query data based on dynamic route parameters. You now know that Remix promotes data fetching at the route module level. This allows us to execute `loader` functions in parallel and avoid request waterfalls. You further understand the importance of moving as much logic as possible to the server to reduce the size and complexity of the client bundle. Finally, you practiced optimizing `loader` functions to make independent requests in parallel. Next, we'll learn about data mutations.

Mutating data

Creating and updating data is just as important as fetching data. In this section, we will add an expense creation form and learn how to mutate data in Remix.

Mutating data without JavaScript

Remember the three-step process for building web UIs from Ryan Florence that we discussed in *Chapter 1*? The first step is to make the user experience work without JavaScript. After that, we add JavaScript to enhance the experience but ensure that the baseline implementation still works. This process is called **progressive enhancement**.

In this section, we use Remix's `action` function to handle incoming form submissions on the server. In the `action` function, we will validate the user data and write the new expense object to the database. Let's see how we can use the native form element to submit user data, without the need for client-side JavaScript:

1. First, create a new route module for the expense creation form: `app/routes/dashboard.expenses._index.tsx`.

   We add the expense creation form to the index route of the `/dashboard/expenses/` path. This leads to the following route hierarchy:

   - `/dashboard/expenses/`: Shows the expenses list and the expense creation form
   - `/dashboard/expenses/$id`: Shows the expenses list and the expense details for the expense with the `id` identifier

2. Add a route component to `dashboard.expenses._index.tsx` that contains an HTML form element:

   ```
   export default function Component() {
     return (
       <form method="POST" action="/dashboard/expenses/?index">
       </form>
     );
   }
   ```

   The HTML form element allows us to set `method` and `action` attributes. `method` defines the submission method (`POST` or `GET`), and `action` sets the path name for the submission.

   We set the method to `POST` as we are mutating data.

   > **POST to mutate, GET to load**
   >
   > HTML forms use the HTTP verbs `POST` and `GET` for submissions. It's best to use a `POST` request for mutations and a `GET` request to read data from the server.

   We want to submit the data to the `dashboard.expenses._index.tsx` route module (the route module of the form element). Note that this is the default behavior, so we could also omit the attribute declaration. However, for educational purposes, we set `action` to `/dashboard/expenses?index` as the pathname for the action.

   Note the `?index` search parameter that is added to the action's pathname. Index route modules and their parent route modules both match the same URL. When defining an `action` function, that action can live in either `dashboard.expenses.tsx` or `dashboard.expenses._index.tsx`. The `?index` search parameter tells Remix to submit to the index route module, not the parent module.

3. Next, let's add input fields for the expense data:

```
export default function Component() {
  return (
    <form method="post" action="/dashboard/expenses/?index">
      <label className="w-full lg:max-w-md">
        Title:
        <input type="text" name="title" placeholder="Dinner for
          Two" required />
      </label>
      <label className="w-full lg:max-w-md">
        Description:
        <textarea name="description" />
      </label>
      <label className="w-full lg:max-w-md">
        Amount (in USD):
        <input type="number" defaultValue={0} name="amount"
          required />
      </label>
      <button type="submit">Create</button>
    </form>
  );
}
```

The `route` module component now renders a simple HTML form with fields for the expense data. It doesn't look pretty without CSS. We will solve this in the next step. For now, let's focus on the content of the form.

We add `name` attributes to the input and textarea elements. On form submission, the form data includes key-value pairs for every named input field. The `name` attributes are used as the keys of the form data. Finally, a button of the `submit` type is used to submit the form data on click.

4. Next, add an `action` function to the route module:

```
import type { ActionFunctionArgs } from '@remix-run/node';

export async function action({ request }: ActionFunctionArgs) {
  // TODO
}
```

We use `loader` functions to handle HTTP GET requests. Remix's `action` function is called for all other HTTP requests to the route, including POST requests.

Both functions receive a couple of parameters. You already know about the `params` parameter, which lets us access dynamic route segments. Now, we're using the `request` parameter, which gives us access to the `Request` object (https://developer.mozilla.org/en-US/docs/Web/API/Request).

We type `loader` function parameters with the `LoaderFunctionArgs` type and `action` function parameters with the `ActionFunctionArgs` type.

5. Use the `request` parameter to parse the request body into form data:

```
export async function action({ request }: ActionFunctionArgs) {
  const formData = await request.formData();
  const title = formData.get('title');
  const description = formData.get('description');
  const amount = formData.get('amount');
}
```

Remix follows the Fetch API specification. On incoming HTTP requests, we have access to the `Request` object.

By calling the `formData` function, we parse the request body into a `FormData` object that provides us with access to the key-value pairs of the form input data. You can find more information about form data in the MDN Web Docs: `https://developer.mozilla.org/en-US/docs/Web/API/FormData`.

6. Import our database client and the `redirect` function from Remix:

```
import { redirect } from '@remix-run/node';

import { db } from '~/modules/db.server';
```

7. Validate the form data before using it to create a new expense:

```
export async function action({ request }: ActionFunctionArgs) {
  const formData = await request.formData();
  const title = formData.get('title');
  const description = formData.get('description');
  const amount = formData.get('amount');
  if (typeof title !== 'string' || typeof description !== 'string' || typeof amount !== 'string') {
    throw Error('something went wrong');
  }
  const amountNumber = Number.parseFloat(amount);
  if (Number.isNaN(amountNumber)) {
    throw Error('something went wrong');
  }
  const expense = await db.expense.create({
    data: {
      title,
      description,
      amount: amountNumber,
      currencyCode: 'USD',
```

```
        },
      });
      return redirect(`/dashboard/expenses/${expense.id}`);
    }
```

This is quite a bit of boilerplate code. However, remember that we implemented a full-stack data mutation, including basic input validation.

It's a must to validate user input data on the server. Later in this book, we will use the `zod` library to help validate user input. For now, we keep it simple and manually validate the data using `if` stamtents.

Note that, once again, we co-locate the server-side HTTP handler and the associated client-side UI together in one file.

8. Review the return statement of the `action` function. We redirect to the expense details page of the created expense to communicate success:

   ```
   redirect(`/dashboard/expenses/${expense.id}`);
   ```

   Like `loader` functions, `action` functions must return a `Response` object or plain JSON (which Remix wraps in a `Response` object for us).

   We utilize Remix's `redirect` helper function to create a redirect response object.

9. Open the `/dashboard.expenses.$id.tsx` route module in your editor and add a quick link to the expense creation page:

   ```
   import { FloatingActionLink } from '~/components/links';

   export default function Component() {
     const expense = useLoaderData<typeof loader>();
     return (
       <>
         <div className="w-full h-full p-8">
           <H2>{expense.title}</H2>
           <p>${expense.amount}</p>
         </div>
         <FloatingActionLink to="/dashboard/expenses/">Add expense</FloatingActionLink>
       </>
     );
   }
   ```

   The `FloatingActionLink` component wraps Remix's `Link` component. The quick link from the expense details page to the creation form allows for a convenient workflow:

- Expense creation redirects to the created expense.

- The expense details page offers a quick link back to expense creation.

10. Execute `npm run dev` to start the dev server.

11. Navigate to the expenses overview page (`http://localhost:3000/dashboard/expenses/`) and test the implementation. Create your first expense!

What do you notice? When submitting the native HTML form element, the browser executes a full-page reload. This is the browser's default behavior on form submissions. Furthermore, you might notice that the created expense appears in the expense list after completing the submission.

A full-page reload triggers a refresh of the full page. Remix renders the HTML on the server and triggers all active loader functions. The expense overview is reloaded on submission.

The form element provides a **declarative way** of describing a fetch request. We use the `FormData` API and use named input fields to declare what fields should be sent to the server. Form submissions trigger `POST` requests to the `action` function. We use the `Request` object to parse the submitted form data. This happens on the server. So far, our implementation uses no client-side JavaScript.

In a React SPA, we often call `event.preventDefault` in `onSubmit` handlers to prevent the browser's default behavior. Here, we initiate a client-side fetch request. This may look something like this:

```
function CreateExpenseForm() {
  const [title, setTitle] = React.useState('');
  const [description, setDescription] = React.useState('');
  const [amount, setAmount] = React.useState(0);
  const [isSubmitting, setIsSubmitting] = React.useState(false);

  const handleSubmit = async (event: React.FormEvent<HTMLFormElement>) => {
    event.preventDefault();
    setIsSubmitting(true);
    await fetch('/dashboard/expenses/?index', {
      method: 'POST',
      body: JSON.stringify({ title, description, amount }),
    });
    setIsSubmitting(false);
  };

  return (
    <form onSubmit={handleSubmit}>
      <Input
        label="Title:"
        placeholder="Dinner for Two"
        required
        value={title}
        onChange={(event) => setTitle(event.target.value)}
```

```
      />
      <Textarea label="Description:" value={description}
        onChange={(event) => setDescription(event.target.value)} />
      <Input
        label="Amount (in USD):"
        type="number"
        required
        value={amount}
        onChange={(e) => setAmount(e.target.valueAsNumber)}
      />
      <Button type="submit" isPrimary disabled={isSubmitting}>
        Create
      </Button>
    </form>
  );
}
```

By doing so, we avoid full-page reloads and gain control over what pieces of the React state should be updated by the mutation. However, without supporting native form submissions, we lose the ability to fall back to the browser's default behavior. Worse, implementing this ourselves forces us to develop custom solutions for pending states, error handling, and state revalidation after mutation.

Making it work without JavaScript enables us to support user interactions before JavaScript has loaded or in case it fails to load. This is a powerful feature we get when using Remix's primitives and conventions. However, Remix also scales upward. Let's add JavaScript to enhance the experience.

Mutating data with JavaScript

Remix provides a `Form` component that progressively enhances the experience. All we need to do is replace the native HTML form element through Remix's `Form` component:

1. Import the `Form` component from Remix:

   ```
   import { Form } from '@remix-run/react';
   ```

2. Use it to replace the native HTML form element:

   ```
   export default function Component() {
     return (
       <Form method="post" action="/dashboard/expenses/?index">
         ...
       </Form>
     );
   }
   ```

3. Now, test the implementation again and create some more expenses.

   What changed? You may be able to notice a few things:

   - When using Remix's `Form` component, Remix prevents the browser's default behavior and executes a client-side fetch request to submit the form, avoiding the full-page reload. This works out of the box without us adding an `onSubmit` handler.
   - Our custom page loading indicator is triggered, indicating that form submissions also affect Remix's global navigation object.
   - After submission, the app still executes a redirect and transitions the user to the expense details page.
   - After submission, the new expense appears in the expense overview list as part of the `/dashboard/expenses/` route's loader data. Remix emulates the browser's default behavior of refreshing all content on the page.

Remember how Remix's `NavLink` and `Link` components enhance anchor tag navigations? By replacing the native form element with Remix's `Form` component, we get client-side data fetching, progressive enhancement, and client-side state revalidation out of the box.

We now take advantage of JavaScript on the client, but that JavaScript is provided through Remix's `Form` component, and no custom boilerplate code is required. Remix's `Form` component sets the global navigation object's state to `submitting` and `loading` for managing pending UIs. Using Remix's `Form` component further ensures the refetching of all active `loader` functions after mutation.

> **Remix revalidates loader data after every action**
>
> Remix refreshes all loader data by re-fetching from all active `loader` functions after executing an `action` function, just like a full-page reload would do on a HTML form submission.

Data revalidation is a powerful feature that lets us avoid stale data on the client or having to develop custom logic to synchronize client and server states.

Nice! In this section, we implemented an expense creation form and associated `action` function. You learned how Remix removes boilerplate code by providing the `Form` component, which does the heavy lifting under the hood. You practiced declaring a fetch request using named input fields and Remix's `Form` component.

Before moving on, let's style our form by bringing in some of the prepared UI components:

1. Import the `Textarea`, `Input`, and `Form` components from the `components` folder:

   ```
   import { Form, Input, Textarea } from '~/components/forms';
   ```

2. Remove the import of Remix's `Form` component since we will be using our custom wrapper component instead.

3. Replace the native label, input, and textarea elements with our styled counterparts:

```
export default function CreateExpensePage() {
  return (
    <Form method="post" action="/dashboard/expenses/?index">
      <Input label="Title:" type="text" name="title"
        placeholder="Dinner for Two" required />
      <Textarea label="Description:" name="description" />
      <Input label="Amount (in USD):" type="number"
        defaultValue={0} name="amount" required />
      <button type="submit">Create</button>
    </Form>
  );
}
```

4. Also, import the styled `Button` component from the `components` folder:

```
import { Button } from '~/components/buttons';
```

5. Replace the native button element with our wrapper component and add the `isPrimary` property:

```
<Button type="submit" isPrimary>
  Create
</Button>
```

6. Run BeeRich locally. The form should look much nicer now.

Make sure you implement the invoice creation form and replicate what we did for the expense routes. Start by implementing the functionality without JavaScript. Then, enhance the experience with Remix's `Form` component. I encourage you to keep the **Network** tab open while running BeeRich locally. Filter by `Fetch/XHR` network requests and inspect how Remix revalidates all loader data after each form submission. If you get stuck working on the income routes, you can find the final solution for this chapter on GitHub: `https://github.com/PacktPublishing/Full-Stack-Web-Development-with-Remix/tree/main/05-fetching-and-mutating-data/bee-rich/solution`.

Summary

Reading and writing data are important aspects of modern web application development. Remix provides primitives, conventions, and levers for both.

This chapter introduced you to Remix's server-side `loader` and `action` functions. You learned that `loader` and `action` functions are route-level HTTP request handlers that get and mutate data. Loaders handle HTTP `GET` requests, while `action` functions receive all other incoming HTTP requests.

Initially, Remix renders our app on the server. All further page transitions happen on the client. On the initial request, loader data is used during server-side rendering. On all subsequent navigations, Remix fetches loader data via fetch requests and only re-renders the changing parts of the route hierarchy on the client.

Next, you learned that route-level data fetching allows us – among other things – to flatten request waterfalls that may occur with component-level fetching. Remix also executes `loader` functions in parallel to reduce response times.

By completing this chapter, you should now understand how Remix uses the HTML form element to work with mutations declaratively. Remix provides progressive enhancement out of the box. By default, Remix executes client-side fetch requests to perform data mutations. However, if JavaScript isn't available (hasn't loaded yet, failed to load, or is disabled), then Remix can fall back to the browser's default behavior.

In this chapter, we added an `action` function to validate request data and create a new expense object. Remix automatically refetches all loader data after every mutation. With Remix, we get data revalidation out of the box.

Remix's data loading and mutations work with and without JavaScript. This allows us to enhance the experience progressively and make our application accessible to more users. In the next chapter, we will learn more about progressively enhancing the experience. We will formalize what we learned in this chapter and learn about more tools to enhance the experience in our Remix apps.

Further reading

The Remix documentation outlines the full stack data flow in Remix here: `https://remix.run/docs/en/2/discussion/data-flow`.

You can find Remix's documentation about data loading here: `https://remix.run/docs/en/2/guides/data-loading`.

You can find Remix's documentation about mutations here: `https://remix.run/docs/en/2/guides/data-writes`.

The Remix team has created an amazing video series called Remix Singles that goes in depth into how to work with data in Remix. The series starts with a video about data loading, which you can find here: `https://www.youtube.com/watch?v=NXqEP_PsPNc`.

MDN Web Docs is a great place to learn more about the HTTP protocol: `https://developer.mozilla.org/en-US/docs/Web/HTTP/Basics_of_HTTP`.

6
Enhancing the User Experience

Remix enables us to build applications with progressive enhancement in mind. In Remix, enhancing the user experience can be achieved by making additive changes. This allows us to follow a simple step-by-step process to build our applications.

In *Chapter 5, Fetching and Mutating Data*, we added data loading and mutations to our BeeRich application. When building out the create expense form, we first implemented the UI to work without JavaScript and then enhanced the browser's default behavior with JavaScript. By doing so, we progressively enhanced the experience.

In this chapter, we'll cover the following topics:

- Understanding progressive enhancement
- Prefetching data
- Working with action data
- Handling concurrent mutations

First, we will formalize how progressive enhancement works in Remix. After that, we will focus on advanced data loading and mutation topics, including how to prefetch loader data and assets. Next, we will learn how to access action data to display mutation feedback. Finally, we will learn how to support concurrent mutations in Remix.

After reading this chapter, you will understand the benefits of working with progressive enhancement in mind. You will also learn how to prefetch data, work with action data, and handle multiple form submissions simultaneously.

Technical requirements

Before you start this chapter, follow the instructions in the README.md file in this chapter's folder on GitHub. You can find the code for this chapter here: https://github.com/PacktPublishing/Full-Stack-Web-Development-with-Remix/tree/main/06-enhancing-the-user-experience.

Understanding progressive enhancement

In this section, we will learn more about the motivation behind progressive enhancement and introduce best practices for working with progressive enhancement in mind.

Progressive enhancement is a design philosophy that aims to create a baseline user experience for users on older devices and browsers. Building with progressive enhancement in mind is like designing mobile first; you start with a minimal UI for small screens and progress from there.

A less frequently used term is **graceful degradation**. Graceful degradation describes a similar idea: striving for the best experience possible while supporting older browsers and devices. Progressive enhancement works upward, while graceful degradation works downward.

Progressive enhancement in Remix

Remix allows us to build highly dynamic user experiences by utilizing web standards. Remix, by default, works without JavaScript. When working with progressive enhancement in mind, we can enhance the experience upward but still keep it accessible and usable when JavaScript is still loading, fails to load, or is disabled.

In *Chapter 4, Routing in Remix*, we learned about Remix's `Link` and `NavLink` components. These components enhance the browser's default behavior with JavaScript. Without JavaScript, Remix's `Link` and `NavLink` components still render an anchor tag that the browser can work with.

If JavaScript is available, `Link` and `NavLink` perform client-side navigations and fetch loader data and assets from the server without re-requesting the full HTML document. Client-side navigations aim to reduce response times by avoiding downloading the entire HTML document repeatedly.

Remix also supports progressive enhancement for data mutations. When using Remix's `Form` component, we again let Remix enhance the experience. If JavaScript is available, Remix prevents the browser's default behavior and initiates a fetch request to the specified action. However, without JavaScript, we still render a form element that the browser can work with. Remix is capable of falling back to native form submissions.

Remix provides the tools to create highly dynamic but progressively enhanced experiences. When working with progressive enhancement in mind, the first step is to make it work without JavaScript.

Making it work without JavaScript

Making it work without JavaScript lets us keep things simple and take advantage of the browser's default behavior.

There are several reasons why JavaScript might not be available on the client:

- JavaScript is still loading, or React is still hydrating when the user interacts with the page. This frequently happens on slower network connections.

- JavaScript failed to load due to a network error.
- JavaScript failed to be interpreted, executed, or hydrated due to an error in the bundle.
- JavaScript is disabled on the browser by the user.
- JavaScript is not supported in the user's environment.

When our application works without JavaScript, we may be able to reach more people on slower networks or further away from our server locations. We may also be able to better serve assistive technologies that rely on the browser's default behavior.

Starting without JavaScript also ensures that our application logic lives on the server whenever possible, reducing our client bundle size and keeping our client application simple.

There are several ways to disable JavaScript in a Remix app to emulate such an environment. For one, we can disable JavaScript in the browser's developer tools. Alternatively, we can open the `app/root.tsx` file in an editor and remove the `Scripts` component:

```
<body>
  <Outlet />
  <ScrollRestoration />
  <Scripts />
  <LiveReload />
</body>
```

Removing the `Scripts` component removes all script tags from the server-side rendered HTML document. By disabling JavaScript or not loading any JavaScript, we are forced to move logic from the client to our server-side `actions` and `loader` functions. Working with progressive enhancement in mind is a great way to reduce client-side code complexity for the baseline user experience. Once the baseline experience is implemented, we can add client-side JavaScript.

Making it worse before making it better

Once we make it work without JavaScript, we can think about further enhancing the experience with JavaScript. One thing to note is that enabling JavaScript will make the experience worse, not better. By default, the browser indicates page loads by showing a loading spinner in the browser window's title tab. Full page reloads also reset client-side states such as form inputs and revalidate the UI with the latest server data. By preventing the browser's default behavior, we get rid of these features.

If we skip refreshing client-side states, resetting forms, and showing loading indicators during transitions or submissions, the user experience suffers. Therefore, we need to add these features back using JavaScript when we stop the browser from doing its default actions.

Enhancing the User Experience

We already added custom loading indications in *Chapter 4*, *Routing in Remix*. However, whenever we add a new form to our application, we should investigate the experience and see whether additional pending indications are necessary.

Testing on slow networks

Testing on slow networks is a great way to check an application's user experience. It is especially helpful when testing pending states. Take the expense creation form as an example; you might not have noticed the missing loading indication with the application running on your local machine.

Your browser's developer tools offer a toggle to throttle your connection to a preset or custom bandwidth. Setting throttling to **Slow 3G** allows you to test your application in a way not possible when developing on fast Wi-Fi.

Let's test BeeRich on a slow 3G connection:

1. Run BeeRich by executing `npm run dev` in the project's root folder.
2. Make sure JavaScript is enabled in case it was previously disabled.
3. Open the application in your browser.
4. Open the developer tools and navigate to the **Network** tab.
5. Look for the throttling functionality and select **Slow 3G**.
6. Open the expense form in your browser window (`http://localhost:3000/dashboard/expense/`).
7. Fill out the form and click **Submit**.

    Note that the **Submit** button remains active and can be clicked again. It is not perfectly clear to the user that the form is currently being submitted.

8. Open the `dashboard.expenses._index.tsx` route module in your editor.
9. Update the route component so that it uses the `useNavigation` hook to derive the current transition state of our application:

    ```
    import { useNavigation } from '@remix-run/react';

    export default function Component() {
      const navigation = useNavigation();
      const isSubmitting = navigation.state !== 'idle' &&
    navigation.formAction === '/dashboard/expenses/?index';
      return (
        <Form method="POST" action="/dashboard/expenses/?index">
          <Input label="Title:" type="text" name="title" placeholder="Dinner for Two" required />
          <Textarea label="Description:" name="description" />
    ```

```
      <Input label="Amount (in USD):" type="number"
defaultValue={0} name="amount" required />
      <Button type="submit" disabled={isSubmitting} isPrimary>
        {isSubmitting ? 'Creating...' : 'Create'}
      </Button>
    </Form>
  );
}
```

Here, we updated the button text to indicate the ongoing submission. The altered text communicates the loading state to the user. We also disabled the **Submit** button on submission. This helps us avoid accidental re-submits.

Note that we ensure that the current submission (if any) submits a form to this form's action by using the navigation object's `formAction` property. We only want to show the pending UI for this form if this form is being submitted.

10. Test the new pending UI with the throttled network connection.

Notice how our changes to the **Submit** button enhance the experience. Submitting the expense creation form on a slow connection may take a few moments. Now, we have a clear loading indication.

Progressive enhancement is about making an application accessible to as many users as possible. Working with progressive enhancement in mind ensures that the baseline user experience stays simple enough to be used on older browsers and devices.

It turns out that building with progressive enhancement in mind creates a simpler mental model for building great user interfaces. First, we create the baseline implementation without JavaScript. Once the baseline implementation works, we focus on enhancing the experience with JavaScript. We test the application by throttling the network. This forces us to build a resilient user experience that scales up and down. Remix supports us by providing primitives and conventions that let us make additive changes to enhance the experience until we are satisfied.

We're just getting started! Remix can scale up to highly dynamic experiences. Next, we'll learn how to prefetch data with Remix to reduce page transition times.

Prefetching data

In this section, we will learn how to prefetch assets and loader data in Remix and how to utilize prefetching to speed up transition times.

Remix compiles the `routes` folder into a routing hierarchy at build time. The hierarchy information is stored in an asset manifest in the `public` folder. This asset manifest is used by both Remix's frontend and backend applications.

Since Remix has access to the asset manifest on the client, Remix knows in advance which `loader` functions to call to transition to a route. This allows Remix to prefetch loader data (and route assets) before the transition.

Enabling prefetching in Remix is as easy as setting a prop on the link we want to prefetch data for:

1. Open the `/app/routes/dashboard.tsx` file in your editor.
2. Add the `prefetch` property to the **Income** and **Expenses** navigation links:

```
<ul className="mt-10 w-full flex flex-row gap-5">
  <li className="ml-auto">
    <NavLink
      to={firstInvoice ? `/dashboard/income/${firstInvoice.id}`
        : '/dashboard/income'}
      prefetch="intent"
    >
      Income
    </NavLink>
  </li>
  <li className="mr-auto">
    <NavLink
      to={firstExpense ? `/dashboard/expenses/${firstExpense.id}` : '/dashboard/expenses'}
      prefetch="intent"
    >
      Expenses
    </NavLink>
  </li>
</ul>
```

The optional `prefetch` property of Remix's `Link` and `NavLink` components can be set to one of the following four values:

- `none`
- `render`
- `intent`
- `viewport`

By default, `prefetch` is set to `none`, which means data and assets won't be prefetched for this link. If `prefetch` is set to `render`, then the loader data and assets for the link are fetched once this link is rendered on the page. If `prefetch` is set to `viewport`, then Remix starts prefetching once the link is within the user's viewport on the screen. If `prefetch` is set to `intent`, then Remix starts prefetching once the user focuses or hovers over the link; that is, the user shows an intent to use the link. For now, we will set `prefetch` to `intent`.

3. Visit the income overview page (http://localhost:3000/dashboard/income) in your browser window.
4. Open the **Network** tab of your developer tools.
5. Clear the list of requests and filter for **All** requests.
6. Now, hover over the **Expenses** link in the navigation.
7. Inspect the **Network** tab. It should now list four prefetch requests, as visible in *Figure 6.1*:

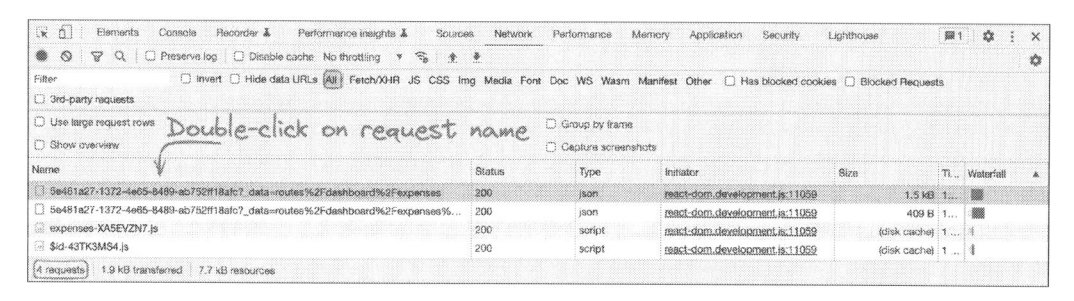

Figure 6.1 – Inspecting prefetch requests

A transition to /dashboard/expenses/$id from the income route matches the following route modules:

- dashboard.tsx
- dashboard.expenses.tsx
- dashboard.expenses.$id.tsx

The dashboard.tsx route module is already active on the page, and there is no need to reload it. Remix only loads assets and loader data for the other two route modules. We can see four prefetch requests in *Figure 6.1*. There are two requests of the JSON content type to fetch the required loader data and two requests to fetch the code-split JavaScript bundles of the two new route modules.

8. Inspect the requests by clicking on them in the **Network** tab. This should open a request detail view. Inspect the nested **Preview** and **Response** tabs. The JSON responses contain the loader data of the two route modules.

Prefetching data is optional. With prefetching, we pull a lever to reduce request times but introduce a risk of fetching unnecessary data if the user does not visit the link.

Prefetching on render is the most aggressive strategy while prefetching on intent is based on the user's actions on the page.

> **Remix provides levers**
>
> Prefetching is a lever we can pull. Using prefetching reduces response times by increasing the risk of downloading unnecessary data over the network. Remix allows us to optimize our application for our use cases and requirements by providing levers.

Now that we've learned about prefetching, let's dive deeper into mutations.

Working with action data

The `loader` and `action` functions contain most of the business logic of our Remix application. This is where we fetch, filter, and update data. Both functions must return a `Response` object. You know about the `redirect` and `json` helper functions, which let us create specific `Response` objects, and you have already practiced working with loader data. In this section, we will learn how to work with action data. For that, we will update the expense details view and implement an edit expense form:

1. Open the `dashboard.expenses.$id.tsx` route module in your editor.

2. Take the current code from `dashboard.expenses._index.tsx`. Can you modify the code to edit an existing expense? Give it a try!

   The final code for this chapter is available in the `/bee-rich/solution` folder on GitHub for this chapter. As we move forward, we'll help you align your work with this final solution.

3. Make sure to update the form's `action` property using the `expense` object from the loader data:

   ```
   <Form method="POST" action={`/dashboard/expenses/${expense.id}`}
   ```

4. If you haven't already, update the `isSubmitting` constant's `formAction` check:

   ```
   const navigation = useNavigation();
   const isSubmitting = navigation.state !== 'idle' && navigation.formAction === `/dashboard/expenses/${expense.id}`;
   ```

   We again use the `useNavigation` hook to compute whether we should add pending indications to the form. Note that, again, we ensure that the submitted form action matches this form's `action` property.

5. Next, update the route component's form fields:

   ```
   <Input label="Title:" type="text" name="title" defaultValue={expense.title} required />
   <Textarea label="Description:" name="description" defaultValue={expense.description || ''} />
   <Input label="Amount (in USD):" type="number" defaultValue={expense.amount} name="amount" required />
   <Button type="submit" name="intent" value="update" disabled={isSubmitting} isPrimary>
     {isSubmitting ? 'Save...' : 'Save'}
   ```

```
          </Button>
```

We use the `defaultValue` property to set the form's initial values. Compare this to setting the `value` property, which also requires us to register `onChange` event handlers and work with React states. Since we use Remix's `Form` component, we don't need to keep track of the input field value changes, which greatly simplifies our client-side code.

Note that we added `name` and `value` properties to the **Submit** button. We can use a button to contain form data. This is convenient if we want to handle several different actions with the same `action` function. We use the `intent` value on the server to know which action to execute.

6. Next, add React's `key` property to the `Form` component to ensure that React reconstructs the content of the form every time we transition between different expense details pages:

   ```
   <Form method="POST" action={`/dashboard/expenses/${expense.id}`}
   key={expense.id}>
   ```

   This is necessary to distinguish different expense forms. Without this change, React may not reset the `defaultValue` value of the input fields when loading a new expense details page.

   To better understand this, remove the `key` property and navigate between different expenses. You will see that the form does not update with the new expense data if we don't tell React that each form is unique based on the expense identifier.

7. Add the following `action` function to the route module:

   ```
   import type { ActionFunctionArgs, LoaderFunctionArgs } from '@
   remix-run/node';

   export async function action({ params, request }:
   ActionFunctionArgs) {
     const { id } = params;
     if (!id) throw Error('id route parameter must be defined');

     const formData = await request.formData();
     const intent = formData.get('intent');
     if (intent === 'delete') {
       // up in the next section!
     }
     if (intent === 'update') {
       return updateExpense(formData, id);
     }
     throw new Response('Bad request', { status: 400 });
   }
   ```

   We use the `$id` route parameter to decide which expense to update. Furthermore, we throw an error if the route parameter is not defined.

We utilize the value on the **Submit** button to specify which action we want to execute. This way, we can handle several different form submissions with the same `action` function.

As you can see, we will add a deletion action in the next section. For now, let's focus on the update functionality.

8. Add the missing `updateExpense` function to the route module file:

    ```
    async function updateExpense(formData: FormData, id: string):
    Promise<Response> {
      const title = formData.get('title');
      const description = formData.get('description');
      const amount = formData.get('amount');
      if (typeof title !== 'string' || typeof description !==
    'string' || typeof amount !== 'string') {
        throw Error('something went wrong');
      }
      const amountNumber = Number.parseFloat(amount);
      if (Number.isNaN(amountNumber)) {
        throw Error('something went wrong');
      }
      await db.expense.update({
        where: { id },
        data: { title, description, amount: amountNumber },
      });
      return json({ success: true });
    }
    ```

    Like the create expense action, we validate the user's input and then use the database client to persist the changes. However, this time, instead of redirecting the user, we return JSON data in the `action` function. Like in `loader` functions, we can return JSON data in `action` functions. This is useful when communicating error or success states to the user after the mutation.

    In this case, we return a success state after successfully updating the expense.

9. Import the `useActionData` hook:

    ```
    import { useActionData, useLoaderData, useNavigation } from '@
    remix-run/react';
    ```

10. Call `useActionData` in the route module's component to access the return data of `action`:

    ```
    const actionData = useActionData<typeof action>();
    ```

    We infer the type of the action data by using the `typeof` operator. Note that action data – unlike loader data – can be undefined.

11. Use the action data to display a success message below the **Submit** button:

    ```
    <Button type="submit" name="intent" value="update"
    disabled={isSubmitting} isPrimary>
      {isSubmitting ? 'Save...' : 'Save'}
    </Button>
    <p aria-live="polite" className="text-green-600">
      {actionData?.success && 'Changes saved!'}
    </p>
    ```

    Whenever the `action` data is present and the `success` property is `true`, we will show the user a **Changes saved!** message.

12. Run the app and test out the updated expense form!

Awesome! Just like that, we can leverage `action` data to communicate successful mutations. Make sure you implement the same functionality on the `income` routes. Try to adapt the income route modules without looking at the instructions. This will help you better understand the lessons of this chapter. If you get stuck, review the instructions of this chapter. You can also find the solution code for this chapter on GitHub.

> **Use useActionData only within the same route module**
>
> Note that a form submission creates a navigation to the location of the `action` function. `useLoaderData` can only access loader data of the same route's loader. Similarly, `useActionData` must be used in the route module of the `action` function that the form submits to.

Remix also provides advanced data mutation utilities. Next, we'll add the ability to delete expenses and learn how to handle concurrent mutations in Remix.

Handling concurrent mutations

So far, we have created expense creation and edit forms. Both forms are standalone on their respective pages. This section will teach you how to manage multiple form submissions simultaneously. Let's start by adding a deletion form to every item in the expense overview list.

Adding a form to a list

The goal of this section is to add a deletion form to every list item in the expense overview list. Clicking the item should delete the associated expense. Let's get started:

1. If you haven't already, follow the instructions in the `README.md` file of this chapter on GitHub: `https://github.com/PacktPublishing/Full-Stack-Web-Development-with-Remix/blob/main/06-enhancing-the-user-experience/bee-rich/README.md`.

The `README.md` file includes instructions for how to update the `ListLinkItem` component for this chapter.

2. Next, open the `dashboard.expenses.$id.tsx` route module.

3. Add a `deleteExpense` function to the route module:

   ```
   async function deleteExpense(request: Request, id: string):
   Promise<Response> {
     const referer = request.headers.get('referer');
     const redirectPath = referer || '/dashboard/expenses';

     try {
       await db.expense.delete({ where: { id } });
     } catch (err) {
       throw new Response('Not found', { status: 404 });
     }

     if (redirectPath.includes(id)) {
       return redirect('/dashboard/expenses');
     }
     return redirect(redirectPath);
   }
   ```

   When submitting a deletion request, the `action` URL (`request.url`) contains the `id` parameter of the expense that should be deleted. However, that may not be the expense that's currently displayed in the details route module. We use the `referer` header to derive the route from which the form was submitted. The goal is to keep the user on the current route unless the current route is the details page of the expense that is being deleted. This ensures that deletion does not navigate the user away from the current page unless the current expense is deleted.

4. Call the newly created `deleteExpense` function in the `action` function:

   ```
   if (intent === 'delete') {
     return deleteExpense(request, id);
   }
   ```

5. Inspect the code of the `ListLinkItem` component in `/app/components/links.tsx`.

   The updated `ListLinkItem` component renders a delete (**X**) button if the `deleteProps` property is provided. The **Submit** button also carries `name` and `value` properties to specify the type of `action` function to perform.

6. Next, open the `dashboard.expenses.tsx` file in your editor and pass the `deleteProps` property to the `ListLinkItem` component:

   ```
   <ListLinkItem
     key={expense.id}
   ```

```
      to={`/dashboard/expenses/${expense.id}`}
      deleteProps={{
        ariaLabel: `Delete expense ${expense.title}`,
        action: `/dashboard/expenses/${expense.id}`,
      }}
    >
      ...
    </ListLinkItem>
```

We now render a form for every expense item in the expense list.

7. Let's also add an indication about which list item is currently active in the details view. Import `useParams` from Remix inside the `dashboard.expenses.tsx` route module:

```
import { Outlet, useLoaderData, useNavigation, useParams } from
'@remix-run/react';
```

The `useParams` hook can be used to access route parameters on the client. We use this hook to calculate the `isActive` property of the `ListLinkItem` component.

8. Use the `useParams` hook in the route module component to access the `id` route parameter of the expense details page:

```
const { id } = useParams();
```

9. Add the `isActive` property to the `ListLinkItem` component:

```
<ListLinkItem
  key={expense.id}
  to={`/dashboard/expenses/${expense.id}`}
  isActive={expense.id === id}
  deleteProps={{
    ariaLabel: `Delete expense ${expense.title}`,
    action: `/dashboard/expenses/${expense.id}`,
  }}
>
  ...
</ListLinkItem>
```

Earlier, the `ListLinkItem` component used the `NavLink` component's `isActive` parameter from the `className` property to update the styling. The new implementation requires custom logic as the `ListLinkItem` component now renders more than just a `NavLink`. We use the `useParam` hook to access the current `id` parameter and then derive whether the `href` attribute of `ListLinkItem` points to the currently displayed expense.

10. Let's try out our implementation. Run the app locally, visit the expense overview page, and delete an expense object by clicking the **X** button.

The `action` function handles the submission and redirects the user back to the current page or the expense overview page. After the mutation, Remix refetches the loader data, which triggers a re-render. The expense object disappears from the expenses list.

Great! Each list item in the expenses list now contains a form to delete an expense. Next, let's indicate pending states on deletion.

Supporting multiple pending states

We already know that we can use the `useNavigation` hook to access the global navigation object. The navigation object's state property indicates the current transition state of our app. Let's use the `useNavigation` hook to indicate pending deletion for the deletion forms:

1. Import `useNavigation` in `/app/components/links.tsx`:

   ```
   import { Form, Link as RemixLink, NavLink as RemixNavLink,
     useNavigation } from '@remix-run/react';
   ```

2. Next, use the hook to access the navigation object inside the `ListLinkItem` function body:

   ```
   const navigation = useNavigation();
   ```

3. Derive whether the form is currently submitting or loading:

   ```
   const isSubmitting =
     navigation.state !== 'idle' &&
     navigation.formAction === deleteProps?.action &&
     navigation.formData?.get('intent') === 'delete';
   ```

   Note that we are playing extra safe here. We check whether there is currently a page navigation happening and whether `formAction` matches this form's `action` function. Finally, we also make sure that the form's `intent` value matches this form's submit button's `intent` value. This ensures that we only show the pending state if this delete button is clicked.

4. Finally, use `isSubmitting` to disable the **Submit** button and indicate the pending submission conditionally:

   ```
   <button
     type="submit"
     aria-label={deleteProps.ariaLabel}
     name="intent"
     value="delete"
     disabled={isSubmitting}
     className={
       isSubmitting
         ? 'animate-spin duration-1000'
   ```

```
            : 'hover:text-primary focus:text-primary dark:hover:text-
   darkPrimary dark:focus:text-darkPrimary'
    }
 >
```

We disable the delete button and showcase a spinner animation if `isSubmitting` is `true`. Based on our previous experience with the navigation object, this should suffice. Let's test it out and see it in action.

5. Run the application in development mode and open `http://localhost:3000/dashboard/expenses` in a browser window.

6. Open the **Network** tab of the browser developer tools and set throttling to **Slow 3G**. This helps us experience the pending UI for longer. Also, make sure to filter by **Fetch/XHR** requests.

7. Try deleting several expenses at once to see whether you spot any issues.

   You may notice a flaw in the current implementation: deleting an expense seems to cancel all other ongoing deletions.

Can you reason why this is the case? Remix's navigation object captures the global navigation state of our application. There can only be one page navigation at a time. If the user submits a second form, then Remix cancels the first navigation, as visible in *Figure 6.2*. The navigation object is updated, reflecting the second form submission:

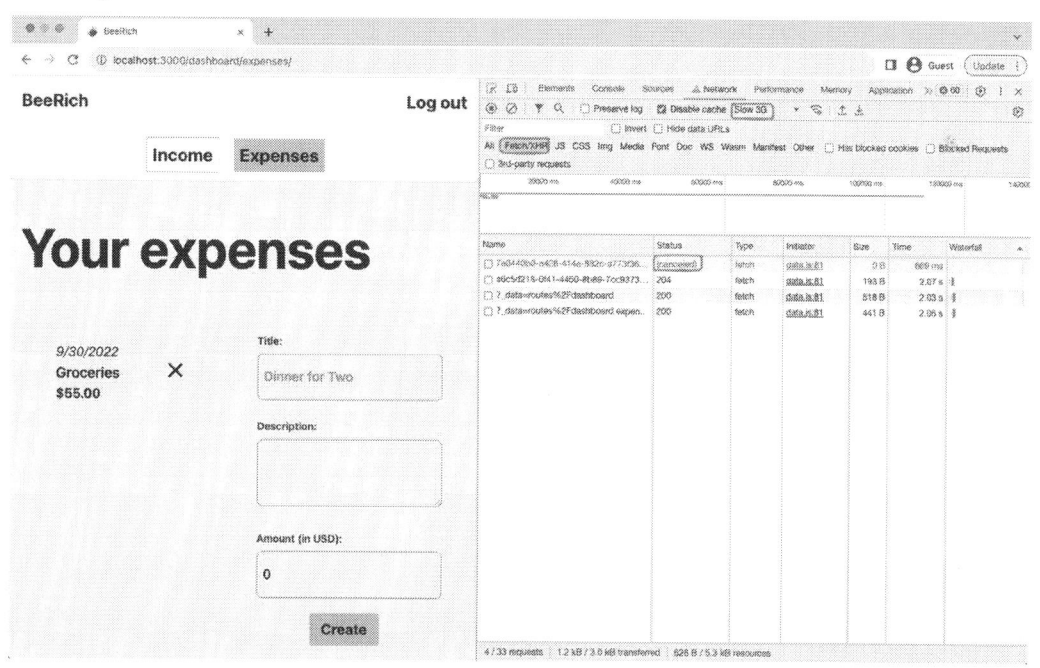

Figure 6.2 – Canceling fetch requests

Note that the deletions are not aborted; we only lose the pending indications. On the client, Remix cancels the current submission and updates the navigation object accordingly. However, the fetch request to delete the expense still reaches the server, and the action is performed. Remix also ensures that the loader data is only revalidated after every submission has been executed to avoid stale data in case the latest submission finishes faster than previous submissions.

> **Remix tracks all ongoing submissions but only handles the last navigation**
>
> Remember that Remix aims to emulate the browser's default behavior. There can only ever be one page navigation. On concurrent form submissions, the last user action determines the final page navigation. In the background, Remix keeps track of all ongoing submissions to manage loader data revalidation.

Let's fix the lost pending indications. We want to show the pending UI for every currently pending deletion. Luckily, Remix provides us with another way to declare a form. Remix's `useFetcher` hook can declare a `Form` component with an isolated submission state:

1. Import `useFetcher`, replacing the `useNavigation` and `Form` imports, in in `/app/components/links.tsx`:

    ```
    import { Link as RemixLink, NavLink as RemixNavLink, useFetcher
    } from '@remix-run/react';
    ```

2. Replace the `useNavigation` hook declaration in the `ListLinkItem` component with a call to `useFetcher`:

    ```
    const fetcher = useFetcher();
    ```

3. Next, update the assignment of the `isSubmitting` constant:

    ```
    const isSubmitting = fetcher.state !== 'idle';
    ```

    The fetcher object that's returned from `useFetcher` has an isolated submission lifecycle and navigation state. The state is unaffected by other submissions or loading activities in the app.

    Note that a `useFetcher` form submission still triggers all active `loader` functions to reload after mutation. This sets the global navigation state to `loading`. However, a `useFetcher` form submission does not set the global navigation object's state to `submitting`.

4. Replace Form with `fetcher.Form`:

    ```
    <fetcher.Form className="p-8 ml-auto" method="POST"
    action={deleteProps.action}>
      ...
    </fetcher.Form>
    ```

A `useFetcher` object provides several different ways to fetch and mutate data. It offers a `load` function to fetch data from a `loader` outside the app's navigation lifecycle. It also offers a `submit` function to call an `action` function programmatically. Finally, `useFetcher` also provides a `Form` component.

There are plenty of use cases for `useFetcher`. Here, we use the hook to create isolated forms for every item in a list.

Since `useFetcher` is a hook, we must follow React's rules for hooks. When working with a list and `useFetcher`, we must declare a new `useFetcher` object for each list element. This ensures that each item has its own navigation state. Usually, this is done by creating a list item component where each list item manages its `useFetcher` object. Conveniently, we are already doing this with the `ListLinkItem` component.

5. Now, create a few expenses using the expense creation form.
6. Open the developer tools and navigate to the **Network** tab.
7. Throttle to **Slow 3G**.
8. Filter for **Fetch/XHR** requests.
9. Now, click the delete (**X**) button of a few expenses as quickly as possible.

   Now, we can create an expense and delete several expenses simultaneously, and it will show the loading spinners correctly for each pending form.

   Note that Remix no longer cancels the previous submission when using `useFetcher`.

> **Loading and mutating data without page navigations with `useFetcher`**
>
> Data mutations through the `Form` component navigate the user to the `action` function's location. This is the browser's default behavior for form submissions.
>
> The `useFetcher` hook allows us to load and mutate data without triggering page navigations; `useFetcher` has an isolated navigation state and does not trigger page navigations if JavaScript is loaded.

One thing to note is that `useFetcher` still honors redirect responses from `action` functions. Also, in case JavaScript is not available, `useFetcher.Form` falls back to the native form element's behavior.

There are plenty of use cases for `useFetcher`. You can read more about `useFetcher` in the Remix documentation: `https://remix.run/docs/en/2/hooks/use-fetcher`.

Next, practice what you've learned and use the updated `ListLinkItem` component for the `income` routes. This will help you study this section's newly introduced concepts.

Amazing! We've covered much ground in this chapter.

Please note that we are currently facing an issue with our user experience. If you are on an expense details page (`dashboard/expenses/$id`) and quickly delete all expenses in one go, you may end up on a not found page. We will address this issue together in the next chapter, *Chapter 7, Error Handling in Remix*.

Summary

In this chapter, we learned about progressive enhancement. Progressive enhancement is a design philosophy that aims to create a baseline user experience for users on older devices and browsers.

You learned that Remix's primitives work with and without JavaScript. This allows us to progressively enhance the experience and make our application accessible to more users. By building with progressive enhancement in mind, we ensure a simple but resilient experience for as many devices and browsers as possible. Once we ensure a baseline experience, we can enhance the experience with JavaScript.

Next, you learned that Remix can scale both up and down. We can start simple and even disable JavaScript, but by making additive changes, we can create highly dynamic experiences with concurrent mutations, data revalidation, and prefetching.

Remix provides levers to optimize the experience for what is important to us. We can decide how aggressively we want to prefetch data by setting the `prefetch` property to `render`, `viewport`, `intent`, or `none`. You further learned about action data, which can be used to communicate error or success states after a mutation.

Finally, you learned how Remix manages concurrent form submissions. You know that there can only ever be one active page navigation. Remix cancels all pending navigations and updates the global navigation object accordingly.

If we want to manage concurrent pending indications and isolated action data, then we can use Remix's `useFetcher` hook. This can be used to programmatically submit forms, but also offers a `useFetcher.Form` component that does not trigger a page navigation if JavaScript is available.

The `useFetcher` hook is especially useful to allow the submission of several forms concurrently while communicating the pending state of each of them in parallel. This is usually the case when rendering a list of forms, as we saw with the expense overview list in BeeRich.

In the next chapter, we will focus on handling errors and see how we can use Remix to provide a great user experience, even when something goes wrong.

Further reading

The Remix team has created an amazing video series called Remix Singles that goes in depth into how to work with data in Remix. I recommend that you watch the entire series. Most notably for this chapter, the series has a video about concurrent mutations with `useFetcher` that you can find here: `https://www.youtube.com/watch?v=vTzNpiOk668&list=PLXoynULbYuEDG2wBFSZ66b85EIspy3fy6`.

The Remix documentation includes a page about progressive enhancement: `https://remix.run/docs/en/2/discussion/progressive-enhancement`

You can also read more about progressive enhancement in the MDN Web Docs: `https://developer.mozilla.org/en-US/docs/Glossary/Progressive_Enhancement`.

You can find more information about the `useFetcher` hook in the Remix documentation: `https://remix.run/docs/en/2/hooks/use-fetcher`.

7
Error Handling in Remix

Error handling is an important part of building resilient user experiences. We can distinguish two kinds of errors:

- Unexpected errors, such as network timeouts
- Expected failures (exceptions) thrown on purpose

Remix provides primitives and conventions to handle both unexpected and expected errors uniformly. This chapter covers the following topics:

- Dealing with unexpected errors
- Handling thrown responses
- Handling page-not-found (404) errors

First, we will fabricate some unexpected errors and learn how to handle them. Next, we will review the difference between returning and throwing `Response` objects in `loader` and `action` functions. We will see how we can handle thrown responses with Remix's `ErrorBoundary`. Finally, we will add not-found error handling to BeeRich.

After reading this chapter, you will understand how to manage both unexpected and expected failures in Remix declaratively using Remix's `ErrorBoundary` component. You will also know how throwing responses fits into Remix's exception-handling story and know the difference between throwing and returning responses. Finally, you will know how to handle not-found errors with Remix.

Technical requirements

You can go ahead and use the solution from the previous chapter. No additional setup steps are required for this chapter. If you get stuck, you can find the solution code for this chapter here: https://github.com/PacktPublishing/Full-Stack-Web-Development-with-Remix/tree/main/07-error-handling-in-remix.

Dealing with unexpected errors

During runtime, a Remix application is executed both in the browser and on the server. A lot can go wrong, and unexpected errors can happen both on the client and server. It is important to consider the error case to provide a resilient user experience. In this section, we will investigate how to handle unexpected errors in Remix both at the root level and in nested routes.

Invoking client and server errors

In *Chapter 2, Creating a New Remix App*, we provided a troubleshooting guide and investigated how Remix handles errors on both the client and server uniformly. Let's review Remix's default error handling again by invoking some "unexpected" errors:

1. Open your BeeRich application in an editor.
2. Open the `dashboard.tsx` route module inside the `app/routes` folder.
3. Add the following code inside the `loader` function body before the return statement:

    ```
    throw Error('Something went wrong!');
    ```

    By throwing an error in a `loader` function, we prevent the application from handling incoming requests. This creates an unexpected failure on the server.

4. Execute `npm run dev` in a terminal to run the app.
5. Visit the BeeRich dashboard by opening `http://localhost:3000/dashboard` in a new browser window.

    Throwing an error in a `loader` function renders Remix's error page, as visible in *Figure 7.1*:

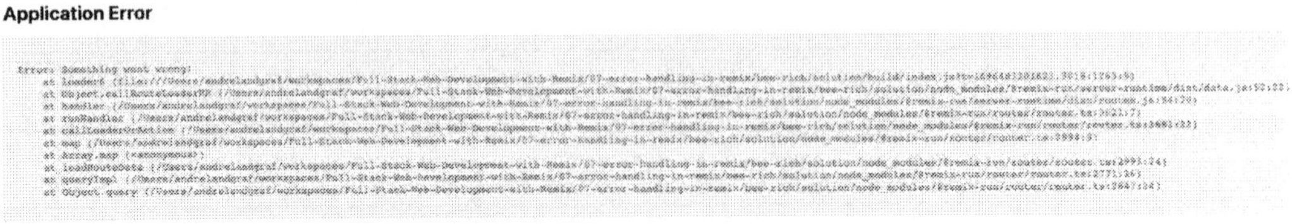

Figure 7.1 – Application error in the loader function

Figure 7.1 showcases Remix's default behavior when handling unexpected errors. We can see our error message stating "Something went wrong!" on the screen and the stack trace of the `loader` function that failed to execute.

6. Now, let's throw an error in a route component. Move the error from the `loader` function inside the `dashboard.tsx` route component:

    ```
    export default function Component() {
      throw Error('Something went wrong!');
    ```

7. Refresh the browser window.

   By reloading the page, we trigger a full-page reload. Remix handles initial document requests on the server. Hence, the dashboard route module component is first called on the server, and we again throw an error on the server.

   The error stack trace changes, but Remix still displays "Something went wrong!" on the screen.

8. Now, wrap the error inside a `useEffect` hook to ensure that the error is executed on the client instead:

   ```
   import { useEffect } from 'react';

   export default function Component() {
     useEffect(() => {
       throw Error('Something went wrong!');
     }, []);
   ```

   React's `useEffect` hook only executes on the client, not the server. This is because the hook is executed after the initial render, and on the server, we only render once.

9. Refresh the browser window one more time. You should see yet another stack trace on the page. This time, the stack trace originates from client-side scripts.

   As visible in *Figure 7.2*, notice that the filenames in the stack trace include hashes. This means the files have been bundled and are part of the client bundle:

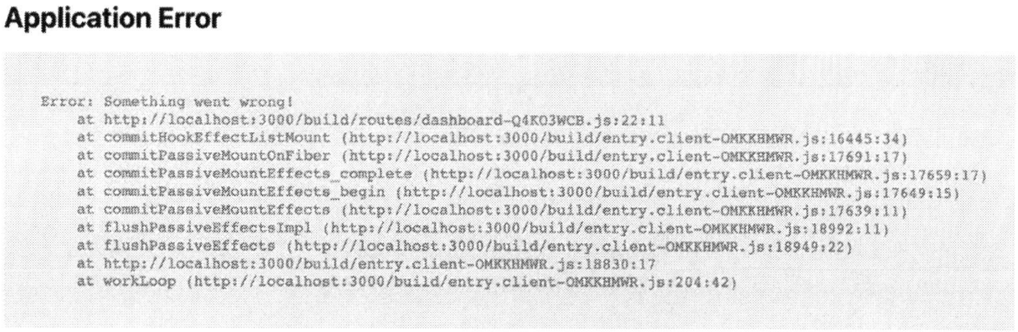

Application Error

```
Error: Something went wrong!
    at http://localhost:3000/build/routes/dashboard-Q4KO3WCB.js:22:11
    at commitHookEffectListMount (http://localhost:3000/build/entry.client-OMKKHMWR.js:16445:34)
    at commitPassiveMountOnFiber (http://localhost:3000/build/entry.client-OMKKHMWR.js:17691:17)
    at commitPassiveMountEffects_complete (http://localhost:3000/build/entry.client-OMKKHMWR.js:17659:17)
    at commitPassiveMountEffects_begin (http://localhost:3000/build/entry.client-OMKKHMWR.js:17649:15)
    at commitPassiveMountEffects (http://localhost:3000/build/entry.client-OMKKHMWR.js:17639:11)
    at flushPassiveEffectsImpl (http://localhost:3000/build/entry.client-OMKKHMWR.js:18992:11)
    at flushPassiveEffects (http://localhost:3000/build/entry.client-OMKKHMWR.js:18949:22)
    at http://localhost:3000/build/entry.client-OMKKHMWR.js:18830:17
    at workLoop (http://localhost:3000/build/entry.client-OMKKHMWR.js:204:42)
```

Figure 7.2 – Application error on the client

This experiment tells us that Remix provides the same default experience for both browser and server errors. Next, let's replace Remix's default error page with custom UIs.

Handling errors with the root error boundary

In React, failures during rendering can be handled through error boundaries. Error boundaries are class components that implement the error boundary life cycle methods. Remix builds on top of React's error boundaries and extends its capabilities to handle server-side errors. Instead of nesting React error boundaries inside our component tree, we declare them through Remix's route module API by exporting an `ErrorBoundary` component in our route modules.

The `ErrorBoundary` component in the `root.tsx` route module is the topmost error boundary of our application. To replace Remix's default error page, we need to export an `ErrorBoundary` component from `root.tsx`:

1. Open the `app/root.tsx` route module in your editor.
2. Import the `useRouteError` hook from Remix:

    ```
    import {
      Links,
      LiveReload,
      Meta,
      Outlet,
      Scripts,
      ScrollRestoration,
      useRouteError,
    } from '@remix-run/react';
    ```

3. Export a new React component named `ErrorBoundary` and add the following code to it:

    ```
    import { H1 } from './components/headings';
    import { ButtonLink } from './components/links';

    export function ErrorBoundary() {
      const error = useRouteError();
      let errorMessage = error instanceof Error ? error.message : null;
      return (
        <section className="m-5 lg:m-20 flex flex-col gap-5">
          <H1>Unexpected Error</H1>
          <p>We are very sorry. An unexpected error occurred. Please
            try again or contact us if the problem persists.</p>
          {errorMessage && (
            <div className="border-4 border-red-500 p-10">
              <p>Error message: {errorMessage}</p>
            </div>
          )}
          <ButtonLink to="/" isPrimary>
    ```

```
            Back to homepage
        </ButtonLink>
      </section>
    );
}
```

The `ErrorBoundary` component is part of Remix's route API and replaces the route module component in case of an error. We can access the error that caused the failure by calling `useRouteError`. We further use the error object to display an error message.

4. Fabricate an unexpected error and refresh the browser window to inspect the updated error page:

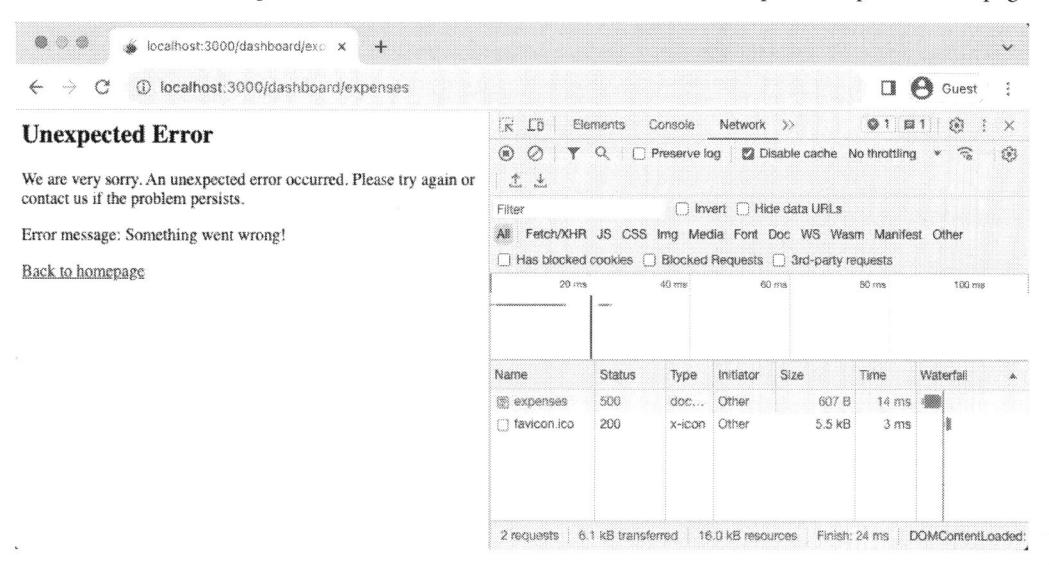

Figure 7.3 – Custom root ErrorBoundary component

As visible in *Figure 7.3*, we now render a custom error page for our application.

5. Investigate the code of the `ErrorBoundary` component in `root.tsx`. Notice that we render our styled `H1` and `ButtonLink` components. Why are our custom styles not applied to the page?

6. Review the **Network** tab, as visible in *Figure 7.3*. Note that we are not loading a stylesheet or any client-side JavaScript. Why is that?

Remix exposes the `Meta`, `Links`, and `Scripts` components to append our meta and link tags and the client-side JavaScript scripts to the HTML document. This happens in the route module component in `root.tsx`. However, on error, we do not render the route module component but the `ErrorBoundary` component.

Remix wraps the content of our error boundary in an HTML body tag by default. However, we can also provide a custom HTML document. Let's update the code so that we render the `Meta`, `Links`, and `Scripts` components in the `root.tsx` file's `ErrorBoundary` component.

7. Create a new `Document` component in `root.tsx` so that we can reuse code between the `App` and `ErrorBoundary` components:

   ```
   function Document({ children }: { children: React.ReactNode }) {
     return (
       <html lang="en">
         <head>
           <meta charSet="utf-8" />
           <meta name="viewport" content="width=device-
             width,initial-scale=1" />
           <Meta />
           <Links />
         </head>
         <body className="bg-background dark:bg-darkBackground
           text-lg text-text dark:text-darkText">
           <PageTransitionProgressBar />
           {children}
           <ScrollRestoration />
           <Scripts />
           <LiveReload />
         </body>
       </html>
     );
   }
   ```

   The reusable `Document` component renders the JSX from the `App` component. We just replaced `Outlet` with `children`.

8. Now, update the App component so that it uses `Document`:

   ```
   export default function App() {
     return (
       <Document>
         <Outlet />
       </Document>
     );
   }
   ```

   The content of the App component remains unchanged. We just moved the code into the reusable Document component.

9. Next, wrap the content of the error boundary inside the Document component as well:

```
export function ErrorBoundary() {
  const error = useRouteError();
  let errorMessage = error instanceof Error ? error.message :
   null;
  return (
    <Document>...</Document>
  );
}
```

By using our custom Document component, the error boundary now includes our application's scripts, stylesheets, and custom html and head elements:

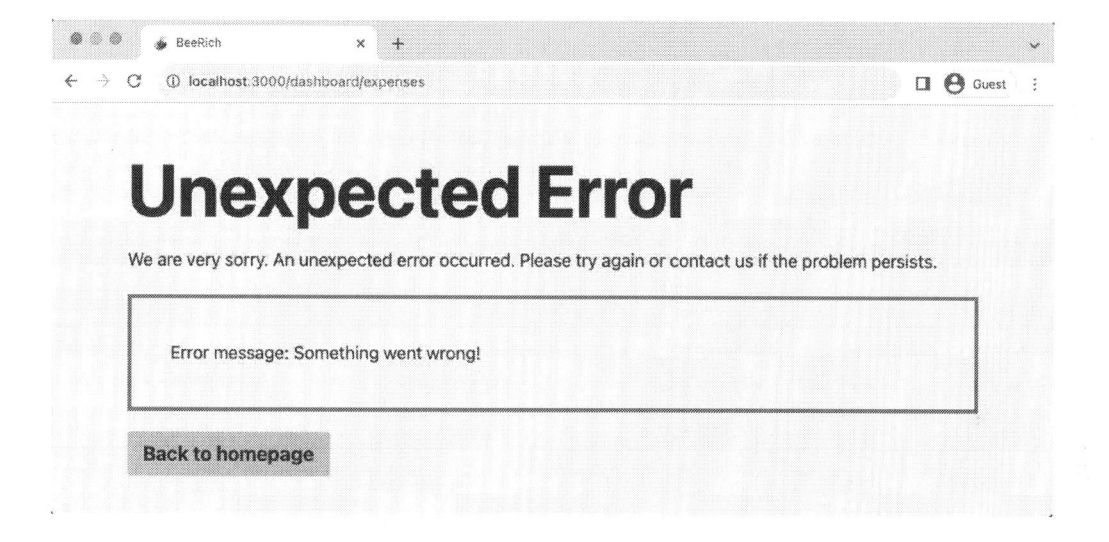

Figure 7.4 – Styled root ErrorBoundary component

Amazing! Now, we can utilize client-side JavaScript and our custom styles in the root ErrorBoundary component. One thing that we must keep in mind when reusing components for our ErrorBoundary component is that we can't call the useLoaderData hook. Be sure not to render components that access loader data, as loader data is not defined when the ErrorBoundary component is rendered.

> **Error boundaries don't have access to useLoaderData**
>
> An error boundary is rendered if an error occurs within the loader or action function of the route module. Conclusively, loader data is not available in the error boundary.

The top-level `ErrorBoundary` component in BeeRich does not render any navigation bar or other layout components. Keeping the top-level `ErrorBoundary` component simple ensures that it renders even in the case of an unexpected failure.

Next, let's see how we can improve error handling further by declaring nested error boundaries.

Nested error handling

Error boundaries can be nested. When an error is thrown, it bubbles upward through the route hierarchy until Remix finds the nearest error boundary. Nested error boundaries let us contain errors.

Let's add a nested error boundary to the dashboard route module:

1. Open the `dashboard.tsx` route module inside the `app/routes` folder.
2. Add a simple `ErrorBoundary` export to the page:

   ```
   export function ErrorBoundary() {
     return <p>Error contained in dashboard.tsx</p>;
   }
   ```

3. Now, throw an error in the `dashboard.tsx` route module's `loader` function:

   ```
   throw Error('Something went wrong!');
   ```

4. Run the app and visit the dashboard by opening `http://localhost:3000/dashboard` in a new browser window.

   Note that we are not rendering the root error boundary but the one nested in `dashboard.tsx`. Remix uses the closest error boundary available and renders it within the parent route component's `Outlet`.

5. Let's make the error boundary look nice. Like we did in `root.tsx`, we want to share markup between the `ErrorBoundary` component and the route component. Refactor the route component so that it's a reusable `Layout` component. First, remove `export default` from the function definition and add a `LayoutProps` type to specify the properties the component expects:

   ```
   import type { Expense, Invoice } from '@prisma/client';
   import type { SerializeFrom } from '@remix-run/node';

   type LayoutProps = {
     children: React.ReactNode;
     firstExpense: SerializeFrom<Expense> | null;
     firstInvoice: SerializeFrom<Invoice> | null;
   };
   ```

```
function Layout({ firstExpense, firstInvoice, children }:
LayoutProps) {
  ...
}
```

The new `Layout` component expects three props: React `children`, `firstExpense`, and `firstInvoice`. To type the props correctly, we wrap the `Expense` and `Invoice` types from Prisma with Remix's `SerializeFrom` type.

Prisma (our database ORM) generates the `Expense` and `Invoice` types based on our Prisma database schema. Remix's `SerializeFrom` type transforms the `Expense` and `Invoice` types into their serialized versions. This is necessary as the data travels over the network, serialized as JSON. For instance, the `createdAt` field is of the `Date` type on the server but serialized as `string` once accessed via `useLoaderData`.

6. Remove the `useLoaderData` call from the `Layout` function body. Since error boundaries cannot call `useLoaderData`, we must pass the loader data as optional props. As visible in `LayoutProps`, we ensure that the `Layout` component also accepts `null` as a value for `firstExpense` and `firstInvoice`. This can be the case if we don't find any expenses or invoices in our database or when the error boundary is rendered.

7. Replace the rendering of `Outlet` with `children`:

   ```
   <main className="p-4 w-full flex justify-center items-
   center">{children}</main>
   ```

8. Create a new route component that uses `Layout`:

   ```
   export default function Component() {
     const { firstExpense, firstInvoice } = useLoaderData<typeof
   loader>();
     return (
       <Layout firstExpense={firstExpense}
   firstInvoice={firstInvoice}>
         <Outlet />
       </Layout>
     );
   }
   ```

   The route component renders the same content as before. We just moved some code to the new `Layout` component.

9. Next, update the `ErrorBoundary` component in `dashboard.tsx`:

   ```
   import { Link as RemixLink, Outlet, useLoaderData, useLocation,
   useRouteError } from '@remix-run/react';

   import { H1 } from '~/components/headings';
   ```

```
export function ErrorBoundary() {
  const error = useRouteError();
  const errorMessage = error instanceof Error && error.message;
  return (
    <Layout firstExpense={null} firstInvoice={null}>
      <Container className="p-5 lg:p-20 flex flex-col gap-5">
        <H1>Unexpected Error</H1>
        <p>We are very sorry. An unexpected error occurred.
          Please try again or contact us if the problem
          persists.</p>
        {errorMessage && (
          <div className="border-4 border-red-500 p-10">
            <p>Error message: {error.message}</p>
          </div>
        )}
      </Container>
    </Layout>
  );
}
```

Great! We created a nice-looking error boundary that shares markup with the route component to create the same look and feel. Let's test our implementation.

10. Remove the thrown error from the `loader` function for a moment.
11. Run the app and visit the `http://localhost:3000/dashboard` page.

    Without throwing an error, we should see the expense overview page. If you can't remember why this is happening, look inside the `dashboard._index.tsx` route module. If the dashboard's index route is active, it redirects to the expense overview page.

12. Next, throw an error in any `loader` function or React component that is active inside the dashboard:

    ```
    throw Error('Something went wrong!');
    ```

    The browser window should now render the styled nested error boundary. As visible in *Figure 7.5*, adding an error boundary to the dashboard route lets us isolate the error and render all parent routes correctly:

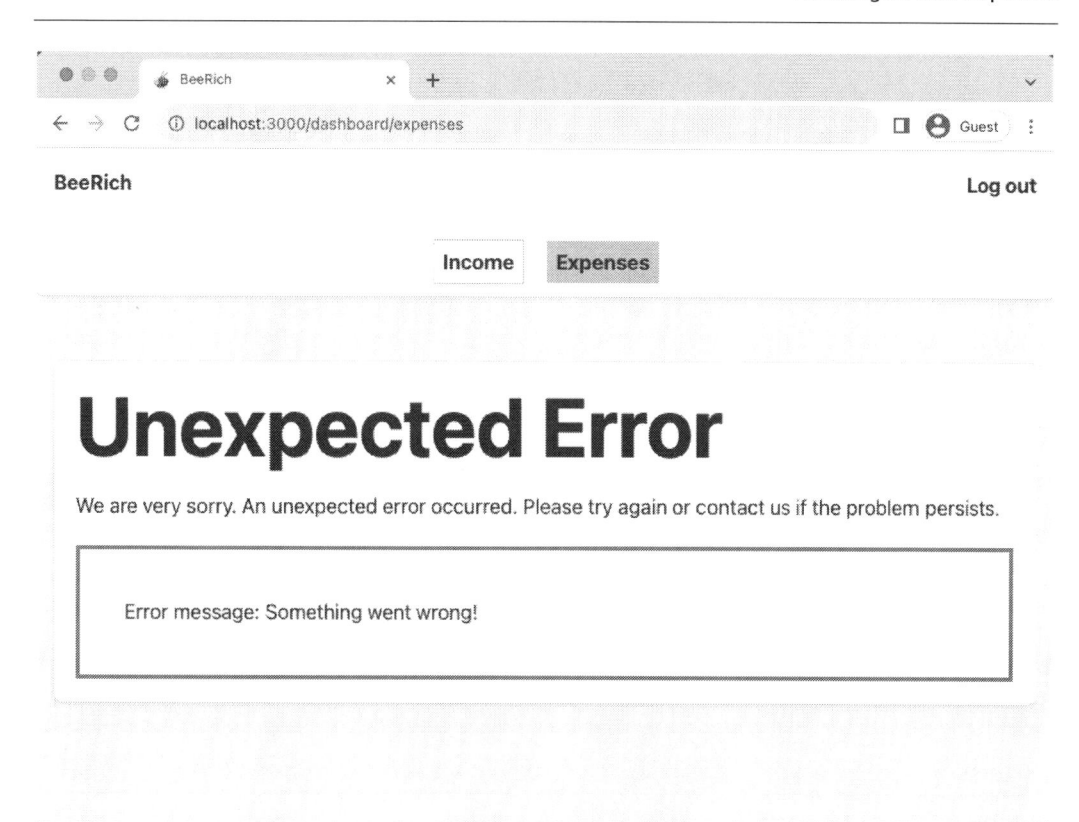

![Figure 7.5 screenshot showing BeeRich dashboard with Unexpected Error message]

Figure 7.5 – Nested dashboard ErrorBoundary component

Nested error boundaries allow us to contain errors within a subset of the route hierarchy. This ensures that the parent routes render as expected. The closer the error boundary is to the error that occurred, the more contained the error will be.

In this section, you learned how to handle unexpected errors in Remix using Remix's `ErrorBoundary` component. Next, let's look at how to use the `ErrorBoundary` component to handle expected exceptions.

Handling thrown responses

We already take advantage of throwing `Response` objects in BeeRich. For instance, in *Chapter 4, Routing in Remix*, we added the following `loader` function to the `dashboard.expenses.$id.tsx` route module:

```
export function loader({ params }: LoaderFunctionArgs) {
  const { id } = params;
  const expense = data.find((expense) => expense.id === Number(id));
```

```
    if (!expense) throw new Response('Not found', { status: 404 });
    return json(expense);
}
```

In the `loader` function, we throw a `Response` object if we cannot find the expense for the `id` route parameter. This creates an expected failure during `loader` function execution. Let's investigate Remix's default behavior when an expected exception occurs.

Throwing responses

In JavaScript, the `throw` statement is used to throw user-defined exceptions. A `catch` block can then catch the thrown exception. We can throw any value, including `Response` objects. Remix takes advantage of this, offering a convention to stop `action` and `loader` functions early with exception responses. Let's invoke the not-found response that was thrown in the expense details `loader`:

1. Run BeeRich on localhost by executing `npm run dev`.
2. Visit the expense overview page by opening `http://localhost:3000/dashboard/expenses` in a new browser window.
3. Now, click on an expense in the overview list. This will redirect us to the expense details page.
4. Replace the `id` route parameter in the URL with a fake one: `http://localhost:3000/dashboard/expenses/fake-id`. Then, reload the browser window.

This should render our dashboard error boundary to the page.

Remix lets us handle unexpected errors and thrown responses uniformly with the `ErrorBoundary` component. Any `Response` object thrown in a `loader` or `action` function triggers the `ErrorBoundary` component.

Thrown responses allow us to retrieve additional information, such as the status code from the error in the `ErrorBoundary` component. For that, we need to check whether the thrown error object is a `Response` object or an unexpected error.

Handling exceptions with error boundaries

Let's add a third error boundary, this time for the nested expense details page:

1. Open the `dashboard.expenses.$id.tsx` route module.
2. Import Remix's `useRouteError` and `isRouteErrorResponse` helpers:

```
import {
  isRouteErrorResponse,
  useActionData,
  useLoaderData,
```

```
    useNavigation,
    useParams,
    useRouteError,
} from '@remix-run/react';
```

3. Create a new `ErrorBoundary` export and add the following code:

```
export function ErrorBoundary() {
  const error = useRouteError();
  const { id } = useParams();
  let heading = 'Something went wrong';
  let message = `Apologies, something went wrong on our end,
please try again.`;
  if (isRouteErrorResponse(error) && error.status === 404) {
    heading = 'Expense not found';
    message = `Apologies, the expense with the id ${id} cannot
be found.`;
  }
  return (
    <>
      <div className="w-full m-auto lg:max-w-3xl flex flex-col
items-center justify-center gap-5">
        <H2>{heading}</H2>
        <p>{message}</p>
      </div>
      <FloatingActionLink to="/dashboard/expenses/">Add
expense</FloatingActionLink>
    </>
  );
}
```

This time, we also use Remix's `useParams` hook to access the expense `id` route parameter. Then, we use Remix's `isRouteErrorResponse` helper to check whether the error object is a `Response` object. If yes, then we can read the status code and other fields of the `Response` object to provide a more specific error message.

4. Next, test the implementation. Navigate to an expense details page and use a fake `id` route parameter in the URL. You should now see the nested `ErrorBoundary` component rendered on the page.

Notice how we still render the expense overview list; this is the power of nested error handling!

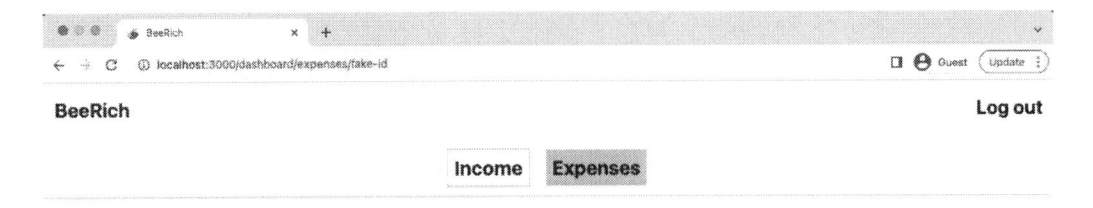

Figure 7.6 – Nested expense details ErrorBoundary component

Now that we've implemented a nested error boundary for the expense details page, go ahead and implement the same experience for the income details page.

Once you've finished working on the income details page, we'll revisit the unpleasant experience from *Chapter 6, Enhancing the User Experience*.

Creating a resilient experience

Do you remember that we created an unpleasant experience in *Chapter 6, Enhancing the User Experience*, when introducing the expense deletion form? If you are on an expense details page (`dashboard/expenses/$id`) and quickly delete all expenses in one go, you may end up on a not-found page. This is because of our redirect logic in the `dashboard/expenses/$id deleteExpense` function:

```
async function deleteExpense(request: Request, id: string):
Promise<Response> {
```

```
  const referer = request.headers.get('referer');
  const redirectPath = referer || '/dashboard/expenses';

  try {
    await db.expense.delete({ where: { id } });
  } catch (err) {
    throw new Response('Not found', { status: 404 });
  }

  if (redirectPath.includes(id)) {
    return redirect('/dashboard/expenses');
  }
  return redirect(redirectPath);
}
```

We use the `referer` header, if available, to redirect the user back to the current route after deletion. This is meant to improve the user experience. If the user is currently on the details page, `/dashboard/expenses/1`, and deletes the expense with `id 2`, then we do not want to redirect the user away from `/dashboard/expenses/1`. However, we also have an `if` condition in the `deleteExpense` function to make sure that we do redirect the user if the user is currently on the details page of the expense that is being deleted.

This logic fails when we quickly delete several expenses. Triggering many expense deletions simultaneously creates a race condition between the different action requests. It is going to be the response of the last triggered `action` that decides where the user is going to be redirected. However, by that time, we might have already deleted the expense that we currently have in the details view.

Let's say we are on the details page, `/dashboard/expenses/1`, and quickly delete the expenses with `id 1` and then also with `id 2`. In the `deleteExpense` function handling the deletion of expense 1, we return a redirect to `/dashboard/expenses` since we know that expense 1 has been deleted. However, in the `deleteExpense` function handling the deletion of expense 2, we will return a redirect to `/dashboard/expenses/1` (the current page). Remix takes the response of the last user action and commits to the redirect to `/dashboard/expenses/1`. We throw a 404 not-found error in the `loader` function as the expense with `id 1` cannot be found (it has been deleted).

As shown in *Figure 7.6*, we've enhanced the user experience by introducing the nested `ErrorBoundary` component for expense details. Nice! Now, if there's a 404 error, the user stays on the expenses overview page, and the error is contained in the nested `ErrorBoundary`. We avoid showing the user a full-screen error message and instead gracefully display the not-found error as part of the dashboard UI.

> **Declarative error handling**
> Remix's error boundaries let us handle errors and exceptions declaratively. By adding nested error boundaries, we can handle edge cases gracefully for a resilient user experience.

Now that we've ensured a resilient user experience with nested error boundaries, let's enhance the root error boundary with custom error messages for common HTTP status codes. In the next section, we will handle page-not-found errors.

Handling page-not-found (404) errors

We can also handle thrown responses in the root `ErrorBoundary` component. One special case that can only be handled in the root `ErrorBoundary` component is the page-not-found exception thrown by Remix. Let's revisit the root error boundary to handle thrown responses at the root level:

1. Run BeeRich on localhost by executing `npm run dev`.
2. Visit a non-existing page such as `http://localhost:3000/cheesecake` in a new browser window.

   When visiting a non-existing route, Remix throws a response with HTTP status code 404 at the root level. We can use `isRouteErrorResponse` to render a 404 page using the root error boundary.

3. Open the `root.tsx` file in an editor.
4. Import `isRouteErrorResponse` from Remix:

   ```
   import {
     isRouteErrorResponse,
     Links,
     LiveReload,
     Meta,
     Outlet,
     Scripts,
     ScrollRestoration,
     useRouteError,
   } from '@remix-run/react';
   ```

5. Update the function body of the `ErrorBoundary` export in `root.tsx`:

   ```
   const error = useRouteError();
   let heading = 'Unexpected Error';
   let message =
     'We are very sorry. An unexpected error occurred. Please try again or contact us if the problem persists.';
   if (isRouteErrorResponse(error)) {
     switch (error.status) {
       case 401:
         heading = '401 Unauthorized';
   ```

```
            message = 'Oops! Looks like you tried to visit a page that
    you do not have access to.';
            break;
        case 404:
            heading = '404 Not Found';
            message = 'Oops! Looks like you tried to visit a page that
    does not exist.';
            break;
    }
}
let errorMessage = error instanceof Error ? error.message :
null;
```

We now create the error message dynamically based on the response status code.

6. Finally, replace the hardcoded H1 and p texts with the `heading` and `message` values:

```
<H1>{heading}</H1>
<p>{message}</p>
{errorMessage && (
  <div className="border-4 border-red-500 p-10">
    <p>Error message: {errorMessage}</p>
  </div>
)}
```

7. Revisit `http://localhost:3000/cheesecake`.

   You should now see the 404 not-found page shown in *Figure 7.7*:

   # 404 Not Found

   Oops! Looks like you tried to visit a page that does not exist.

   Back to homepage

   Figure 7.7 – Screenshot of BeeRich's 404 page

Great! We've added root and nested error boundaries to BeeRich. Note that we can throw custom 404 responses in `loader` and `action` functions. Nested error boundaries can handle these thrown exceptions. Remix throws a root-level 404 response if the requested URL does not match any routes. Since the exception is thrown at the root level, we use the root error boundary to handle the global 404 not-found page in Remix.

Summary

In this chapter, you learned that Remix lets us handle both expected and unexpected failures declaratively using Remix's `ErrorBoundary` component.

The root `ErrorBoundary` export handles thrown responses and errors if no other nested error boundary has handled them yet. Both errors and thrown responses bubble upward through the route hierarchy.

Then, you learned that error boundaries do not have access to loader data. It is important not to render any components in the boundaries that access the `useLoaderData` hook.

Using error boundaries makes the application more resilient toward errors. Tight error boundaries keep parts of our application functional if an unexpected error only affects a nested route module.

In the next chapter, we will throw some more responses – 401 responses, to be precise – as we implement an authentication flow and learn more about state management with Remix.

Further reading

You can find a list of all HTTP status codes on MDN: `https://developer.mozilla.org/en-US/docs/Web/HTTP/Status`.

If you want to learn more about exception and error handling, I recommend that you check out Shawn Wang's (@swyx) blog post *Errors Are Not Exceptions*: `https://www.swyx.io/errors-not-exceptions`.

You can find more information about the `ErrorBoundary` route module export in the Remix documentation: `https://remix.run/docs/en/2/route/error-boundary`.

The Remix docs also contain a guide with more information about not-found error handling, which you can find here: `https://remix.run/docs/en/2/guides/not-found`.

8
Session Management

Session management describes the process of preserving data across different user interactions and request-response roundtrips. Session management is crucial to provide personalized experiences on the web. In this chapter, we will work with Remix's primitives to manage application state and user session data. This chapter covers the following topics:

- Working with search parameters
- Creating user sessions with cookies
- Authenticating access to user data

First, we will work with Remix's primitives to tie application states to URL search parameters. Then, we will utilize HTTP cookies to persist user session data. Finally, we will use the session cookie to authenticate users in `loader` and `action` functions.

After reading this chapter, you will understand how to work with search parameters to control application states in Remix. You will also know how to submit forms programmatically using Remix's `useSubmit` hook. You will further practice working with Remix's session cookie helpers and learn how to implement login, signup, and logout functionalities in Remix. Finally, you will understand how to authenticate users on the server and how to access loader data globally across your application.

Technical requirements

You can find the code for this chapter here: `https://github.com/PacktPublishing/Full-Stack-Web-Development-with-Remix/blob/main/08-session-management/`.

Before starting this chapter, follow the instructions in the `README.md` file in this chapter's `bee-rich` folder on GitHub. This README file guides you through adding a `User` model to the database schema of the BeeRich application. It further helps you initiate a `session.server.ts` file with some useful helper functions. Note that following the README guide will temporarily break the create and edit expense and income form actions. We will update the code in this chapter. Until then, use the seed data to populate the database for testing purposes.

Working with search parameters

The URL stores information about the user's current location. We already utilize dynamic route parameters for expense and invoice identifiers. Similarly, we can use URL search parameters to store additional application states.

A URL is the perfect place to persist state that concerns only one or a few pages. In this section, we will use URL search parameters to create a search filter on the expense overview page in BeeRich.

Did you know that Google uses a search parameter to implement search queries? Open google.com and use the search input field to start a new Google search. After pressing *Enter*, Google navigates you to the search results page. If you inspect the URL, you will see that Google uses a search parameter called q (short for query probably) to store your search query: https://www.google.com/search?q=Using+search+params+in+Remix.run.

Search parameters are key-value pairs that are added to the URL after the pathname following a question mark (?) and appended via ampersands (&). Search parameters allow us to store additional optional application states outside of the URL path.

Let's build an experience similar to Google Search in BeeRich to filter the expense list through a search filter.

Reading search parameters in loader functions

The expenses list is fetched and rendered in the dashboard.expenses.tsx route module. Now, we want to allow users to filter the list by using a search input field.

We can divide the work into two steps:

- Update the database query so that it filters by a search query.
- Provide the user with the UI so that they can enter search queries.

First, let's update the loader function. The goal is to update the loader function so that it only fetches expenses that match the query string provided through the request URL:

1. Open the dashboard.expenses.tsx route module in your editor and inspect the module's loader function.
2. First, add the request parameter to the loader function arguments:

   ```
   import type { LoaderFunctionArgs } from '@remix-run/node';

   export async function loader({ request }: LoaderFunctionArgs)
   ```

3. Next, access the URL string of the request to create a new URL object and get the q search parameter:

```
export async function loader({ request }: LoaderFunctionArgs) {
  const url = new URL(request.url);
  const searchString = url.searchParams.get('q');
  const expenses = await db.expense.findMany({
    orderBy: {
      createdAt: 'desc',
    },
  });
  return json(expenses);
}
```

Following Google's implementation, we call the parameter q - short for query. You can find more information about the URL interface in the MDN Web Docs: https://developer.mozilla.org/en-US/docs/Web/API/URL.

4. Update the database query so that it only returns the expenses where the title contains the search string:

```
const expenses = await db.expense.findMany({
  orderBy: {
    createdAt: 'desc',
  },
  where: {
    title: {
      contains: searchString ? searchString : '',
    },
  },
});
```

If the URL does not contain a query string, we search against an empty string, which matches all expenses. In this case, the `loader` function behaves as before.

5. Run BeeRich in development mode by executing `npm run dev` in a terminal and navigate to the expenses overview page (http://localhost:3000/dashboard/expenses).

Since we didn't include a query string in the URL, we still return the full list of expenses.

6. Next, update the URL in the URL bar by adding a query string such as http://localhost:3000/dashboard/expenses?q=Groceries and refresh the page. It should now display a filtered list of expenses.

Great! The `loader` function now handles the q search parameters when present and returns a filtered list of expenses. Next, let's add a search input field to let the user search for specific expenses.

Updating search parameters with form submissions

Next, we'll provide the user with a search input field:

1. Optionally, disable JavaScript to ensure the base implementation works without client-side JavaScript.

   You can disable JavaScript in your browser's developer tools or by removing the `Script` component in `root.tsx`.

2. Import Remix's `Form` component from `@remix-run/react`:

   ```
   import { useNavigation, Outlet, useLoaderData, useParams, Form }
   from '@remix-run/react';
   ```

3. Import BeeRich's styled `Input` component:

   ```
   import { Input } from '~/components/forms';
   ```

4. Next, use the `Form` and `Input` components to implement a search input field between the **All expenses** screenreader heading and the unordered list of expenses:

   ```
   <h2 className="sr-only">All expenses</h2>
   <Form method="GET">
     <Input name="q" type="search" label="Search by title" />
   </Form>
   <ul className="flex flex-col">
   ```

Note that the search form does not mutate data. We use the form to navigate to a new page with the q search parameter. For this, we set the form method to `GET` to perform an HTTP GET request.

Conveniently, by default, a form submission appends the form data as search parameters to the request URL. We add the `name` attribute to the input field as only named input fields are part of the submission.

We still have one problem to solve: since the search form is rendered on a layout parent route, it is visible on several pages. By default, the form submits and navigates to `/dashboard/expenses`. However, we would like the user to remain on their current page.

Since we are not targeting a specific `action` function, we can point the form action to the current URL path. This ensures that a form submission does not redirect users away from their current page.

5. Import the `useLocation` hook from Remix to access the current URL path:

   ```
   import { Form, Outlet, useLoaderData, useLocation,
   useNavigation, useParams } from '@remix-run/react';
   ```

6. Access the location in the function body of the route component:

   ```
   const location = useLocation();
   ```

7. Use the path of the current location to set the form's action dynamically:

   ```
   <Form method="GET" action={location.pathname}>
   ```

   A submission now creates a GET request to the current page with an updated search parameter to filter the list of expenses.

8. Try out the new search input field by typing a search query and hitting *Enter* to submit the form.

9. Note that the search input field is empty after every full-page reload, even when a q search parameter is set.

10. Import the `useSearchParams` hook from Remix:

    ```
    import { Form, Outlet, useLoaderData, useLocation,
    useNavigation, useParams, useSearchParams } from '@remix-run/
    react';
    ```

11. Retrieve the q search parameter in the route component:

    ```
    const [searchParams] = useSearchParams();
    const searchQuery = searchParams.get('q') || '';
    ```

    Note that the `searchParams` object implements the web's `URLSearchParams` interface that we also use in the `loader` function when accessing the URL's `searchParams`.

12. Use the `searchQuery` value as the `defaultValue` property for the input field:

    ```
    <Input name="q" type="search" label="Search by title"
    defaultValue={searchQuery} />
    ```

    The input field's value is now set to the previous `searchQuery` by default, even during server-side rendering:

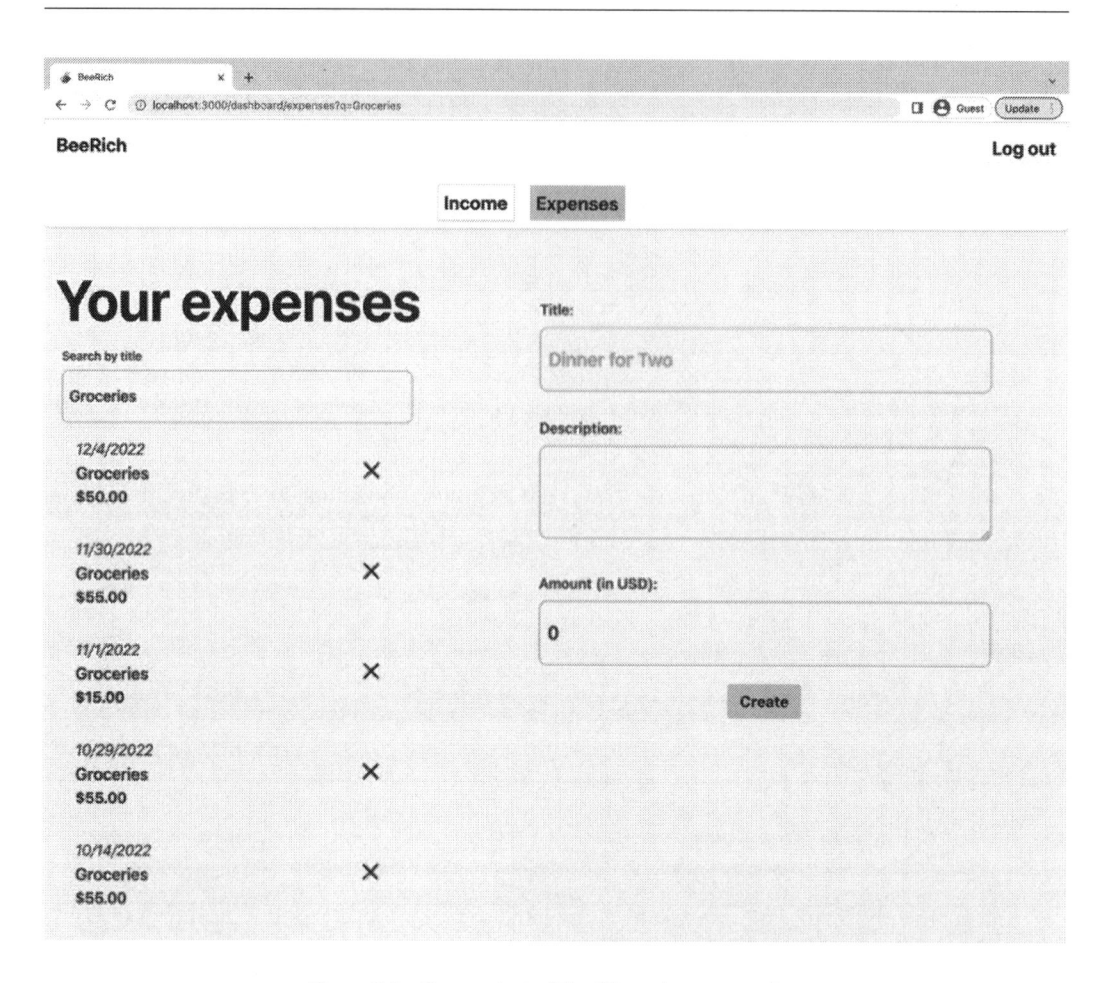

Figure 8.1 – Screenshot of the filtered expenses list

Great! Hitting *Enter* after typing a search query submits the form and updates the URL so that it includes the search query. The `loader` function then returns an updated filtered list of expenses. Note that we didn't use any React state to implement this feature, and as always, the search feature also works without JavaScript.

> **Mapping UIs to URLs**
>
> The advantage of search parameters over React state is that they can be accessed on the server by reading from the request URL. Search parameters persist on full-page reloads and work with the browser's back and forward buttons. Additionally, search parameters create URL variants that CDNs and browsers can cache.

Implement the same behavior for the income overview route. Update the `dashboard.income.tsx` route module's `loader` function and implement the search form to query invoices. Once the income route has been updated, we can enhance the experience with custom JavaScript.

Programmatically submitting forms

Currently, the user needs to press *Enter* to trigger a new search. Let's add a debounced search that submits the form automatically whenever the user changes the value in the input field:

1. First, import `useSubmit` from Remix:

   ```
   import {
     Form,
     Outlet,
     useLoaderData,
     useLocation,
     useNavigation,
     useParams,
     useSearchParams,
     useSubmit,
   } from '@remix-run/react';
   ```

   The `useSubmit` hook lets us submit forms programmatically. You might remember that `useFetcher` also offers a `submit` function. Both `useSubmit` and `useFetcher().submit` allow us to submit forms programmatically.

   Fetcher submissions behave like `fetch` requests and do not trigger global transitions in Remix. They don't affect the global `useNavigation` state or initiate page navigations. The `useSubmit` hook mimics Remix's `Form` behavior.

   In our case, we use Remix's `Form` component for the search and want to retrigger the `/dashboard/expenses` route module's `loader` function so that the loader data updates. For such cases, we want to use the `useSubmit` hook.

2. In the route module's component body, create a new submit function by calling `useSubmit`:

   ```
   const submit = useSubmit();
   ```

3. Add the following change event handler to the search input:

   Replace code example with just this line:

   ```
   onChange={(e) => submit(e.target.form)}
   ```

   On change, we programmatically submit the form using the `submit` function. We pass `submit` the HTML form element, accessing it from the event's target object.

4. Try out the current implementation and type something into the search input field.

   You may notice that we are currently submitting a new form for every change event. This is not very efficient. Instead, we should delay the submission until the user finishes typing. This method of delaying a function call is called debouncing.

5. Replace `Input` with `SearchInput`:

   ```
   import { SearchInput } from '~/components/forms';
   ```

   The `SearchInput` component adds debouncing with a 500-millisecond delay. Refer to the implementation in `/app/components/forms.tsx`.

6. Now, update the JSX so that it renders `SearchInput` instead of the `Input` component:

   ```
   <SearchInput name="q" type="search" label="Search by title"
     defaultValue={searchQuery} />
   ```

   The `SearchInput` component uses Remix's `useSubmit` hook to programmatically submit the form that it is embedded in after a timeout once the user finishes typing.

7. Since the submission is now handled inside the `SearchInput` component, remove the `useSubmit` hook from the `dashboard.expenses.tsx` route module.

You now know three ways of submitting data in Remix: the `Form` component, the `useFetcher` hook, and the `useSubmit` hook. This raises the question of when to best use which utility.

> **When to use Remix data fetching primitives**
>
> Use the `Form` component for the main interactions on the page. The `Form` component is the most straightforward way to implement a form interaction in Remix. Stick with the `Form` component for all simple use cases.
>
> Use the `useSubmit` hook when you want to programmatically submit a `Form` component (for example, on change). You can add `useSubmit` to `Form` implementations to enhance the experience progressively.
>
> Remember that there can only ever be one active navigation at a time. Use the `useFetcher` hook to implement a list of forms, or aside user interactions, that should support concurrent submissions. Aside interactions are usually not meant to trigger page navigations and should have access to isolated navigation states and action data. Whenever you want to trigger a `useFetcher` hook's `Form` component programmatically, you can use `useFetcher.load` and `useFetcher.submit`.

In this section, you learned how to handle application state with the URL. You also learned that forms can execute GET requests by setting the form method to `"GET"`. Finally, you practiced how to programmatically submit a form with `useSubmit`.

Ensure you update the income route to practice what you've learned in this section. Once you've done that, we can start investigating how to handle user sessions with cookies.

Creating user sessions with cookies

A session maintains the state of a user's interactions with a web application across multiple requests. Sessions track information such as user authentication credentials, shopping cart contents, color scheme preferences, and other user-specific data. In this section, we will use Remix's session cookie helpers to create a login and signup flow in BeeRich.

One way to manage sessions is via cookies. Cookies contain small pieces of data and are appended to both document and fetch requests, making them a great way to handle user sessions, personalization, and tracking. Additionally, cookies can be encrypted to securely carry user credentials without client access.

Cookies are part of the HTTP protocol and enable persisting information in the otherwise stateless HTTP protocol. Where URL search parameters are visible to the user and can be bookmarked and shared, cookie data can be encrypted and are then only accessible on the server. Search parameters are handy for storing application states that are not tied to specific users. Cookies are ideal for authenticating users and storing small chunks of private session data.

A web server can append a cookie to the current session by setting the **Set-Cookie** header on the HTTP response. Once a cookie has been set, the browser attaches the cookie using the **Cookie** header to all subsequent requests based on the lifetime specified during cookie setup.

Remix provides two different abstractions to work with cookies:

1. `createCookie` to read and write cookies
2. `createCookieSessionStorage` to implement a session storage using a cookie

In this chapter, we will use Remix's `createCookieSessionStorage` function since our goal is to implement user sessions for authentication and authorization. We will have a look at the `createCookie` helper function in *Chapter 15, Advanced Session Management,* to persist visitor tracking data.

Working with Remix's session helpers

Let's implement the register and login pages in BeeRich:

1. First, follow the `README.md` file in this chapter's folder on GitHub to prepare BeeRich for this section.
2. Once you've followed the setup guide in the `README.md` file, open the `modules/session/session.server.ts` file in your editor.

3. Next, import the `createCookieSessionStorage` and `redirect` helper functions from Remix:

   ```
   import { createCookieSessionStorage, redirect } from '@remix-run/node'
   ```

   Remix provides session helper functions for different session management strategies. The `createCookieSessionStorage` helper function builds on top of Remix's cookie helpers to store session data in a cookie.

   Refer to the Remix documentation for alternative session helpers. For example, `createMemorySessionStorage` manages session data in the server's memory; `createSessionStorage` is more generic and allows us to retrieve session data from a custom storage implementation while storing only the session identifier in a cookie.

4. Now, add the following code below the already existing `registerUser` and `loginUser` functions:

   ```
   const sessionSecret = process.env.SESSION_SECRET;
   if (!sessionSecret) {
     throw new Error('SESSION_SECRET must be set');
   }

   const { getSession, commitSession, destroySession } =
   createCookieSessionStorage({
     cookie: {
       name: 'bee-rich-session',
       secure: process.env.NODE_ENV === 'production',
       secrets: [sessionSecret],
       sameSite: 'lax',
       path: '/',
       maxAge: 60 * 60 * 24 * 30,
       httpOnly: true,
     },
   });
   ```

   We use the `createCookieSessionStorage` helper function to create a session storage object. The object contains three functions to help us manage the lifecycle of our user sessions.

   The `createCookieSessionStorage` function expects a cookie configuration object to set the session cookie's lifetime (`maxAge`), its access rules (`secure`, `sameSite`, `path`, and `httpOnly`), and signing secrets (`secrets`). You can refer to the Remix documentation for more information about the configuration options.

   We set the cookie to expire after 30 days, meaning it will be automatically deleted after that period. By setting `httpOnly` to `true`, we ensure that the cookie cannot be read by the client, enhancing security. We also use secrets to sign the cookie, adding an extra layer of verification.

5. Open the `.env` file in your project's root folder and add a `SESSION_SECRET` environment variable:

   ```
   SESSION_SECRET="[A secret string]"
   ```

   HTTP cookie signing involves adding a cryptographic signature to a cookie using a secret key known only to the server. When the client sends this signed cookie back in future requests, the server uses the secret key to verify that the cookie has not been tampered with. This adds an extra layer of security.

   We read the environment variables when first starting our server environment. Make sure you restart your development server in case it is currently running to ensure the new environment variable is picked up.

6. Finally, add the following helper function to the `session.server.ts` file:

   ```
   export async function createUserSession(user: User, headers =
   new Headers()) {
     const session = await getSession();
     session.set('userId', user.id);
     headers.set('Set-Cookie', await commitSession(session));
     return headers;
   }
   ```

   We use `createUserSession` to initiate the session cookie after successful registration or login.

   `createUserSession` expects a user object and an optional `headers` parameter. The function then calls `getSession` to create a new session object for the current user. We add `userId` to the session object and use `commitSession` to parse the object into a cookie value. We set the cookie to the **Set-Cookie** header and return the `Headers` object.

   Note that cookies can only store a small amount of data (a few KB). Hence, we only store `userId`. When storing more data, it might make sense to store the session data in a database and only store a session identifier in the session cookie (for example, using the `createSessionStorage` helper).

Now that we can create new user sessions, let's implement a signup flow to register new users.

Adding a user registration flow

In this section, we will apply what we have learned thus far to implemnet a registration form and associated `action` function. Before reading through the solution, I encourage you to try it yourself. Start by updating the signup route module component. Then, add an `action` function and parse the form data.

Now, let's go through the implementation step by step:

1. Open the `_layout.signup.tsx` route module and update the route module component:

   ```
   import { useNavigation } from '@remix-run/react';

   import { Button } from '~/components/buttons';
   import { Card } from '~/components/containers';
   import { Form, Input } from '~/components/forms';
   import { H1 } from '~/components/headings';

   export default function Component() {
     const navigation = useNavigation();
     const isSubmitting = navigation.state !== 'idle' &&
       navigation.formAction === '/signup';
     return (
       <Card>
         <Form method="POST" action="/signup">
           <H1>Sign Up</H1>
           <Input label="Name:" name="name" required />
           <Input label="Email:" name="email" type="email" required
            />
           <Input label="Password:" name="password" type="password"
            required />
           <Button disabled={isSubmitting} type="submit" isPrimary>
             {isSubmitting ? 'Signing you up...' : 'Sign up!'}
           </Button>
         </Form>
       </Card>
     );
   }
   ```

   Note that we use some reusable components to add our custom styles. Also, note that we set the form method to POST. A signup flow mutates data and must not be a GET request. Finally, we again utilize the `useNavigation` hook to add pending indicators when the form is submitting.

2. Next, add an `action` function to handle registration form submissions:

   ```
   import type { ActionFunctionArgs } from '@remix-run/node';
   import { json, redirect } from '@remix-run/node';

   import { createUserSession, registerUser } from '~/modules/
   session/session.server';

   export async function action({ request }: ActionFunctionArgs) {
     const formData = await request.formData();
   ```

```
    const { name, email, password } = Object.fromEntries
      (formData);
    if (!name || !email || !password) {
      return json({ error: 'Please fill out all fields.' });
    }
    if (typeof name !== 'string' || typeof email !== 'string' ||
     typeof password !== 'string') {
      throw new Error('Invalid form data.');
    }
    try {
      const user = await registerUser({ name, email, password });
      return redirect('/dashboard', {
        headers: await createUserSession(user),
      });
    } catch (error: any) {
      return json({ error: error?.message || 'Something went
        wrong.' });
    }
  }
}
```

First, we parse the form data from the request object. Then, we validate the form data and ensure that all required fields are present and of type `string`.

Once the data has been validated, we call the `registerUser` function to create a new user object or throw an error if the user already exists in the database. If the creation is successful, we call `createUserSession` to add the session cookie to the response headers. Otherwise, we return an error response.

On success, we redirect the user to the dashboard. On error, we return the error message as action data. Next, let's display the error message to the users.

3. Import `useActionData` from Remix:

    ```
    import { useActionData, useNavigation } from '@remix-run/react';
    ```

4. Access the error message action data in the route component:

    ```
    const actionData = useActionData<typeof action>();
    ```

5. Import our styled inline error component:

    ```
    import { InlineError } from '~/components/texts';
    ```

6. Render the `InlineError` component below the submit button to display any error messages:

    ```
    <InlineError aria-live="assertive">{actionData?.error &&
    actionData.error}</InlineError>
    ```

7. Try out the registration flow by running the application with `npm run dev` and visiting the `/signup` page.

   After form submission, you should be redirected to the dashboard. Great! But what if we want to log out? For now, we can clear the cookie using the developer tools.

8. Open the developer tools in your browser window and navigate to the **Application** tab:

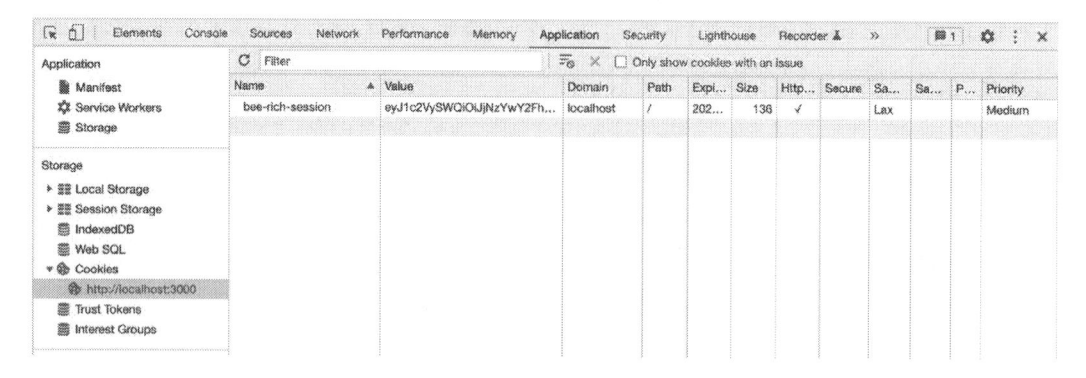

Figure 8.2 – The Application tab of the developer tools

Under **Cookies**, you should find the session cookie for BeeRich. Note that the cookie value is encrypted because of the `httpOnly` flag.

Right-click on the cookie and select **Delete**.

This allows us to play around with the registration form a bit more before we implement our logout flow.

9. Try to register the same email address again. You should now see an inline error. Awesome!

   Feel free to spend more time on this section and investigate the code flow through the `action` function and the `session.server.ts` file. Use the `debugger` or `console.log` statements to review what happens during signup.

Once you feel comfortable with the added code, delete the cookie using the developer tools. This will let us implement and test the login flow.

Adding a user login flow

Copy and paste the route module component from the registration flow and see whether you can update it to make it work for the login page. Maybe try the same for the `action` function.

Once you have tried it out, let's go through the implementation together:

1. Add the following code to update the `_layout.login.tsx` route component:

    ```
    import { useActionData, useNavigation } from '@remix-run/react';

    import { Button } from '~/components/buttons';
    import { Card } from '~/components/containers';
    import { Form, Input } from '~/components/forms';
    import { H1 } from '~/components/headings';
    import { InlineError } from '~/components/texts';

    export default function Component() {
      const navigation = useNavigation();
      const isSubmitting = navigation.state !== 'idle' &&
        navigation.formAction === '/login';
      const actionData = useActionData<typeof action>();
      return (
        <Card>
          <Form method="POST" action="/login">
            <H1>Log In</H1>
            <Input label="Email:" name="email" type="email" required />
            <Input label="Password:" name="password" type="password" required />
            <Button disabled={isSubmitting} type="submit" isPrimary>
              {isSubmitting ? 'Logging you in...' : 'Log in!'}
            </Button>
            <InlineError aria-live="assertive">{actionData?.error &&
              actionData.error}</InlineError>
          </Form>
        </Card>
      );
    }
    ```

    The login and signup forms are nearly identical; only the number of input fields differs.

2. Next, add the `action` function to handle the login form submissions:

    ```
    import type { ActionFunctionArgs } from '@remix-run/node';
    import { json, redirect } from '@remix-run/node';

    import { createUserSession, loginUser } from '~/modules/session/session.server';

    export async function action({ request }: ActionFunctionArgs) {
      const formData = await request.formData();
    ```

```
    const email = formData.get('email');
    const password = formData.get('password');
    if (!email || !password) {
      return json({ error: 'Please fill out all fields.' });
    }
    if (typeof email !== 'string' || typeof password !== 'string')
{
      throw new Error('Invalid form data.');
    }
    try {
      const user = await loginUser({ email, password });
      return redirect('/dashboard', {
        headers: await createUserSession(user),
      });
    } catch (error: any) {
      return json({ error: error?.message || 'Something went
      wrong.' });
    }
  }
```

We parse the form data from the request, validate the form data, and log the user in using the `loginUser` helper function. If the user can be found in the database and the password matches, we create the session cookie and add it to the response. Otherwise, we use the error message to return a JSON response.

3. Try out the login flow using the email address you used during the registration flow. You should now be able to register and log in to BeeRich.

So far, we have utilized session helper functions to create a user session after successful registration or login. By inspecting the developer tools, we ensured that the browser registered the cookie. Next, we'll add a logout flow that removes the session cookie.

Deleting a session during logout

Removing a session cookie is straightforward. In `session.server.ts`, we have access to three session life cycle methods: `getSession`, `commitSession`, and `destroySession`. Follow these steps:

1. Let's add a helper function to `session.server.ts` to get the current user session from an incoming request:

```
function getUserSession(request: Request) {
  return getSession(request.headers.get('Cookie'));
}
```

The `getUserSession` function is a helper that we will utilize to access the current session object from the cookie header of a request.

Remix's `getSession` function parses the cookie header and returns a session object we can use to access the stored data. Once we have the session object, we can read from it or destroy it using the `destroySession` life cycle method.

2. Add a logout function to `session.server.ts`:

    ```
    export async function logout(request: Request) {
      const session = await getUserSession(request);
      return redirect('/login', {
        headers: {
          'Set-Cookie': await destroySession(session),
        },
      });
    }
    ```

    The `logout` function parses the current session object from the incoming request and then redirects the user to the login page. The returned response uses the **Set-Cookie** header to clear the current session cookie.

3. Now, create a new `_layout.logout.tsx` route module and add the following code:

    ```
    import type { ActionFunctionArgs } from '@remix-run/node';
    import { redirect } from '@remix-run/node';
    import { logout } from '~/modules/session/session.server';

    export function action({ request }: ActionFunctionArgs) {
      return logout(request);
    }

    export function loader() {
      return redirect('/login');
    }
    ```

    The logout route module has an `action` function that executes the `logout` function. This removes the session cookie and redirects the user to `login`. The logout route module also has a `loader` function to redirect all traffic to `login`. This is convenient if a user accidentally navigates to the logout page.

    Remember that Remix refetches all loader data from all active `loader` functions after an `action` function executes. Since `logout` mutates the server state (the user session), we use an `action` function and not a `loader` function to implement `logout`. After logging out, we want to remove all user-specific data from the page by revalidating all loader data.

    Note that the logout route module does not export a route component. Thus, it is not a document but a resource route.

4. Open the `dashboard.tsx` route module and locate the current logout link in the navigation bar:

   ```
   <RemixLink to="/404">Log out</RemixLink>
   ```

   Currently, the logout button is a placeholder linking to a non-existent page.

5. Import `Form` from Remix and replace the code to create a form that submits a POST request to the logout route:

   ```
   <Form method="POST" action="/logout">
     <button type="submit">Log out</button>
   </Form>
   ```

   Clicking the **Log out** link submits a form to the logout action function, redirecting the user to log in and removing the current user session cookie. And with that, we have successfully implemented a logout flow in BeeRich.

In this section, we practiced creating and deleting session cookies using Remix's session cookie helpers. Next, we will read from the session cookie to authenticate the user and return user-specific data from our `loader` functions.

Authenticating access to user data

We can access cookies in our `loader` and `action` functions as cookies are appended to every HTTP request to the web server. This makes cookies a great tool for managing sessions. In this section, we will read from the session cookie to authenticate users and query user-specific data.

Accessing cookie data on the server

Once we append a cookie to a response, we can access the cookie data on every following request to the server. This lets us build personalized and session-based user experiences. Let's add some helper functions to make this task easier:

1. Add the following code to the `session.server.ts` file:

   ```
   export async function getUserId(request: Request) {
     const session = await getUserSession(request);
     const userId = session.get('userId');
     if (!userId || typeof userId !== 'string') return null;
     return userId;
   }

   export async function getUser(request: Request) {
     const userId = await getUserId(request);
     if (typeof userId !== 'string') {
       return null;
   ```

```
  }
  try {
    return db.user.findUnique({
      where: { id: userId },
      select: { id: true, name: true, email: true, createdAt:
true, updatedAt: true },
    });
  } catch {
    throw logout(request);
  }
}
```

On register and login, we call `createUserSession` to write `userId` to the session cookie.

The `getUserId` function expects a `Request` object and returns `userId` from the session cookie if it's present, or null otherwise. We use `getUserSession` to get the current session object from the cookie header of the `Request` object.

We also add a `getUser` function that uses the `getUserId` function under the hood and returns the user object from the database. To avoid exposing the user's password hash, we ensure not to query the password field from the database.

Let's see how we can use `getUserId` to check whether a user is logged in.

2. Add the following `loader` functions to the login and signup route modules:

```
import type { LoaderFunctionArgs } from '@remix-run/node';
import { redirect } from '@remix-run/node';

import { getUserId } from '~/modules/session/session.server';

export async function loader({ request }: LoaderFunctionArgs) {
  const userId = await getUserId(request);
  if (userId) {
    return redirect('/dashboard');
  }
  return {};
}
```

Once a user is logged in, we ensure they are redirected away should they visit the login and signup pages.

If a session cookie is appended to the request and `userId` exists, then we can be sure that the user has already been authenticated. In this case, we redirect to the dashboard. Otherwise, we show the login or signup page.

Note that we return an empty object for our base case in the `loader` function. This is because a `loader` function cannot return `undefined`.

Session Management

In this section, we implemented the `getUserId` and `getUser` helper functions. We use `getUserId` to check whether a user is logged in. Next, we will use `getUser` to get the user object of the currently logged-in user, if any.

Working with user data on the client

In this section, we will use `getUser` to work with the user object of the currently logged-in user:

1. First, import `LoaderFunctionArgs` and `getUser` in root.tsx.

   ```
   import type { LinksFunction, LoaderFunctionArgs, MetaFunction }
   from '@remix-run/node';
   import { getUser } from './modules/session/session.server';
   ```

2. Next, add a `loader` export to `root.tsx`, querying and returning the current user object:

   ```
   export async function loader({ request }: LoaderFunctionArgs) {
     const user = await getUser(request);
     return { user };
   }
   ```

   Note that `getUser` returns a user object without the password property. This is important as we forward the user object to the client. We must not leak user or app secrets to the client application.

   We can now access the user object with `useLoaderData` in `root.tsx`. However, we likely want to have access to the user object throughout our application. Let's see how we can do this with Remix.

3. Create a `session.ts` file in `app/modules/session`.

   We plan to create a small React hook to access the root loader user data across our React app. Since we also want to access the hook in our React app on the client, we must not put the hook in the `session.server.ts` file as it is only included in the server bundle.

4. Add the following `useUser` hook to `session.ts`:

   ```
   import type { User } from '@prisma/client';
   import { useRouteLoaderData } from '@remix-run/react';

   import type { loader } from '~/root';

   type PublicUser = Omit<User, 'password'>;

   export function useUser(): PublicUser | null {
     const data = useRouteLoaderData<typeof loader>('root');
     if (!data || !data.user) return null;
     const deserializedUser: PublicUser = {
       ...data.user,
   ```

```
      createdAt: new Date(data.user.createdAt),
      updatedAt: new Date(data.user.updatedAt),
    };
    return deserializedUser;
}
```

We use Remix's `useRouteLoaderData` hook to access the root loader data user object. We also import the type of the root `loader` function for type inference. We further deserialize the user object to match the `User` type from `@prisma/client` without the password property.

Note that Remix assigns every route module a unique identifier. The ID of the root route module is "root". We must pass `useRouteLoaderData` the ID of the route module of which we want to access the loader data. Remix's route module IDs match the route file name relative to the app folder. You can find more information in the Remix documentation: https://remix.run/docs/en/2/hooks/use-route-loader-data.

We can now call `useUser` throughout our Remix application to access the current user object. You can use the same pattern for any global application state.

Let's try out the hook in action!

5. Use the `useUser` hook in the `_layout.tsx` route component:

    ```
    const user = useUser();
    ```

6. In the unordered list of the navigation, replace the current **Log in** and **Sign in** list items with the following code:

    ```
    {user ? (
      <li className="ml-auto">
        <NavLink to="/dashboard" prefetch="intent">
          Dashboard
        </NavLink>
      </li>
    ) : (
      <>
        <li className="ml-auto">
          <NavLink to="/login" prefetch="intent">
            Log in
          </NavLink>
        </li>
        <li>
          <NavLink to="/signup" prefetch="intent">
            Sign up
          </NavLink>
        </li>
      </>
    )}
    ```

We now conditionally render the **Log in** and **Sign up** links if no user is logged in or a link to **Dashboard** if a user is already logged in.

Note that the user object returned by `useUser` can also be `null`. We try to query a user object if a session exists or return `null` otherwise. However, sometimes, we must ensure that a user is logged in. We'll look at enforcing authentication in the next section.

Enforcing authentication on the server

The dashboard routes of BeeRich are for logged-in users only. Can you think of a way to enforce that a session cookie is present?

Let's implement some authentication logic that redirects the user to the login page if no user session exists:

1. Create another helper function in `session.server.tsx`:

   ```
   export async function requireUserId(request: Request) {
     const session = await getUserSession(request);
     const userId = session.get('userId');
     if (!userId || typeof userId !== 'string') {
       throw redirect('/login');
     }
     return userId;
   }
   ```

   `requireUserId` looks similar to `getUserId`, but this time, we throw a redirect `Response` if no user session was found.

   Note that throwing a redirect `Response` does not trigger the `ErrorBoundary` component. Redirects are a special case where we leave the current route module and navigate to another one instead. The final `Response` of a redirect is the document response of the redirected route module.

2. Next, add the following line to the top of all `loader` and `action` functions in the dashboard route modules:

   ```
   await requireUserId(request);
   ```

   The `requireUserId` call ensures that the user is redirected to the login page in case they are not authenticated.

   Since `loader` functions run in parallel and `action` functions expose API endpoints over the internet, we must add the authentication check to every single `loader` and `action` function that requires authentication.

   We must also ensure that we only retrieve data associated with the current `userId`. A user should not be able to view the expenses and invoices of other users. Let's update our `loader` and `action` functions further.

3. Open the `dashboard.tsx` route module and update the `loader` function to require a user session and use `userId` to query user-specific expense and income objects:

```
import type { LoaderFunctionArgs, SerializeFrom } from '@remix-
run/node';

import { requireUserId } from '~/session.server';

export async function loader({ request }: LoaderFunctionArgs) {
  const userId = await requireUserId(request);
  const expenseQuery = db.expense.findFirst({
    orderBy: { createdAt: 'desc' },
    where: { userId },
  });
  const invoiceQuery = db.invoice.findFirst({
    orderBy: { createdAt: 'desc' },
    where: { userId },
  });

  const [firstExpense, firstInvoice] = await Promise.all([expenseQuery, invoiceQuery]);
  return json({ firstExpense, firstInvoice });
}
```

By requiring `userId`, we ensure that a session cookie is present. If no session cookie is present, `requireUserId` will throw `redirect` to the login route.

We also filter our database queries for user-specific content. We now query for the last expense and invoice objects created by the logged-in user.

4. Open the `dashboard.expenses.tsx` route module and update the `loader` function so that it checks for an existing user session:

```
import { requireUserId } from '~/session.server';

export async function loader({ request }: LoaderFunctionArgs) {
  const userId = await requireUserId(request);
  const url = new URL(request.url);
  const searchString = url.searchParams.get('q');
  const expenses = await db.expense.findMany({
    orderBy: {
      createdAt: 'desc',
    },
    where: {
      userId,
      title: {
```

```
          contains: searchString ? searchString : '',
        },
      },
    });
    return json(expenses);
}
```

Again, we ensure that a user session is present and use the stored `userId` to only filter for user-specific data.

5. Open the `dashboard.expenses._index.tsx` route module and update the `action` function:

```
import { requireUserId } from '~/modules/session/session.server';

export async function action({ request }: ActionFunctionArgs) {
  const userId = await requireUserId(request);
  const formData = await request.formData();
  const title = formData.get('title');
  const description = formData.get('description');
  const amount = formData.get('amount');
  if (typeof title !== 'string' || typeof description !== 'string' || typeof amount !== 'string') {
    throw Error('something went wrong');
  }
  const amountNumber = Number.parseFloat(amount);
  if (Number.isNaN(amountNumber)) {
    throw Error('something went wrong');
  }
  const expense = await db.expense.create({
    data: {
      title,
      description,
      amount: amountNumber,
      currencyCode: 'USD',
      user: {
        connect: {
          id: userId,
        },
      },
    },
  });
  return redirect(`/dashboard/expenses/${expense.id}`);
}
```

On expense creation, we now connect the new expense object to the `userId` parameter that was retrieved from the session cookie.

6. Open the `dashboard.expenses.$id.tsx` route module and update the `loader` function:

    ```
    export async function loader({ request, params }:
    LoaderFunctionArgs) {
      const userId = await requireUserId(request);
      const { id } = params;
      if (!id) throw Error('id route parameter must be defined');
      const expense = await db.expense.findUnique({ where: { id_
        userId: { id, userId } } });
      if (!expense) throw new Response('Not found', { status: 404
    });
      return json(expense);
    }
    ```

    We query for an expense matching the route parameter identifier and the `userId` cookie value. This ensures that a user can't visit different expense detail pages and view the content of other users.

7. Update the `deleteExpense` handler function in `dashboard.expenses.$id.tsx`:

    ```
    async function deleteExpense(request: Request, id: string,
    userId: string): Promise<Response> {
      const referer = request.headers.get('referer');
      const redirectPath = referer || '/dashboard/expenses';

      try {
        await db.expense.delete({ where: { id_userId: { id, userId }
    } });
      } catch (err) {
        throw new Response('Not found', { status: 404 });
      }

      if (redirectPath.includes(id)) {
        return redirect('/dashboard/expenses');
      }
      return redirect(redirectPath);
    }
    ```

    We update the database call to query both by `id` and `userId`. This ensures that a user can only ever delete an expense that was also created by that user.

8. Update the `updateExpense` handler function in `dashboard.expenses.$id.tsx`:

    ```
    async function updateExpense(formData: FormData, id: string,
    userId: string): Promise<Response> {
    ```

```
    const title = formData.get('title');
    const description = formData.get('description');
    const amount = formData.get('amount');
    if (typeof title !== 'string' || typeof description !==
      'string' || typeof amount !== 'string') {
      throw Error('something went wrong');
    }
    const amountNumber = Number.parseFloat(amount);
    if (Number.isNaN(amountNumber)) {
      throw Error('something went wrong');
    }
    await db.expense.update({
      where: { id_userId: { id, userId } },
      data: { title, description, amount: amountNumber },
    });
    return json({ success: true });
}
```

9. Finally, update the `action` function in `dashboard.expenses.$id.tsx`:

```
export async function action({ params, request }:
ActionFunctionArgs) {
  const userId = await requireUserId(request);
  const { id } = params;
  if (!id) throw Error('id route parameter must be defined');

  const formData = await request.formData();
  const intent = formData.get('intent');
  if (intent === 'delete') {
    return deleteExpense(request, id, userId);
  }
  if (intent === 'update') {
    return updateExpense(formData, id, userId);
  }
  throw new Response('Bad request', { status: 400 });
}
```

Again, we call `requireUserId` to enforce an existing user session. Then, we pass `userId` to the `deleteExpense` and `updateExpense` handler functions.

That was quite a bit of code to go through, but by making some minor changes here and there, we have fully authenticated our application's HTTP endpoints and ensured that only authenticated users can visit our dashboard pages.

10. Now is a good time to play around with BeeRich. See whether you can still access any of the dashboard routes without logging in first.

    See whether you can hack into BeeRich by playing around with several tabs. Open the expense creation form in the first tab and log yourself out in the second tab. Can you still successfully create a new expense? Notice how cookies are appended and updated across different tabs.

> **Securing loader and action functions**
> Remix's `loader` functions run in parallel for faster execution. However, their concurrent nature also dictates that we must secure each loader function. Both `loader` and `action` functions are accessible over the internet and must be treated and secured like API endpoints.

We still need to update the income routes. This will be good practice to ensure you understand how to authenticate `loader` and `action` functions. Take your time and go over each `loader` and `action` function in the income routes to practice what you've learned in this chapter.

In this section, you learned how to access state from session cookies in Remix and how to use session cookies to authenticate users in `loader` and `action` functions.

Summary

In this chapter, you learned about session and state management in Remix. First, you learned how to use URL search parameters to persist application state using Remix's `Form` component and the `useSearchParams` hook. The URL is often all we need to handle application state.

You also practiced using `useSubmit` to submit a form programmatically and learned more about Remix's different mutation utilities. We concluded that we use the `Form` component and the `useSubmit` hook for the primary actions on the page; `useFetcher` is used to support concurrent submissions with isolated submission states.

Next, you learned that cookies are part of the HTTP protocol and can be used to persist state across page transitions. Cookies are a great tool for session management. Remix provides helper functions for working with cookies and sessions. Remix's session primitives allow us to manage sessions using different strategies, such as storing session data in memory, files, databases, or cookies.

We utilized Remix's primitives to implement an authentication flow with login, signup, and logout functionalities in BeeRich. You learned how to authenticate users and use session cookies to query for user-specific content.

On register and login, we create and fetch a user object and write `userId` to Remix's session object. The object is then serialized to a string and added as a cookie to the HTTP response using the **Set-Cookie** header. Once a cookie has been set to the response, the browser will append it to all the following requests. This enables us to read the cookie header in `loader` and `action` functions to authenticate user sessions and query user-specific data.

You also learned how to access loader data globally throughout your application using Remix's `useRouteLoaderData` hook. You practiced creating a small custom hook to abstract accessing the user object from the root `loader`.

After reading this chapter, you understand that `action` functions are standalone endpoints and `loader` functions run in parallel. Conclusively, we must authenticate the user in every restricted `loader` and `action` function to prevent unauthorized access.

In the next chapter, you will learn more about working with static assets and files in Remix.

Further reading

Review the MDN Web Docs for more information about URL search parameters and the `URLSearchParams` interface: `https://developer.mozilla.org/en-US/docs/Web/API/URLSearchParams`.

Also refer to the MDN Web Docs if you want to learn more about HTTP cookies: `https://developer.mozilla.org/en-US/docs/Web/HTTP/Cookies` or the `Headers` interface: `https://developer.mozilla.org/en-US/docs/Web/API/Headers`.

Refresh your knowledge about HTML forms by reading through the MDN Web Docs: `https://developer.mozilla.org/en-US/docs/Web/HTML/Element/form`.

Remix provides several primitives for working with sessions. You can find more information in the Remix documentation: `https://remix.run/docs/en/2/utils/sessions`.

Remix also provides lower-level primitives for working with cookies: `https://remix.run/docs/en/2/utils/cookies`.

9
Assets and Metadata Handling

So far, we've practiced routing, data loading and mutations, handling errors, and managing state and sessions in Remix. However, building for the web also involves managing static assets to ensure a smooth and efficient user experience.

In this chapter, we will learn how to manage static assets and meta tags in Remix. This chapter is split into three sections:

- Using meta tags in Remix
- Handling fonts, images, stylesheets, and other assets
- Exposing assets with loader functions

First, we will use Remix's `meta` export to create dynamic meta tags based on loader data. Next, we will investigate how to expose static assets in Remix. We will create a `robots.txt` file, add a custom font, and experiment with nested stylesheets. After that, we will discuss managing images in Remix. Finally, we will see how we can create assets dynamically in `loader` functions.

After reading this chapter, you will understand how to work with meta tags in Remix. You will also know how to expose and access static assets and how to link external resources. Finally, you will know how to expose dynamic assets via `loader` functions.

Technical requirements

You can find the code for this chapter here: `https://github.com/PacktPublishing/Full-Stack-Web-Development-with-Remix/tree/main/09-assets-and-meta-data-handling`. You can go ahead and use the end solution from the previous chapter. No additional setup steps are required for this chapter.

Using meta tags in Remix

Meta tags are used to describe the content of an HTML document. They are important for **Search Engine Optimization** (**SEO**) and are used by web crawlers to understand the content of your site.

Meta tags are also used to configure browser behavior, link previews, and the site's appearance in the bookmark list and search results.

For example, the title, description, and image meta tags are used on link previews and search pages, like Google's search results. The title meta tag is also used together with the favicon to display the website in the bookmark list.

In this section, you will learn how to add meta tags to your Remix application.

Declaring global meta tags

An application usually exposes some global meta tags that must be included on every page. Since Remix allows us to manage the full HTML document in React, including the head, we can inline global meta tags in the root of our application:

```
<head>
  <meta charSet="utf-8" />
  <meta name="viewport" content="width=device-width, initial-scale=1" />
  <Meta />
  <Links />
</head>
```

Review the `Document` component in `root.tsx`. Notice that we export two global meta tags to set the `charSet` attribute and `viewport` meta tag of the application. As always, you can find more information about browser APIs and the web platform in the MDN Web Docs:

- The `viewport` meta tag: https://developer.mozilla.org/en-US/docs/Web/HTML/Viewport_meta_tag
- The `charSet` attribute: https://developer.mozilla.org/en-US/docs/Web/HTML/Element/meta#attributes

Content-aware meta tags, such as `title` and `description`, must be set dynamically for every page. In Remix, we can use the `meta` export to inject meta tags into the head of our application. Let's see how that works.

Exporting the meta function

Every route module in Remix can export a `meta` function. Remix follows the route hierarchy to find the closest `meta` export and injects it into the head of the HTML document. Let's jump into the code of our BeeRich application and investigate how the `meta` export is used to define meta tags:

1. Open the `app/root.tsx` file and look for the `meta` export:

    ```
    export const meta: MetaFunction = () => {
      return [{ title: 'BeeRich' }];
    };
    ```

The `meta` function returns a list of metadata objects. Currently, we only return a title metadata object.

2. Run BeeRich locally with `npm run dev`.
3. Open the app in a browser window by navigating to `http://localhost:3000/`.
4. Inspect the HTML by using the developer tools of your browser. The head element's content should look as follows:

   ```
   <head>
     <meta charset="utf-8">
     <meta name="viewport" content="width=device-width, initial-scale=1">
     <title>BeeRich</title>
     <link rel="stylesheet" href="/build/_assets/tailwind-QJKU32GV.css">
   </head>
   ```

   Notice that the `title` element made it into the head of the HTML document.

5. Add a description metadata object to the `meta` function's return value in `root.tsx`:

   ```
   export const meta: MetaFunction = () => {
     return [
       { title: 'BeeRich' },
       {
         name: 'description',
         content:
           'Bee in control of your finances with BeeRich - the buzzworthy expense and income tracker with a modern interface. Keep your finances organized and make honey with your money!',
       },
     ];
   };
   ```

6. Refresh the browser window and inspect the head element in the developer tools. You can see that the description meta tag was added.

   The question is, how does Remix inject the `meta` export into the head of our app? The answer can be found in the `root.tsx` file.

7. Inspect the JSX of the `Document` component in `root.tsx`:

   ```
   <head>
     <meta charSet="utf-8" />
     <meta name="viewport" content="width=device-width, initial-scale=1" />
   ```

```
    <Meta />
    <Links />
</head>
```

Note that we render Remix's `Meta` component. Remix uses the `Meta` component to add the `meta` exports to our application. The `Meta` component receives the content of the closest `meta` export and injects its content into our React application.

By default, the `Meta` component is rendered in the head of our Remix application. If we were to remove the `Meta` component, the `meta` exports would not end up in our document anymore.

Next, let's investigate how Remix manages nested `meta` exports.

Nesting meta exports

In this section, we'll add some `meta` exports to nested route modules:

1. Open the `_layout.login.tsx` route module and add the following code:

   ```
   import type { ActionFunctionArgs, LoaderFunctionArgs,
   MetaFunction } from '@remix-run/node';

   export const meta: MetaFunction = () => {
     return [
       { title: 'Log In | BeeRich' },
       { name: 'description', content: 'Log into your BeeRich
   account to track your expenses and income.' },
     ];
   };
   ```

2. Run BeeRich locally by executing `npm run dev` in your terminal.

3. Open the login page by navigating to `http://localhost:3000/login` and inspect the content of the head element.

   Note that the title and description defined in `root.tsx` are overridden by the nested `meta` export.

> **Use the meta export in nested route modules to override parent meta tags**
>
> The `meta` route module export lets us define meta tags at any level in the route hierarchy. Remix uses the closest `meta` function return values and adds them to the head of the document by using the `Meta` component. Nested `meta` exports replace parent `meta` exports.

Remix initially renders on the server. The rendered document includes all declared meta tags and ensures that crawlers can inspect all meta tags without the need to execute client-side JavaScript. This is great for SEO.

Often, the content of the meta tags depends on dynamic data. For example, you may want to use the title and summary of an article for the title and description meta tags. Let's see how we can access loader data in `meta` functions.

Using loader data in meta functions

A `meta` function runs both on the client and the server. On initial render, the `meta` function is called during server-side rendering. For all subsequent client-side navigations, the `meta` function is executed on the client after the loader data has been fetched from the server. In both cases, Remix passes the route's loader data and a hash map of all parent loader data to the `meta` function.

In this section, we will add the current user's name to the title of the BeeRich dashboard and explore how we can take advantage of loader data in `meta` functions:

1. Open the `dashboard.tsx` route module in your editor.
2. Update the `loader` function in `dashboard.tsx` to return the current user's name.

   ```
   import { getUser, logout } from '~/modules/session/session.
   server';

   export async function loader({ request }: LoaderFunctionArgs) {
     const user = await getUser(request);
     if (!user) return logout(request);
     const expenseQuery = db.expense.findFirst({
       orderBy: { createdAt: 'desc' },
       where: { userId: user.id },
     });
     const invoiceQuery = db.invoice.findFirst({
       orderBy: { createdAt: 'desc' },
       where: { userId: user.id },
     });

     const [firstExpense, firstInvoice] = await Promise.
   all([expenseQuery, invoiceQuery]);
     return json({ firstExpense, firstInvoice, username: user.name
   });
   }
   ```

   Previously, the `requireUserId` helper function was used to get `userId` from the session cookie and authenticate the user.

   Now, we replace the usage of `requireUserId` with `getUser` and `logout`. We use the `getUser` helper functions to query for the user object. We then check whether the user object exists; otherwise, we call `logout` to clear the session. Finally, we return the user name as part of the loader data.

3. Next, add the following `meta` function export to the route module:

```
import type { LoaderFunctionArgs, MetaFunction, SerializeFrom }
from '@remix-run/node';

export const meta: MetaFunction<typeof loader> = ({ data }) => {
  const title = data?.username ? `${data.username}'s Dashboard | BeeRich` : 'Dashboard | BeeRich';
  return [{ title }, { name: 'robots', content: 'noindex' }];
};
```

We access the route's loader data using the `data` property. Then, we read the `username` property to dynamically create a `title` tag.

We also set the `robots` meta tag to `noindex` as the dashboard is hidden behind a login page. Web crawlers should not attempt to index our dashboard pages. All nested routes will inherit the `noindex` value if they don't export a `meta` function themselves.

Great! Just like that, we can use dynamic data to create metatags. However, one question remains: Why do we use the `?` operator to check whether the (loader) `data` property is defined before accessing `username`?

Note that the `meta` function is also executed if an error occurs. This ensures our meta tags are added even when an error boundary is rendered. If we render an error boundary, then the loader data won't be available. Conclusively, in `meta`, we must always check whether the `data` property is defined before accessing its properties.

> **Meta functions run on the client, the server, and on error**
>
> A `meta` function runs even if the route's `loader` function throws an error. Hence, it is important to check whether the expected loader data exists before accessing it. Additionally, we must ensure that our `meta` functions can be safely executed on both the client and the server since they run in both environments. Any server-side logic must be executed in the `loader` functions (on the server), and any required data should be forwarded to the `meta` function via loader data.

Web crawlers use meta tags to understand the content of your page. Remix's declarative approach to managing meta tags in nested route modules ensures the co-location of meta tags and the related loader data. However, sometimes, we can avoid refetching data if that data has already been fetched in another active `loader`. Let's see what that looks like.

Using matches data in meta functions

In Remix, `meta` functions are executed after all loaders have run. This means we have access to all currently active loader data. In this section, we'll learn about Remix's `matches` array and how to access the loader data of other routes in `meta`.

Remember that we already fetch the user data in the `root.tsx` `loader` function:

```
export async function loader({ request }: LoaderFunctionArgs) {
  const user = await getUser(request);
  return { user };
}
```

There is no need to refetch the user object in `dashboard.tsx`. We can optimize our code and access the user object from the root loader data. This way, we avoid querying the database again in the `dashboard.tsx` route module's `loader` function:

1. First, import the root `loader` function from `root.tsx` as a type import:

   ```
   import type { loader as rootLoader } from '~/root';
   ```

   We import the `loader` function as a type import as we only use it for type inference. Note that we must rename the `loader` import to `rootLoader` to avoid a naming collision with the `dashboard.tsx` route module's `loader` function.

2. Next, update the meta function in `dashboard.tsx`, as follows:

   ```
   export const meta: MetaFunction<typeof loader, { root: typeof
   rootLoader }> = ({ matches }) => {
     const root = matches.find((match) => match.id === 'root');
     const userName = root?.data?.user?.name || null;
     const title = userName ? `${userName}'s Dashboard | BeeRich` :
   'Dashboard | BeeRich';
     return [{ title }, { name: 'robots', content: 'noindex' }];
   };
   ```

   `MetaFunction` supports a second generic type parameter that can be used to type the loader data of other routes.

   We pass the following type to `MetaFunction`:

   ```
   { root: typeof rootLoader }
   ```

   We specify that a route exists with `root` as the `id` parameter, of which the loader data is of the type returned by the `rootLoader` function.

   Next, we use the `matches` parameter to find the matching route with the `id` parameter of `root` and retrieve its (loader) data. The `matches` array contains a list of route objects that currently match the URL and are active on the page.

   Remix assigns every route module a unique identifier. These identifiers are based on the route module filenames, but the easiest way to identify a route module identifier is by logging the matches array during development.

3. Now that we're using the loader data of another matching route, revert the changes to the `dashboard.tsx` route module's `loader` function. Replace the `getUser` function call with `requireUserId`. This avoids a database query and optimizes our code. Finally, remove the `username` parameter that we added to the `loader` function return object.

In this section, you learned how to type and work with Remix's `matches` array and how to access the loader data of other routes in the `meta` function. Next, let's learn about handling static assets in Remix.

Handling fonts, images, stylesheets, and other assets

Fonts, images, and stylesheets are examples of static assets that need to be efficiently managed when building for the web. To ensure a fast user experience, it is necessary to optimize, minimize, and cache these assets. Proper management of static assets can significantly improve page load times and enhance the overall user experience. In this section, you will learn how to access and manage static assets in Remix. Let's start by reviewing how to access a simple static file in Remix.

Working with static assets

We can host static assets on our web server so that our client application can access them. As we learned previously, Remix is not a web server but an HTTP request handler. As such, Remix does not offer a built-in way to serve static assets. It's the underlying web server's responsibility to set up access for public assets.

Luckily, Remix's starter templates follow the common pattern of offering a `public` folder to expose static assets over the web and come with the required boilerplate code to do so. For instance, BeeRich – which was bootstrapped via the `create-remix` CLI tool using the Express.js adapter – contains a bootstrapped `server.js` file that sets up Express.js to serve static assets:

```
app.use(express.static('public', { maxAge: '1h' }));
```

So far, the `public` folder of the BeeRich application contains a `favicon.ico` file, which serves as the favicon of our site. Let's also add a `robots.txt` file:

1. Create a `robots.txt` file in the `/public` folder and add this content:

   ```
   User-agent: *
   Disallow: /dashboard/
   Allow: /login
   Allow: /signup
   Allow: /$
   ```

   Web crawlers request the `/robots.txt` file from your web server to find directives for which content to crawl on your site.

We specify that web crawlers are allowed to crawl the login, signup, and index pages of our application. However, since the dashboard is behind a login page, we prevent crawlers from attempting to crawl any of our dashboard pages.

2. Now, run BeeRich with `npm run dev`.
3. Visit `http://localhost:3000/robots.txt` in your browser. You should now see the content of the `robots.txt` text file displayed in your browser.

We use the underlying web server to serve the static contents of our Remix app. Similarly, we can expose fonts, images, stylesheets, third-party scripts, and any other static assets by simply placing them as files in the `public` folder.

Note that some assets, such as images, should be optimized before you access them from the browser. Usually, images and other big assets are better off hosted and optimized in dedicated services such as CDNs and static file storage.

Third-party assets, such as third-party stylesheets and fonts, can also be referenced by using HTML link tags so that we don't have to manage them ourselves in the `public` folder. Let's learn about exposing link tags in Remix.

Managing links in Remix

HTML `link` elements are used to reference third-party resources such as stylesheets and fonts. In Remix, links can be declared via the `links` route module export.

Remix offers a `Links` component to inject all `links` return values into the head of the HTML document. You may have already noticed the `Links` component previously when inspecting the Document component in `root.tsx`:

```
<head>
  <Meta />
  <Links />
</head>
```

So far, we only have one `links` export in BeeRich in the `root.tsx` route module to link to our global Tailwind CSS stylesheet:

```
import tailwindCSS from './styles/tailwind.css';

export const links: LinksFunction = () => [{ rel: 'stylesheet', href: tailwindCSS }];
```

Let's add a font from Google Fonts to practice working with the `links` export:

1. Visit `https://fonts.google.com/specimen/Ubuntu` to inspect the **Ubuntu** font that we want to use. Google Fonts lists the required link tags that we need to add to our application.

   Copy the link tags from `fonts.google.com` and update the return value of the `links` function in `root.tsx`:

   ```
   export const links: LinksFunction = () => [
     { rel: 'stylesheet', href: tailwindCSS },
     { rel: 'preconnect', href: 'https://fonts.googleapis.com' },
     { rel: 'preconnect', href: 'https://fonts.gstatic.com',
   crossOrigin: 'anonymous' },
     {
       rel: 'stylesheet',
       href: 'https://fonts.googleapis.com/
   css2?family=Ubuntu:ital,wght@0,300;0,400;0,
   500;0,700;1,300;1,400;1,500;1,700&display=swap',
     },
   ];
   ```

   Google Fonts specifies three links that we need to add to our `links` function.

2. Next, update the `` `tailwind.config.ts` `` file in the project's root to make **Ubuntu** the default sans serif font:

   ```
   import defaultTheme from 'tailwindcss/defaultTheme';

   export default {
     content: ['./app/**/*.{ts,tsx,jsx,js}'],
     darkMode: 'media', // or 'media' or 'class'
     theme: {
       extend: {
         colors: {
           ...
         },
         fontFamily: {
           sans: ['Ubuntu', ...defaultTheme.fontFamily.sans],
         },
       },
     },
     plugins: [],
   } satisfies Config;
   ```

3. Next, run BeeRich locally by executing `npm run dev` in your terminal.
4. Open BeeRich in a browser window. The new font should now be applied to all text on the page.
5. Open the developer tools to inspect the application's network activity.
6. Refresh the page to reset the displayed activities on the **Network** tab and review the displayed results:

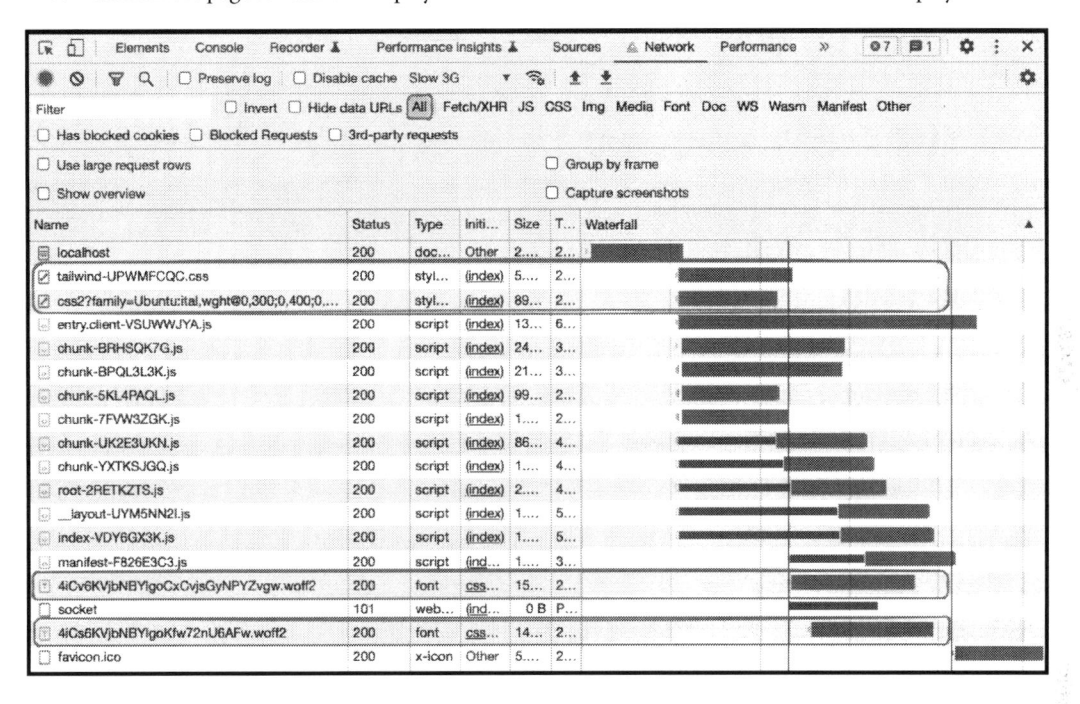

Figure 9.1 – Screenshot of the Network tab downloading a Google font

As visible in *Figure 9.1*, the `links` export works as expected. We make a request for our global Tailwind CSS stylesheet and a request to `fonts.googleapis.com/css2`. The request to `fonts.googleapis` then triggers the download of the required font assets.

Just like that, the `links` export lets us declare external resources declaratively within our nested route hierarchy.

In BeeRich, we use one global Tailwind CSS stylesheet for our application. However, Remix's `links` exports also work well when managing route-specific stylesheets. Let's see how we can use the `links` export for modular stylesheets in Remix.

Styling in Remix

Remix supports any styling solution that exposes a stylesheet. This includes popular choices such as PostCSS, Tailwind CSS, and vanilla-extract. Once we have a path to a stylesheet, we can reference it with a `link` element.

In BeeRich, we use Tailwind CSS. Tailwind outputs one global stylesheet, which we can reference in a global link tag for our application. Remix also provides built-in support for compiling the Tailwind CSS stylesheet. You can read more about Remix's Tailwind CSS integration here: `https://remix.run/docs/en/2/styling/tailwind`.

Additionally, Remix offers support for working with modular CSS solutions. Let's review how that works.

Route-scoped stylesheets

Let's experiment with nested `links` exports by creating a scoped CSS stylesheet for our login page:

1. Create a stylesheet called `login.css` in `app/styles`.
2. Add the following content to the file:

    ```css
    * {
      background-color: beige;
    }
    ```

    We use this global CSS rule as an example for some custom styling that we only want to apply to the login route. Other routes, such as the signup route, should be unaffected by this CSS.

3. Import the stylesheet in the `_layout.login.tsx` route module:

    ```
    import loginCSS from '~/styles/login.css';
    ```

4. Create a new `links` export and add the content of the stylesheet import to it:

    ```
    import type { ActionFunctionArgs, LinksFunction,
    LoaderFunctionArgs, MetaFunction } from '@remix-run/node';

    export const links: LinksFunction = () => [{ rel: 'stylesheet',
    href: loginCSS }];
    ```

5. Run BeeRich locally by executing `npm run dev`.
6. Visit the login route in a browser window and open the **Network** tab of the developer tools to inspect what's going on (`http://localhost:3000/login`).

    Make sure you log out first before visiting the login route as you will be redirected away otherwise.

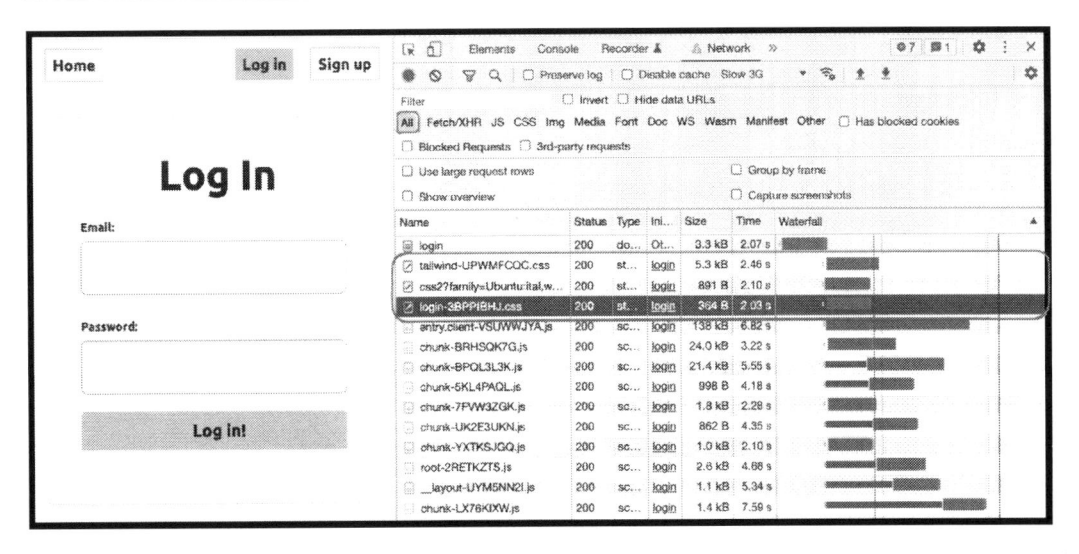

Handling fonts, images, stylesheets, and other assets   185

Figure 9.2 – Loading a nested stylesheet for the login route

Notice that the nested stylesheet loads in parallel with our global linked resources. Remix merges the return values of all `links` functions together and uses the `Links` component to inject the content into the head of the HTML document.

Our login page now has the questionable appearance we wanted. But what happens if we navigate to another URL?

7. Click the **Sign up** button in the top-right corner to trigger a client-side transition away from the login route.

   Notice that the beige background color disappears.

For nested `links` exports, Remix unmounts all resources once we leave the associated route. This is particularly useful when working with nested stylesheets. Remix makes it easy to scope stylesheets to a specific nested route or subset of routes.

Since Remix knows of all `links` exports, it can also prefetch linked resources when using the `Link` export's `prefetch` property, which we will review in the next section.

Prefetching linked resources

Let's investigate how Remix prefetches linked resources:

1. Open the `_layout.tsx` route module in your editor.
2. Add the `prefetch` property to all `NavLink` components rendered in the route's component and set its value to `"intent"`:

   ```
   <NavLink to="/" prefetch="intent">
     Home
   ```

```
</NavLink>
<NavLink to="/dashboard" prefetch="intent">
  Dashboard
</NavLink>
<NavLink to="/login" prefetch="intent">
  Log in
</NavLink>
<NavLink to="/signup" prefetch="intent">
  Sign up
</NavLink>
```

Note that we redacted other markup from the `_layout.tsx` route module component for readability.

As discussed in *Chapter 6, Enhancing the User Experience*, we can add the `prefetch` property to Remix's `Link` and `NavLink` components to prefetch the content of the new matching route modules. Setting `prefetch` to `intent` prefetches the content of all newly matching route modules on hover or focus.

3. Now, visit the signup page in your browser window (`http://localhost:3000/signup`).
4. Open the **Network** tab and clear any logged entries for better visibility.
5. Next, hover over or focus the **Log in** anchor tag in the navigation bar and inspect the **Network** tab:

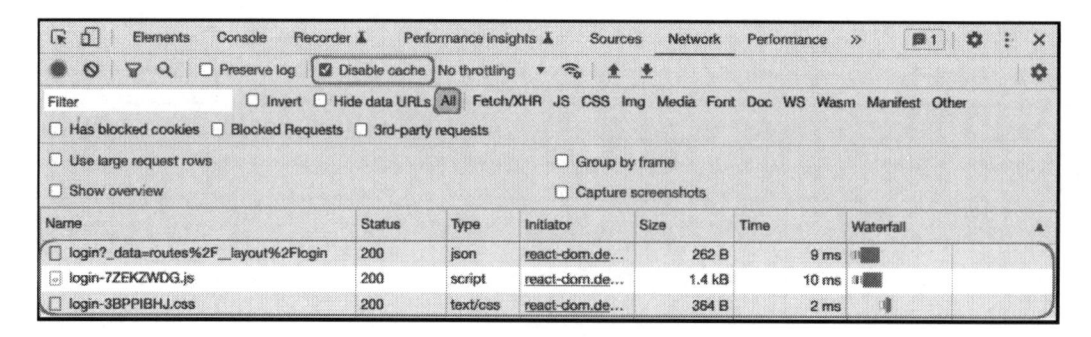

Figure 9.3 – Prefetching linked resources

Notice that Remix prefetches linked resources together with the loader data and the login route JavaScript module. Based on the request waterfall, we can tell that Remix first fetches the loader data and JavaScript modules before prefetching the linked resources.

Remix must first fetch the new route's loader data and JavaScript bundle to know what links to fetch. Once this information has been fetched, Remix prefetches all linked resources in parallel.

Remix allows us to declare meta tags and links in nested route modules. When using the `links` export, Remix enables us to prefetch linked resources together with the loader data and route's JavaScript modules using the `prefetch` property.

Remix also unloads all external resources once the associated route has been unmounted during a transition. This ensures that scoped stylesheets and other resources do not affect other routes.

Next, let's go over some tips for working with images in Remix.

Working with images in Remix

Following best practices to deliver the most performant image to users is no simple task. We need to use web-friendly formats like webp, but also provide fallbacks for browsers that don't support them. On top of that, we have to offer different image sizes for various device screens. That's why using a specialized service for handling images is often a better choice than hosting them on your own web server.

Remix doesn't have built-in tools or features specifically for handling images, unlike some other frameworks. You can put images in the public folder just like any other static files. But since images need to be optimized, it's often best to use a dedicated service to manage and deliver them.

While image optimization is not the focus of this book, it's still an important consideration. To help you get started with image optimization in Remix, we recommend checking out the open source `unpic-img` project. `unpic-img` provides a minimal React component that can be set up with several popular CDNs. Check out the project on GitHub at https://github.com/ascorbic/unpic-img to get started.

In this section, you learned how to expose static assets in Remix and how to work with link elements. You practiced using the `links` function to declare external resources. We also experimented with nested stylesheets and discussed the importance of image optimization.

Remix also provides a way to serve assets via `loader` functions in resource routes. In the next section, we will use our `robots.txt` file as an example of how to use resource routes and `loader` functions to expose static assets.

Exposing assets with loader functions

Earlier in this chapter, we created a `robots.txt` file and exposed it by placing it into the `public` folder. However, we can also use `loader` functions in resource routes to expose assets. This is particularly useful when we want to dynamically create these assets on the fly or manage user access. To get started, follow these steps:

1. Delete the existing `robots.txt` file from the public folder as it will override our API route otherwise.

2. Create a new `robots[.txt].tsx` file in the routes folder.

   The square brackets let us escape parts of the route name. Instead of creating a `.txt` file, we create a `.tsx` file but ensure that the route matches the `robots.txt` path.

3. Add the following content to the newly created resource route:

   ```
   const textContent = `User-agent: *
   Disallow: /dashboard/
   Allow: /login
   Allow: /signup
   Allow: /$`;

   export function loader() {
     return new Response(textContent, { headers: { 'Content-Type': 'text/plain' } });
   }
   ```

Remix lets us return any kind of HTTP response in `loader` functions. Any route without a route component becomes a resource route that can receive HTTP GET requests. The `loader` function in `robots[.txt].tsx` responds to incoming GET requests to `/robots.txt` and returns a text file with the specified text content.

Resource routes and the `Response` API are powerful tools that let us generate PDFs, images, text content, or JSON data on the fly. The bracket annotation (for example, `[.txt]`) is used to escape parts of the route name.

Using `loader` functions to generate assets allows us to run dynamic computations on incoming requests. For example, we can authenticate user sessions or dynamically generate the asset. Our `robots.txt` file is currently static and does not require additional computations. In this case, it is sufficient to store the file in the `public` folder.

Summary

In this chapter, you learned how to handle static assets and meta tags in Remix.

First, we introduced you to the `meta` route module export. You learned that Remix injects the `meta` function's return value into the head of the HTML element by using the `Meta` component. Remix will always use the closest `meta` function export and ignore all other `meta` function exports higher up in the route hierarchy.

You also learned that Remix runs `meta` functions both on the client and server. Remix passes the `meta` function, a `data` property that can be used to access the route's loader data. After following this chapter, you should understand that the `data` property of the `meta` function can potentially be undefined if a `loader` function throws an error. Hence, it is important to only conditionally access loader data in `meta` functions.

You also practiced typing the `matches` parameter and learned how to access other matching route data in the `meta` function.

Next, you learned about handling static assets. You now understand that static assets are served by the underlying web server and not by Remix directly. Remix's starter templates set up a `public` folder and the necessary server code.

You also learned about the `links` route module export. You now know that Remix prefetches linked resources when using the prefetch property on `Link` and `NavLink` components. You also practiced creating route-scoped CSS stylesheets by declaring nested `links` exports.

After reading this chapter, you know the importance of image optimization and where you can get started. You understand that images must be optimized before being served. You also know that CDNs and other services can be used to handle image optimization for us.

Finally, you learned that you can use resource routes to serve static assets. We used the square bracket notation to escape sections of a route name (for example, `[.txt]`). With that, we created a resource route that matches the `/robots.txt` path and implemented a `loader` function that returns a text file response.

In the next chapter, we will add file-uploading capabilities to BeeRich and use a resource route to manage user access to user files. This will conclude part two of this book and enable us to kick off advanced topics in part three.

Further reading

You can find more information about meta tags in the MDN Web Docs: `https://developer.mozilla.org/en-US/docs/Web/HTML/Element/meta`.

You can learn more about Remix's route module meta export in the Remix documentation: `https://remix.run/docs/en/2.0.0/route/meta`.

You can read more about `robots.txt` files in the Google documentation: `https://developers.google.com/search/docs/crawling-indexing/robots/intro`.

Review the MDN Web Docs if you want to learn more about link tags: `https://developer.mozilla.org/en-US/docs/Web/HTML/Element/link`.

You can find more information about handling styling in Remix in the Remix documentation: `https://remix.run/docs/en/2/styling/css`.

You can learn more about working with resource routes in the Remix documentation: `https://remix.run/docs/en/2/guides/resource-routes`.

10
Working with File Uploads

Uploading files is something we do all the time on the web. The web provides built-in support for uploading files. However, uploading and processing files as part of a form submission still requires some additional considerations that we will cover in this chapter. This chapter is split into four sections:

- Using multi-part form data in Remix
- Processing files on the server
- Authorizing access to assets with resource routes
- Forwarding files to third-party services

In this chapter, we will iterate on BeeRich to support file uploads. First, we will update the creation and edit forms to allow adding and removing attachments. Next, we will refactor the `action` functions to process the attached files on the server. Further, we will investigate how to authorize access to uploaded files. Finally, we will learn about file size considerations and discuss different file storage solutions.

After reading this chapter, you will understand how to work with multi-part form data in Remix. You will know how to use Remix's file upload helpers and how to use resource routes to authorize access to uploaded files. You will have also gained a theoretical understanding of what to consider when processing files and how to forward files to third-party services.

Technical requirements

You can find the code for this chapter here: `https://github.com/PacktPublishing/Full-Stack-Web-Development-with-Remix/blob/main/10-working-with-file-uploads/`.

Before starting this chapter, follow the instructions in the README.md file in this chapter's folder on GitHub to clean up the experiments from *Chapter 9, Assets and Metadata Handling*.

Using multi-part form data in Remix

By default, form data is encoded using the `application/x-www-form-urlencoded` encoding type. URL-encoded form data appends the form data as key-value pairs to the request URL as search parameters. To attach files to HTML forms, we need to change the form's encoding type. Appending form data to the URL is not the right approach when transferring binary data such as files. In this section, you will learn how to use multi-part encoding to support file uploads.

There are three different encoding types for HTML form elements:

- `application/x-www-form-urlencoded`
- `multipart/form-data`
- `text/plain`

`text/plain` is not what we are looking for. Plaintext encoding is not used for client-server communication as it submits the data in a human-readable format. Instead, we want to use `multipart/form-data` encoding, which places the form data into the request body, making it possible to include and stream binary files.

Let's update the expense creation and edit forms to allow users to attach files. First, let's go ahead and make the changes to the expense creation form:

1. Open the `dashboard.expenses._index.tsx` route module in an editor.

    The route component currently renders a form with input fields for the expense's title, description, and amount.

2. Update the form encoding type to `multipart/form-data` and add a file input field:

    ```
    <Form method="POST" action="/dashboard/expenses/?index"
    encType="multipart/form-data">
      <Input label="Title:" type="text" name="title"
    placeholder="Dinner for Two" required />
      <Textarea label="Description:" name="description" />
      <Input label="Amount (in USD):" type="number" defaultValue={0}
    name="amount" required />
      <Input label="Attachment" type="file" name="attachment" />
      <Button type="submit" disabled={isSubmitting} isPrimary>
        {isSubmitting ? 'Creating'...'': 'Cre'te'}
      </Button>
    </Form>
    ```

    The `encType` property sets the encoding type for the HTML form element. The default value, `application/x-www-form-urlencoded`, is what we've used thus far in BeeRich. For file uploads, we must update `encyType` to `multipart/form-data`.

Note that the input element's `multiple` property can be used to attach several files to one input field. By default, the input element's `multiple` property is set to `false`. This means the input field lets the user attach only one file.

3. Now, run the app locally (`npm run dev`) and inspect the updated UI.

   As visible in *Figure 10.1*, the expense creation form now contains an attachment input field.

4. Fill out and submit the expense creation form.

   Note that the form submission still works. The `request.formData` function can parse both URL-encoded and multi-part form data. One downside of `request.formData` is that it loads all the form data into server memory. We will see what alternatives we have later in this chapter:

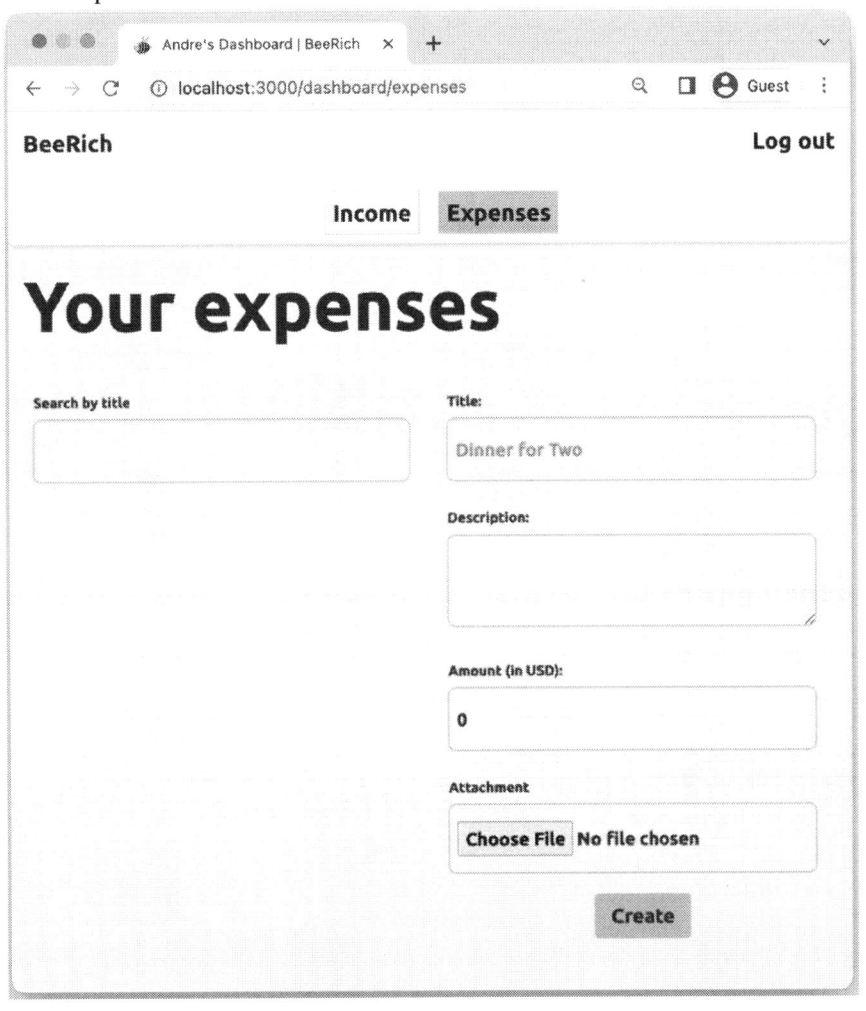

Figure 10.1 – Screenshot of a form with an attachment input field

Great! Just like that, we added an attachment to the expense creation form. As always, apply the same changes to the invoice creation form.

The expense creation form can now include an optional file attachment. In the next section, we will read the uploaded file on the server and persist it to the filesystem. However, we also need to associate saved attachments with the expenses. Let's update the database schema so that it supports adding attachments to expenses and invoices:

1. First, open the `prisma/schema.prisma` file in your editor.
2. Add the following line to the `Expense` and `Invoice` database models:

   ```
   attachment String?
   ```

   In our database, we only store the filename of the attachment and not the attachment data itself. Most databases can store files, but usually, it is recommended to have a dedicated file storage, as storing files in the database may affect the overall query performance of the database.

   Note that the `attachment` field is marked as optional since we added a question mark symbol after the data type.

3. Save the changes and run `npx prisma format` in the terminal at the project's root to format the `schema.prisma` file.
4. Next, execute `npm run build` to update the Prisma client and types.

   Under the hood, Prisma generates types based on the `schema.prisma` file. After running `npm run build`, the expense and invoice types include the optional `attachment` property.

5. Finally, run `npm run update:db` to synchronize your local SQLite database schema with the updated Prisma schema.

Once an expense has been created, we want to let users view and remove their current attachment. If no attachment is set, we further want users to be able to upload a new attachment. Next, let's update the expense edit form to add this functionality:

1. Open the `dashboard.expenses.$id.tsx` route module in your editor.
2. Update the route component's form encoding type so that it supports file uploads:

   ```
   <Form method="POST" action={`/dashboard/expenses/${expense.id}`}
     key={expense.id} encType="multipart/form-data">
   ```

3. Next, inspect the `loader` function's return value.

   We need to access the `expense.attachment` property on the client. Note that we already return the full expense object. This automatically includes the new `expense.attachment` property. We can go ahead and read the property in the route's component without changing the `loader` function.

4. Open the `app/components/forms.tsx` file in your editor and inspect the implementation of the `Attachment` component.

   The `Attachment` component expects a `label` property and an `attachmentUrl` property and renders an anchor tag linking to the attachment. It further includes a submit button and a hidden input field named `attachmentUrl`.

   Let's use the `Attachment` component within the edit forms to let users view and delete their expense and invoice attachments.

5. Import the reusable `Attachment` component in `dashboard.expenses.$id.tsx`:

   ```
   import { Attachment, Form, Input, Textarea } from '~/components/
   forms';
   ```

6. Add the following code below the last input field in `dashboard.expenses.$id.tsx`, right before the submit button:

   ```
   {expense.attachment ? (
     <Attachment
       label="Current Attachment"
       attachmentUrl={`/dashboard/expenses/${expense.id}/
   attachments/${expense.attachment}`}
     />
   ) : (
     <Input label="New Attachment" type="file" name="attachment" />
   )}
   ```

   If the expense object has an attachment, then we render the `Attachment` component, which displays a link to the attachment and a submit button to remove the attachment. Otherwise, we display the same input field as in the expense creation form so that users can add a new attachment.

   Notice that the `attachmentUrl` property value points to a new path: `dashboard/expenses/$id/attachments/$`.

7. Run the application locally and inspect the new file input field on the expense edit form.

We need to add a new route module that handles access to file attachments. The new route module will be a resource route nested within the `dashboard/expenses/$id` path. Let's create the necessary route structure for the new route module:

1. Rename the `dashboard.expenses.$id.tsx` file to `dashboard.expenses.$id._index.tsx`.

   The route module still matches the same path as before. As an index route, it now acts as the default child route for the `$id` path segment.

2. Update the `action` attribute on all forms that are submitted to `dashboard.expenses.$id._index.tsx`.

   We moved the `action` function in `dashboard.expenses.$id.tsx` to `dashboard.expenses.$id._index.tsx`. This changes the `action` function's path.

   A. Open the `dashboard.expenses.tsx` parent route module and update the `deleteProps` property of the `ListLinkItem` component:

   ```
   deleteProps={{
     ariaLabel: `Delete expense ${expense.title}`,
     action: `/dashboard/expenses/${expense.id}?index`,
   }}
   ```

   We added the `?index` flag to tell Remix that the `action` function can be found in the index file instead of the layout parent route module.

   B. Open the new `dashboard.expenses.$id._index.tsx` route module and add the `?index` search parameter to the form's `action` prop:

   ```
   <Form
     method="POST"
     action={`/dashboard/expenses/${expense.id}?index`}
     key={expense.id}
     encType="multipart/form-data"
   >
   ```

   This sets the action of the expense edit form to the updated route module path. Alternatively, we could omit the action path here. Remix ensures that, by default, every route module submits to its own `action` function.

3. Next, create a new splat route module named `dashboard.expenses.$id.attachments.$.tsx`.

   Splats are wildcard route parameters that match the rest of the URL path starting from its location. Regardless of what subpath follows `/dashboard/expenses/$id/attachments/`, the splat parameter matches and stores the subpath in `params['*']`.

   For instance, if a user visits the `/dashboard/expenses/$id/attachments/bees/cool-bees.png` URL path, then the `params['*']` splat parameter contains the `bees/cool-bees.png` string.

4. Add the following code to the `dashboard.expenses.$id.attachments.$.tsx` splat route module:

   ```
   import type { LoaderFunctionArgs } from '@remix-run/node';

   export async function loader({ request, params }:
   LoaderFunctionArgs) {
   ```

```
    const { id } = params;
    const slug = params['*'];
    if (!id || !slug) throw Error('id and slug route parameters
must be defined');
    console.log({ id, slug });
    return new Response('Coming soon!');
}
```

For now, we read the splat route and expense identifier parameters. Then, we log the route parameters to the terminal and return a text response.

We will update this code later in this chapter once we've taken care of persisting attachments on the server.

5. Now, run the app locally (`npm run dev`) and open the application in a new browser window.
6. Sign or log in to BeeRich and create a new expense.
7. Navigate to an expense details page by clicking on an expense in the expense overview list on the dashboard.
8. Append the: `/attachments/bees/cool-bees.png` path to the URL in the browser window.

   You should see the **Coming soon** text in your browser window. Resource routes allow us to return any kind of response from `loader` functions, not just data for our route components.

9. Investigate the terminal and review the output of `console.log({ id, slug })`. Change the URL in the browser window to see how the output changes.

Great! We created the required route module structure for our file upload functionality. As always, make sure to update the income route files to practice what you've learned in this section. Run the application locally to debug your implementation.

In this section, you learned how to set the encoding type on an HTML form element and add file input fields. You further practiced working with splat route modules and resource routes. Next, we will utilize Remix's file upload helper functions on the server to write the incoming files to the filesystem.

Processing files on the server

There are several important considerations when handling file uploads on the server, most importantly the file size. In this section, we will learn how to process files in Remix's `action` functions. We will start with a naïve implementation before refactoring the code and taking more concerns into account.

Loading files into memory

Let's get started by implementing some utilities for working with files:

1. Create a new `app/modules/attachments.server.ts` file.

2. Add the following code to `attachments.server.ts`:

```
import fs from 'fs';
import path from 'path';

export async function writeFile(file: File) {
  const localPath = path.join(process.cwd(), 'public', file.name);
  const arrayBufferView = new Uint8Array(await file.arrayBuffer());
  fs.writeFileSync(localPath, arrayBufferView);
}
```

The added `writeFile` function accepts a file and writes it to the `public` folder. Note that this is not our end solution but an intermediate step.

The way we access the filesystem depends on the underlying server runtime. BeeRich runs on a Node.js runtime. Hence, in BeeRich, we use Node.js libraries to write to the filesystem.

3. Open the `dashboard.expenses._index.tsx` route module.

4. Update the route module's `action` function, as follows:

```
import { writeFile } from '~/modules/attachments.server';

export async function action({ request }: ActionFunctionArgs) {
  const userId = await requireUserId(request);
  const formData = await request.formData();
  const file = formData.get('attachment');
  if (file && file instanceof File) {
    writeFile(file);
  }
  ...
}
```

We access the `attachment` form data entry, check whether it is a file, and then pass it to the `writeFile` function. Currently, `writeFile` writes the uploaded file to the `public` folder for easy public access.

5. Run BeeRich locally to test the current implementation.

6. Fill out the expense creation form, attach a file, and click **Create**.

You should see the selected file pop up in the `public` folder in your editor. Just like that, we can upload a file to the server and write it to the filesystem.

7. You can now access the file by navigating to `http://localhost:3000/$file-name`. Note that you must also add the file extension to the path.

Theoretically, we could now read the filename on the server and save it to the expense object in the database. Since all files in the `public` folder are already accessible over the web, we could let users access their files by linking to `/$filename`.

Unfortunately, there are some limitations to the current naïve implementation:

- Filename collisions
- File size limitations
- Privacy concerns

With the current implementation, we do not manage filenames to avoid collisions. What if two users upload a file with the same name? We also don't handle file size limitations. Large files can easily eat up the runtime memory on a server. Hence, it is important that we either limit the file size a user can upload or better implement the file upload handler in a way that it processes the incoming file as a stream of data where the file is handled in chunks rather than trying to load the whole file into memory at once.

Further, by storing files in the `public` folder, we make the files publicly accessible. Anyone can try to guess filenames until they are lucky and able to access a file of another user – this is a huge security concern, especially when we are talking about sensitive data such as invoices and expenses.

Luckily, we can solve all these problems by taking advantage of Remix's primitives and conventions. Let's solve the first two concerns first using Remix's upload handler helper functions.

Using Remix's upload handler helper functions

Remix offers a set of helper functions to manage file uploads. We will use the following ones to improve the current naïve implementation:

- `unstable_composeUploadHandlers`
- `unstable_createFileUploadHandler`
- `unstable_createMemoryUploadHandler`
- `unstable_parseMultipartFormData`

Note that the functions currently include an `unstable_` prefix. This means their implementation may be up to change in future releases.

Let's get started:

1. First, create a new folder in the project's root called `attachments`. This is where we will store all attached files on the server.
2. Next, open the `app/modules/attachments.server.ts` file in your editor.

3. Remove the `writeFile` function.
4. Instead, use the `unstable_createFileUploadHandler` function to create a new file upload handler:

```
import type { UploadHandler } from '@remix-run/node';
import {
  unstable_composeUploadHandlers,
  unstable_createFileUploadHandler,
  unstable_createMemoryUploadHandler,
} from '@remix-run/node';

const standardFileUploadHandler = unstable_createFileUploadHandler({
  directory: './attachments',
  avoidFileConflicts: true,
});
```

The `unstable_createFileUploadHandler` function takes a configuration object to specify where to store the uploaded files. It also lets us set the `avoidFileConflicts` flag to create unique filenames.

The `standardFileUploadHandler` function is responsible for writing the uploaded files to the filesystem. Refer to the Remix documentation for more information about the available configuration options: `https://remix.run/docs/en/2.0.0/utils/unstable-create-file-upload-handler`.

5. Next, create a custom file upload handler function:

```
const attachmentsUploadHandler: UploadHandler = async (args) => {
  if (args.name !== 'attachment' || !args.filename) return null;
  const file = await standardFileUploadHandler(args);
  if (!file) return null;
  if (typeof file === 'string') return file;
  return file.name;
};
```

We wrap `standardFileUploadHandler` to add a bit of helper logic. First, we ensure that we only process file attachments with the `attachment` input name. Then, we make sure to return the filename or `null` if no file was attached.

Notice that `attachmentsUploadHandler` implements Remix's `UploadHandler` type. This allows us to compose it together with Remix's file helper functions.

6. Use Remix's `unstable_composeUploadHandlers` function to compose our `attachmentsUploadHandler` helper function and Remix's `unstable_createMemoryUploadHandler`:

   ```
   export const uploadHandler = unstable_composeUploadHandlers(
     attachmentsUploadHandler,
     unstable_createMemoryUploadHandler(),
   );
   ```

   With that, we've created a higher-level `uploadHandler` helper function composed of two upload handlers.

   `uploadHandler` calls the two handlers for each form data entry. First, we attempt to handle the form data entry with `attachmentsUploadHandler`. If `attachmentsUploadHandler` returns `null`, then we also attempt to handle the form data entry with `unstable_createMemoryUploadHandler`.

   As its name suggests, Remix's `unstable_createMemoryUploadHandler` will handle all other form data fields and upload them to server memory so that we can access it, as usual, using the `FormData` interface.

Great work! Let's update our `action` functions so that they utilize the new upload handler:

1. Open the `dashboard.expenses._index.tsx` route module.

2. Remove the `writeFile` import and naïve implementation in the route module's `action` function:

   ```
   const file = formData.get('attachment');
   if (file && file instanceof File) {
     writeFile(file);
   }
   ```

3. Import `unstable_parseMultipartFormData` from Remix:

   ```
   import { redirect, unstable_parseMultipartFormData } from '@remix-run/node';
   ```

4. Import `uploadHandler` from `app/modules/attachments.server.tsx`:

   ```
   import { uploadHandler } from '~/modules/attachments.server';
   ```

5. Use `parseMultipartFormData` to replace `request.formData()`:

   ```
   const formData = await unstable_parseMultipartFormData(request, uploadHandler);
   ```

   Here, we let `unstable_parseMultipartFormData` handle the multipart form data using our custom `uploadHandler`. `unstable_parseMultipartFormData` calls our higher-order upload handler for every form data entry. The composed upload handler loops through our upload handlers until one of them returns neither `null` nor `undefined`. The attachment form data entry is processed by the file upload handler, returning the file name of the uploaded file, or null if no file has been submitted. `unstable_createMemoryUploadHandler` handles all other form data for us.

6. Next, add the code to read the attachment form data and update the database query:

```
export async function action({ request }: ActionFunctionArgs) {
  const userId = await requireUserId(request);
  const formData = await unstable_
parseMultipartFormData(request, uploadHandler);
  const title = formData.get('title');
  const description = formData.get('description');
  const amount = formData.get('amount');
  if (typeof title !== 'string' || typeof description !==
'string' || typeof amount !== 'string') {
    throw Error('something went wrong');
  }
  const amountNumber = Number.parseFloat(amount);
  if (Number.isNaN(amountNumber)) {
    throw Error('something went wrong');
  }
  let attachment = formData.get('attachment');
  if (!attachment || typeof attachment !== 'string') {
    attachment = null;
  }
  const expense = await db.expense.create({
    data: {
      title,
      description,
      amount: amountNumber,
      currencyCode: 'USD',
      attachment,
      user: {
        connect: {
          id: userId,
        },
      },
    },
  });
  return redirect(`/dashboard/expenses/${expense.id}`);
}
```

We now use a custom upload handler to write the incoming stream of file data chunks to the filesystem and persist the associated filename in the database.

7. Run BeeRich locally and test uploading a file with the expense creation form.

   You should be able to see the attached files in the new `attachments` folder.

   Note that the file upload will fail if the file size exceeds 30 MB. This is Remix's default maximum file size. The file size can be increased by updating the configuration options that are passed to `unstable_createFileUploadHandler`.

Congratulations! You successfully added a file upload to the expense creation form. Make sure you apply the same changes to the income routes before moving on to the next section. Reuse the helper functions in `attachments.server.ts` to update the invoice creation `action` function.

> **Preventing server memory overflows**
>
> When working with file uploads, we must keep memory limitations in mind. Large file sizes can easily overwhelm our servers. This is why it's important to handle incoming files in chunks instead of loading them fully into memory. Remix's file upload helpers help us avoid filenaming collisions and let us stream file data to avoid server memory overflows.

Next, we will update the expense edit form so that it can also handle file uploads:

1. Open the `dashboard.expenses.$id._index.tsx` file in your editor.

2. Again, import `unstable_parseMultipartFormData` and `uploadHandler`:

   ```
   import { json, redirect, unstable_parseMultipartFormData } from
   '@remix-run/node';
   import { uploadHandler } from '~/modules/attachments.server';
   ```

3. Next, update the `action` function with the following code:

   ```
   export async function action({ params, request }:
   ActionFunctionArgs) {
     const userId = await requireUserId(request);
     const { id } = params;
     if (!id) throw Error('id route parameter must be defined');

     let formData: FormData;
     const contentType = request.headers.get('content-type');
     if (contentType?.toLowerCase().includes('multipart/form-
   data')) {
       formData = await unstable_parseMultipartFormData(request,
   uploadHandler);
     } else {
       formData = await request.formData();
     }

     const intent = formData.get('intent');
   ```

```
    if (intent === 'delete') {
      return deleteExpense(request, id, userId);
    }
    if (intent === 'update') {
      return updateExpense(formData, id, userId);
    }
    throw new Response('Bad request', { status: 400 });
  }
```

Notice that the `action` function distinguishes between `delete` and `update` form submissions. The delete form submission originates from the `ListLinkItem` component, while the update submission originates from the expense edit form in the `dashboard.expenses.$id._index.tsx` route module.

Earlier in the chapter, we updated the expense edit form encoding to multi-part encoding, but we did not do the same to the expense deletion form. Hence, the `action` function must be able to support both multipart and URL-encoded form data. For this, we use the `content-type` header to distinguish which form encoding has been used and only use `parseMultipartFormData` for `multipart/form-data`.

4. Next, update the `updateExpense` function so that it reads the `attachment` form data entry and adds the value to the database update query:

```
let attachment: FormDataEntryValue | null | undefined =
  formData.get('attachment');
if (!attachment || typeof attachment !== 'string') {
  attachment = undefined;
}
await db.expense.update({
  where: { id_userId: { id, userId } },
  data: { title, description, amount: amountNumber, attachment
},
});
```

The `updateExpense` function is called when the edit expense form is submitted. Here, we want to ensure that newly uploaded attachments are added to the expense update query.

Note that we already persisted the file to the filesystem when calling `unstable_parseMultipartFormData(request, uploadHandler)`. The `updateExpense` function ensures that the expense entry in the database is updated accordingly.

We must also make sure we clean up the filesystem whenever an attachment is removed or the associated expense is deleted.

5. Add the following function to the `attachments.server.ts` file:

   ```
   import fs from 'fs';
   import path from 'path';

   export function deleteAttachment(fileName: string) {
     const localPath = path.join(process.cwd(), 'attachments', fileName);
     try {
       fs.unlinkSync(localPath);
     } catch (error) {
       console.error(error);
     }
   }
   ```

   `deleteAttachment` receives a `fileName` and deletes the associated file from the `attachments` folder.

6. Import `deleteAttachment` in `dashboard.expenses.$id._index.tsx`:

   ```
   import { deleteAttachment, uploadHandler } from '~/modules/attachments.server';
   ```

7. Next, implement a new `removeAttachment` function, which we will call in the route module's `action` function:

   ```
   async function removeAttachment(formData: FormData, id: string, userId: string): Promise<Response> {
     const attachmentUrl = formData.get('attachmentUrl');
     if (!attachmentUrl || typeof attachmentUrl !== 'string') {
       throw Error('something went wrong');
     }
     const fileName = attachmentUrl.split('/').pop();
     if (!fileName) throw Error('something went wrong');
     await db.expense.update({
       where: { id_userId: { id, userId } },
       data: { attachment: null },
     });
     deleteAttachment(fileName);
     return json({ success: true });
   }
   ```

   `removeAttachment` is called within the route module's `action` function when the submit button carries the `remove-attachment` value, which is implemented in the `Attachment` component.

8. Update the route module's `action` function so that it handles the `remove-attachment` form's action intent:

```
const intent = formData.get('intent');
if (intent === 'delete') {
  return deleteExpense(request, id, userId);
}
if (intent === 'update') {
  return updateExpense(formData, id, userId);
}
if (intent === 'remove-attachment') {
  return removeAttachment(formData, id, userId);
}
throw new Response('Bad request', { status: 400 });
```

If you aren't sure where the `remove-attachment` value originates from, investigate the `Attachment` component in `app/components/forms.tsx`. The Attachment component contains a hidden input field for `attachmentUrl` and a submit button with a value of `remove-attachment`. The component is nested in the `dashboard.expenses.$id._index.tsx` route module's form and submits to the same `action` function.

9. Finally, update the `deleteExpense` function in the same file to remove the attachment when an expense is deleted:

```
const expense = await db.expense.delete({ where: { id_userId: { id, userId } } });
if (expense.attachment) {
  deleteAttachment(expense.attachment);
}
```

10. Now that you've done all the hard work, run `npm run dev` and open a browser window to test the implementation.

11. Create an expense with an attachment. Check the `attachments` folder in your editor.

12. Remove the attachment by clicking the **X** button next to the **Current Attachment** link. Again, investigate the `attachments` folder to see whether the file was deleted successfully.

13. Next, add a new attachment to the same expense using the edit form and investigate the `attachments` folder again.

14. Finally, delete the expense by clicking the **X** button in the expense overview list and check whether the file was deleted:

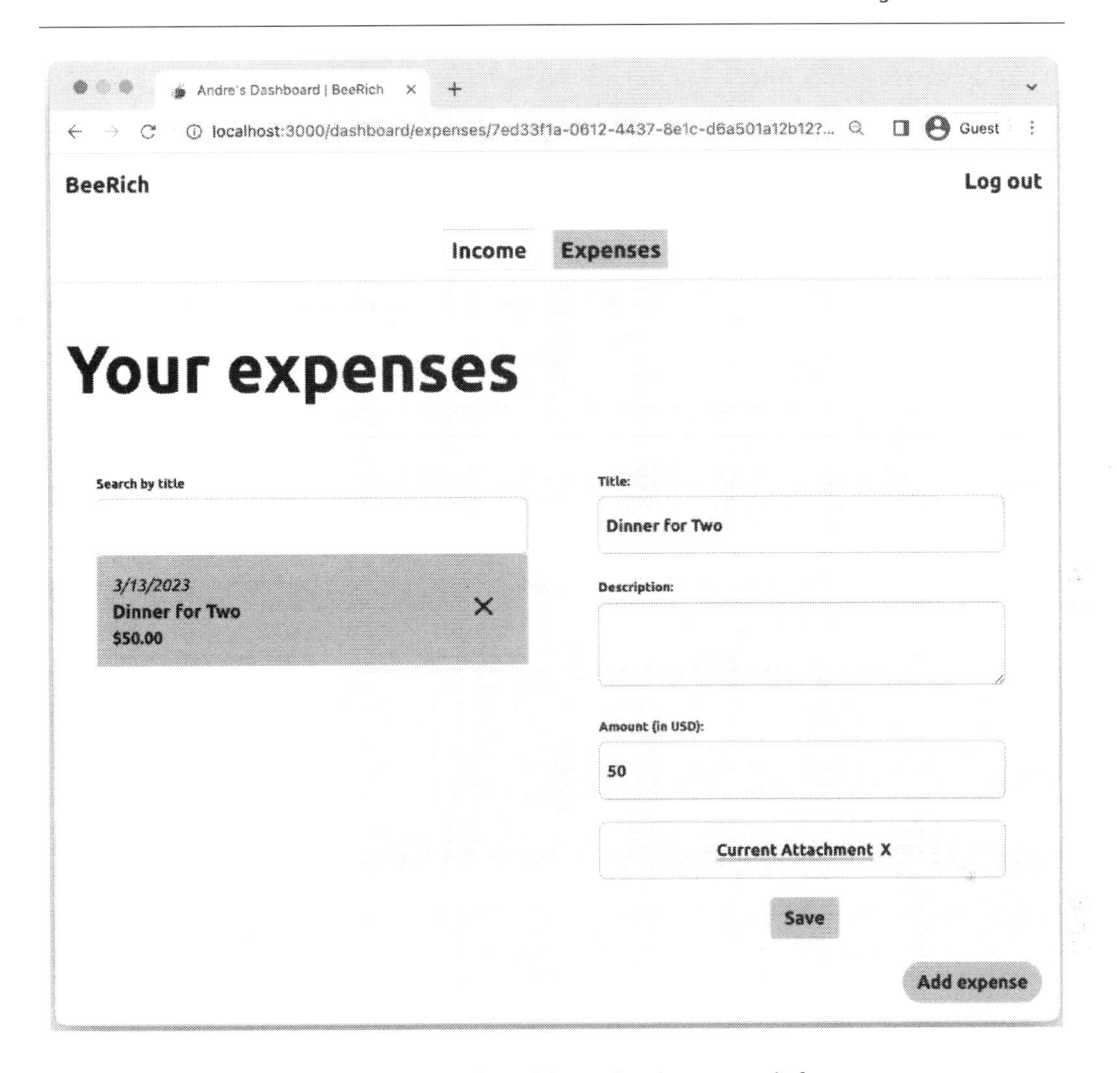

Figure 10.2 – Screenshot of the updated expense edit form

As visible in *Figure 10.2*, the expense edit form should now correctly switch between the current attachment and the attachment input field if no attachment is set. The **X** button next to the **Current Attachment** link should now remove the attachment from the expense database entry and delete the file from the `attachments` folder. Deleting an expense should also remove the associated attached file from the `attachments` folder.

Before moving on, update the `income` routes to practice what you have learned in this section. Once the `income` routes have been updated, you can move on to the next section.

In this section, you learned how to work with Remix's file upload helper functions. You now understand the considerations that come into play when managing file uploads and how to use Remix's utilities to avoid memory and filenaming collisions. Next, we will implement the splat route to give BeeRich users secure access to their attachments.

Authorizing access to assets with resource routes

In *Chapter 9, Assets and Metadata Handling*, you practiced exposing assets via resource routes. We will now expand on that by dynamically creating a file download for the requested expense attachment. We will implement the splat route responsible for exposing the attachments and ensure that only authorized users can access their files:

1. First, let's add one more helper function to the `attachments.server.ts` file:

    ```
    export function buildFileResponse(fileName: string): Response {
      const localPath = path.join(process.cwd(), 'attachments', fileName);
      try {
        const file = fs.readFileSync(localPath);
        return new Response(file, {
          headers: {
            'Content-Type': 'application/octet-stream',
            'Content-Disposition': `attachment; filename="${fileName}"`,
          },
        });
      } catch (error) {
        console.error(error);
        return new Response('Not Found', { status: 404 });
      }
    }
    ```

    The `buildFileResponse` function takes a `fileName` string and attempts to stream the associated file into a `Response` object. The `content-disposition` header ensures that the response is treated as a file download.

    Again, we avoid loading the full file into memory. Instead, we make sure to read the file into a buffer and manage it in chunks to avoid exceeding the server's memory capabilities.

2. Next, open the `dashboard.expenses.$id.attachments.$.tsx` splat route module and replace its content with the following code:

    ```
    import type { LoaderFunctionArgs } from '@remix-run/node';
    import { redirect } from '@remix-run/router';
    ```

```
import { buildFileResponse } from '~/modules/attachments.
server';
import { db } from '~/modules/db.server';
import { requireUserId } from '~/modules/session/session.
server';

export async function loader({ request, params }:
LoaderFunctionArgs) {
  const userId = await requireUserId(request);
  const { id } = params;
  const slug = params['*'];
  if (!id || !slug) throw Error('id and slug route parameters must be defined');

  const expense = await db.expense.findUnique({ where: { id_userId: { id, userId } } });
  if (!expense || !expense.attachment) throw new Response('Not found', { status: 404 });
  if (slug !== expense.attachment) return redirect(`/dashboard/expenses/${id}/attachments/${expense.attachment}`);
  return buildFileResponse(expense.attachment);
}
```

We secure the resource route by requiring a user session. We further query the database by the id parameter of the expense of the requested attachment.

Notice that we query by a combination of expense id and user id. This ensures that a user can only access their own expenses.

We then do some sanity checks before returning the response created by our new buildFileResponse helper function.

3. It's time to test the implementation. Try to download a current attachment. Clicking on the **Current Attachment** link should initiate a file download.

Great work! You implemented a full stack file upload feature in BeeRich that spans several different forms, routes, and utilities.

Before moving on, make sure you implement the income splat route. Repeating this work on the income routes will help you practice all the new concepts.

> **Restricting access to user files**
>
> It is important to remember that files in the public folder are publicly accessible over the internet. We must ensure that private user data is protected by authorization code. In Remix, we can use resource routes to dynamically check access rights before granting access to user files.

In this section, you learned how to create dynamic responses and expose assets via resource routes. You now understand how to authorize users in resource routes to restrict access. Next, we will discuss forwarding files to third-party services.

Forwarding files to third-party services

So far, we are hosting our user files on the server's filesystem. This is sufficient for the educative scope of BeeRich. However, when working with user files, we should also consider hosting them on a dedicated file storage service. This section quickly outlines what else we need to consider when working with user files.

Hosting user files directly on a web server may not be sufficient for most use cases. Hosting files locally may be hard to scale and requires you to secure sensitive user files and backups on your systems. Additionally, reading and writing to disk might create a lot of overhead for the web server that can be avoided by delegating the reads and writes to a third-party service.

Most popular third-party storage services offer APIs to stream files. This allows us to receive the file upload as a stream of data so that we can forward the stream to a third-party service. After the upload is completed, the storage API usually provides a URL to the uploaded file, which we can use in our database to link to the new file.

Remix's upload handler primitives let you create custom handlers for different third-party services. Instead of writing to the local filesystem, we can create an upload handler that streams the data to a cloud provider.

Popular file hosting providers include AWS S3, Cloudflare, Cloudinary, Firebase, and Vercel. You can find an example implementation that uses Cloudinary in the *Further reading* section.

Summary

In this chapter, you learned how to add files to HTML forms and how to handle file uploads in Remix.

HTML forms support different encoding types. Multipart form encoding adds the form data to the response body. This is required when appending binary data, such as files. On the server, we can then stream in the response body and handle the uploaded files in chunks.

By reading this chapter, you now understand that Remix provides a set of file upload utilities for handling file uploads. Remix utilities help us avoid filenaming collisions and allow us to configure file size limits and file streaming. We can further compose several file upload handlers together and implement custom wrappers by implementing the `UploadHandler` type.

Next, you learned how to restrict access to a resource route by authenticating user sessions and ensuring authorized database queries that query for a unique combination of entity `id` and user `id`. We must not place user files in the `public` folder. Instead, we must leverage resource routes and custom authorization logic.

Finally, we discussed the usage of third-party file hosting services. You now understand that using a third-party service may be more scalable and allow us to offload much of the complexity of storing files to a third-party service.

Congratulations! Just like that, you made it through the second part of this book. In the next chapter, we'll kick off the advanced topics of this book and learn more about optimistic UIs. Keep going to unlock the full potential of the web platform with Remix.

Further reading

You can learn more about the HTML form element's `enctype` property via MDN Web Docs: `https://developer.mozilla.org/en-US/docs/Web/API/HTMLFormElement/enctype`.

You can find additional information about HTTP POST requests via MDN Web Docs: `https://developer.mozilla.org/en-US/docs/Web/HTTP/Methods/POST`.

Review this example implementation from Remix's example repository for uploading files to Cloudinary: `https://github.com/remix-run/examples/tree/main/file-and-cloudinary-upload`.

You can learn more about Remix's file upload helpers by reading the Remix documentation:

- `https://remix.run/docs/en/2.0.0/utils/parse-multipart-form-data`
- `https://remix.run/docs/en/2.0.0/utils/unstable-create-file-upload-handler`
- `https://remix.run/docs/en/2.0.0/utils/unstable-create-memory-upload-handler`

Part 3 – Advanced Concepts of Full Stack Web Development with Remix

In this final part, you will practice advanced concepts of full stack web development, such as optimistic UI, caching strategies, HTML streaming, and real-time data updates. You will again iterate on BeeRich to practice the studied concepts. You will also dig deeper into session management and understand what it means to deploy to the edge. Finally, you will learn about migration strategies to Remix and learn how to keep a Remix application up to date.

This part has the following chapters:

- *Chapter 11, Optimistic UI*
- *Chapter 12, Caching Strategies*
- *Chapter 13, Deferring Loader Data*
- *Chapter 14, Real-Time with Remix*
- *Chapter 15, Advanced Session Management*
- *Chapter 16, Developing for the Edge*
- *Chapter 17, Migration and Upgrade Strategies*

11
Optimistic UI

Optimistic UI makes your app feel snappy by giving immediate feedback, even when actions take a bit longer. This is especially useful when you're waiting for a network response. Optimistic updates can make a UI feel more responsive and improve the user experience. In this chapter, you will learn how to add optimistic UI updates with Remix.

This chapter is split into two sections:

- Considering optimistic UI
- Adding optimistic UI updates in Remix

First, we will discuss the trade-offs of using optimistic UI updates and investigate the complexity and risks of client/server state synchronizations and rollbacks. Next, we will review the current state of BeeRich and investigate which mutations to enhance with optimistic UI updates. We will then add optimistic UI updates where it makes sense using Remix's primitives.

After reading this chapter, you will know how to evaluate the usage of optimistic UIs. You will have also practiced implementing optimistic UIs with Remix's primitives, such as `useNavigation` and `useFetcher`. Finally, you will understand how Remix eases the implementation of optimistic UIs by providing a resilient baseline for your application.

Technical requirements

You can find the code for this chapter here: `https://github.com/PacktPublishing/Full-Stack-Web-Development-with-Remix/tree/main/11-optimistic-ui`.

BeeRich has grown quite a bit. Now is a good time to refactor the code. Before starting with this chapter, we want to update the current code. We will also enhance our form validation and parsing using `zod`. Follow the step-by-step guide in the `README.md` file to prepare BeeRich for the upcoming advanced topics.

Considering optimistic UI

The source of truth of a web application is usually stored remotely in a database. We can only be sure that a mutation succeeded after updating the database and receiving confirmation from the server. The UI response to a mutation is thereby delayed until we hear back from the server.

Optimistic UI is a pattern that's used to provide instant feedback to users while waiting for an execution to resolve. When updating the UI optimistically, we apply a UI update before receiving the definitive response from the server. Most of the time, our mutations succeed, so why wait for a server response? In this section, we will discuss some trade-offs of optimistic UI updates.

Communicating rollbacks

Updating the UI optimistically speeds up the perceived response time when the optimistic state aligns with the server response. When the optimistic update does not align with the server response, then optimistic updates need to be rolled back or corrected. This is where the optimistic UI pattern starts to become more complicated.

When something goes wrong with an optimistic mutation, we must communicate the error and highlight the rollback to the user. Otherwise, we risk losing the user's trust and confidence in our application. For instance, after attempting to delete an item, we might have to revert to the optimistic removal of the item and tell the user why the item reappeared again – "*I just deleted that item; why is it back?*"

When considering optimistic UI, it is a good idea to investigate the error rate of a mutation. If the error rate is high, then the number of rollbacks might degrade the user experience more than the increased response times are worth. As always, it depends on the use case, type of application, and user.

We can summarize that error handling with optimistic UI becomes harder to implement as rollbacks have to be communicated correctly. On top of that, optimistic UIs also require re-synchronizing client and server states, leading to more complicated client-side code.

Synchronizing client and server states

One of the biggest risks of optimistic UI is introducing stale states in the UI. When applying optimistic updates, it can become quite challenging to synchronize the UI state with the server response consistently. The resulting logic might be complex and introduce bugs where part of the application's UI is out of sync with the server state.

When adding optimistic updates, we may allow users to submit several updates subsequently. We optimistically update the UI each time. Then, we must deal with the synchronization of the UI with the server responses. When several updates happen simultaneously, this may lead to race conditions and other hard problems that require thorough synchronization logic and error handling.

Optimistic UI updates are optional. When implemented correctly, they may improve the user experience by speeding up the perceived response time. However, there is also the risk that optimistic UI updates may increase the complexity of our application's state management disproportionally and degrade the user experience if not implemented thoroughly.

Optimistic UI updates can lead to stale states, complex client-server state synchronization logic, and a worse user experience if rollbacks aren't communicated properly. Conclusively, we must cautiously evaluate whether a certain mutation would profit from the addition of optimistic UI updates or whether it would disproportionally increase the complexity.

Luckily, Remix provides a great foundation for implementing optimistic UI updates and allows us to implement optimistic UI updates through additive changes to our existing pending UI. Let's remind ourselves of Remix's `loader` revalidation feature.

Synchronizing client and server states in Remix

Remix manages the complexity of optimistic UI out of the box by providing a data revalidation flow. Let's quickly review Remix's built-in `loader` revalidation before jumping into the code.

Whenever we submit a form in Remix and execute an `action` function, Remix will automatically re-fetch the data from all active `loader` functions. This ensures that we always update all data on the page after every data mutation.

When utilizing Remix's `loader` and `action` functions for data reads and writes, we avoid introducing stale data in our UIs and eliminate the main concern of degrading the user experience when implementing optimistic UI updates.

Additionally, Remix's primitives, such as `useNavigation` and `useFetcher`, allow us to read pending submission data without adding custom React states, which keeps the complexity increase of adding optimistic UI at a low. Let's see for ourselves by adding optimistic UI to BeeRich. First, let's review the current mutations in our BeeRich application and investigate whether adding an optimistic UI would improve the user experience.

Adding optimistic UI updates in Remix

In this section, we will review our BeeRich application and discuss which user actions would profit the most from adding optimistic UI updates. Then, we will go ahead and make the required code changes.

Creating an expense

Run BeeRich locally by executing `npm run dev` in the project's root and navigate to the expense overview page (`http://localhost:3000/dashboard/expenses`). Now, create a new expense.

Notice that after submitting the expense creation form, we are redirected to the expense details page. The URL now includes the new expense identifier. After the redirect, we have access to the newly created expense loader data, including the expense identifier. All further updates to the expense require the expense identifier.

Adding optimistic UI updates to the expense creation form may become quite complicated. One way to achieve this would be to optimistically update the look and feel of the creation form so that it looks like the expense update form before redirecting the user to the actual details page. However, we can't execute any subsequent expense update submissions until we receive the expense `id` parameter from the expense creation submission. We could disable all submit buttons until we receive the server response, or we could queue subsequent submissions and submit an update programmatically with the latest changes the user tried to submit. This could become quite complicated.

Things become even more complicated when thinking about the attachment logic. What if we are still waiting on the `id` parameter when the user wants to remove the attached file or tries to upload a new attachment? We could prevent all subsequent changes to the attachment by disabling the attachment actions until we get the expense `id` parameter from the server.

As always, it comes down to trade-offs. How much could we increase the response time and enhance the experience by adding optimistic updates? Is it worth the complexity? Since our application is quite fast, we decided not to add optimistic updates to the expense creation form. Instead, let's move on and investigate the expense update form.

Updating an expense

Navigate to the expense overview page (`http://localhost:3000/dashboard/expenses`) and select an expense. This will navigate us to the expense details page, which renders the expense update form. Now, make some changes to the existing expense and click **Save**. Make sure you test the experience on a throttled network using the **Network** tab of your browser's developer tools. After a successful update, we do not redirect the user and are not awaiting an `id` parameter. Instead, we display a success message: **Changes saved!**.

Technically, the UI already displays optimistic updates as we always show the latest input values to the user. Let's also update the **Save** submit button in the `dashboard.expenses.$id._index.tsx` route module:

1. Remove the `disabled` property and pending "Save..." UI state:

    ```
    <Button type="submit" name="intent" value="update" isPrimary>
      Save
    </Button>
    ```

    It might feel odd at first to remove the pending UI. Let's think this through. The form now supports subsequent updates as we no longer disable the submit button on pending submissions. Since we always show the user-inputted values in the update form, the input state itself is already optimistic. Since we still show the global transition animation and expense details pulse animation on pending navigation, we still communicate that updates are in progress. Additionally, we still display the success message on successful update. This might be a good compromise.

But what about the attachment? Adding an attachment creates a new `expense.attachment` value. We require the attachment filename value for the view and delete attachment actions of the `Attachment` component.

One solution is to add the attachment optimistically but disable the attachment link and the delete button until we receive the server response, which includes the newly added attachment value. Let's make it happen!

2. In the `dashboard.expenses.$id._index.tsx` route module component, use Remix's global navigation object to derive whether an attachment is currently being uploaded:

   ```
   const navigation = useNavigation();
   const attachment = navigation.formData?.get('attachment');
   const isUploadingAttachment = attachment instanceof File &&
   attachment.name !== '';
   ```

   Remix's navigation object has a `formData` property. This property contains the data of the currently submitted form or `undefined` if no submission is in progress. By checking for the `name` property of the `attachment` input value, we can verify whether a file has been appended to the expense update form.

3. Next, update the conditional render clause for the `Attachment` component to render if an attachment is currently being uploaded. Further, pass `disabled` to the `Attachment` component:

   ```
   {(isUploadingAttachment || expense.attachment) ? (
     <Attachment
       label="Current Attachment"
       attachmentUrl={`/dashboard/expenses/${expense.id}/attachments/${expense.attachment}`}
       disabled={isUploadingAttachment}
     />
   ) : (
     <Input label="New Attachment" type="file" name="attachment" />
   )}
   ```

   We now render the `Attachment` component when an upload is still in progress. This is an optimistic update to the UI since the upload is still in progress.

   By disabling the `Attachment` component's actions if an upload is still in progress, we prevent users from viewing or removing a pending attachment.

Remix's `useNavigation` hook and its `formData` property allow us to conditionally update the UI without creating additional custom React states. This is great as we avoid the need for synchronization logic altogether. Remix's `ErrorBoundary` components further ensure a resilient baseline if an error occurs.

Great! Just like that, we added optimistic UI updates when attaching a file and updating an expense. Users can now make multiple updates without having to wait for a response from the server. If an issue arises, Remix will display our `ErrorBoundary`, letting the user know about the error.

As always, implement the same experience for the income routes. This ensures that you revisit the lessons learned before moving on.

Next, let's investigate the expense deletion form for an opportunity to add optimistic UI updates.

Deleting an expense

On the expense overview page, we render a `ListLinkItem` component for every expense. The `ListLinkItem` component in `app/components/links.tsx` uses `useFetcher.Form` to submit the delete mutation. Optimistically removing or adding elements to a list is a great way to provide instant feedback. Let's see how we can add an optimistic UI to our expense deletion forms.

One way to implement optimistic updates on deletion is to hide the list item immediately after entering the pending state. Update the `ListLinkItem` component in `app/components/links.tsx`, as follows:

```
const fetcher = useFetcher();
const isSubmitting = fetcher.state !== 'idle';
if (isSubmitting) {
  return null;
}
```

You already know that the `useFetcher` hook manages its transition life cycle. When trying to implement pending and optimistic UIs with `useFetcher.Form`, we don't use `useNavigation`; instead, we use the `useFetcher` hook's `state` and `formData` properties.

Just like that, we remove the expense item from the list when a submission is pending. Once the `action` function finishes, Remix refreshes the loader data and sets the navigation state back to `idle`. If the mutation was successful, then the updated loader data no longer contains the deleted expense, and our UI update persists. But what happens if an error occurs?

1. Take a look at the `handleDelete` function in the `dashboard.expenses.$id._index.tsx` route module. Right now, we throw a 404 `Response` if deleting an expense doesn't work. This triggers the `ErrorBoundary`. Let's improve this by giving the user direct feedback in the UI if the delete action fails.

2. Update `handleDelete` to return a JSON `Response` if the delete action fails:

    ```
    try {
      await deleteExpense(id, userId);
    } catch (err) {
    ```

```
      return json({ success: false });
   }
```

3. Next, update the `ListLinkItem` component in `components/links.tsx`.

   ```
   const fetcher = useFetcher<{ success: boolean }>();
   const isSubmitting = fetcher.state !== 'idle';
   const hasFailed = fetcher.data?.success === false;
   if (isSubmitting) {
     return null;
   }
   ```

   We access the action data using the fetcher's `data` property. If the action data is present and `success` is `false`, we know that the expense's deletion failed.

4. Finally, update the `className` property on the list element conditionally to style the list item text red in case `hasFailed` is `true`.

   ```
   className={clsx(
     'w-full flex flex-row items-center border',
     isActive
       ? 'bg-secondary dark:bg-darkSecondary border-secondary dark:border-darkSecondary'
       : 'hover:bg-backgroundPrimary dark:hover:bg-darkBackgroundPrimary border-background dark:border-darkBackground hover:border-secondary dark:hover:border-darkSecondary',
     {
       'text-red-600 dark:text-red-400 hover:text-red-700 dark:hover:text-red-500 focus:text-red-700 dark:focus:text-red-500':
           hasFailed,
     },
     className,
   )}
   ```

   If an error occurs, we now avoid rendering the `ErrorBoundary` and instead display error feedback right where the error happened in the UI.

5. Test the changes by throwing an error inside the try-case in `handleDelete` in `dashboard.expenses.$id._index.tsx`:

   ```
   try {
     throw Error('something went wrong while deleting');
     await deleteExpense(id, userId);
   } catch (err) {
     return json({ success: false });
   }
   ```

6. Run BeeRich locally and try to delete an expense. The expense list item text should now turn red and indicate the state rollback.

Great work! Remix's `ErrorBoundary` is a great fallback in case something goes wrong. However, sometimes, it is a good idea to enhance the user experience further by providing inline feedback. This allows the user to retry the failed action immediately, and Remix's loader data revalidation takes care of the rest.

> **Remix provides a great foundation for optimistic UI**
>
> Remix automatically updates loader data after a mutation, keeping the client and server in sync. This greatly simplifies the process of creating optimistic UIs.

Great work! As always, make sure to also update the income routes with the latest changes in this section. This ensures that you practice what you learned before moving on to the next section.

In this part, we added optimistic UI updates for deleting expenses. We also used the fetcher's `data` property to signal when an action fails and needs to be rolled back. Next, let's investigate if we can optimistically remove expense and income attachments.

Removing an attachment

We already optimistically display the `Attachment` component on pending uploads. We should also consider optimistically removing an attachment when clicking the attachment deletion button.

This time, we don't want to display the `Attachment` component on pending removal but instead display the file input. However, we also want to prevent race conditions and we should make sure we disable the input until the server confirms the removal.

Since the attachment deletion form submission uses a `Form` component (instead of `useFetcher.Form`), we know the submission is handled via the global navigation object. Hence, we can detect whether the user deletes an attachment by checking the `formData` property on the global navigation object:

1. Add the following Boolean flag to the `dashboard.expenses.$id._index.tsx` route module component:

    ```
    const isUploadingAttachment = attachment instanceof File &&
      attachment.name !== '';
    const isRemovingAttachment = navigation.formData?.get('intent')
      === 'remove-attachment';
    ```

2. Next, update the conditional to display the `Attachment` component if an upload is pending or an attachment exists on the expense but not if an attachment is currently being removed. Additionally, disable the input field if a submission is pending:

    ```
    {(isUploadingAttachment || expense.attachment) &&
    !isRemovingAttachment ? (
    ```

```
      <Attachment
        label="Current Attachment"
        attachmentUrl={`/dashboard/expenses/${expense.id}/
  attachments/${expense.attachment}`}
        disabled={isUploadingAttachment}
      />
    ) : (
      <Input label="New Attachment" type="file" name="attachment"
  disabled={isSubmitting} />
    )}
```

3. Try out the implementation to verify that everything works as expected. As always, use the **Network** tab to throttle the connection to inspect pending states.

Great! We added optimistic UI updates to the attachment deletion form and the expense update form. You learned that Remix's `useFetcher` and `useNavigation` primitives contain the `formData` property of the form currently being submitted. We can use the `formData` property to optimistically update the UI until the `loader` revalidation synchronizes the UI with the server state.

Summary

In this chapter, you learned how to add optimistic UI updates in Remix. You were introduced to the trade offs of optimistic UI, such as the increased complexity of client-side logic and the necessity of user feedback in case of rollbacks.

Remix's `loader` revalidation is a great starting point for synchronizing the UI with the server state. You now understand that Remix's `loader` revalidation enables us to avoid custom client-server state synchronization and lets us avoid stale states. When relying on the loader data, we get rollbacks out of the box. After each mutation, we receive the latest loader data, and our UI updates automatically.

It is still worth communicating why a mutation failed. With or without optimistic updates, it is important to display an error message to the user. For optimistic updates, it might also make sense to highlight the rolled-back data visually. Remix's `ErrorBoundary` component is a great starting point for recovering from errors. However, if we want more granular feedback, we must add custom error messages and utilize Remix's primitives to highlight rolled-back data.

When implementing optimistic UIs, we usually start by removing pending UIs. Adding and removing pending entities to and from lists is an easy way to show instant feedback.

You also learned how to implement optimistic UI updates using Remix's primitives such as `useNavigation` and `useFetcher`. We can use the `formData` property on the client to display user data before the final response is returned from the server.

In the next chapter, we will learn about different caching strategies to further improve the response times and performance of Remix applications.

Further reading

You can find more information about how to implement optimistic UI in the Remix documentation: `https://remix.run/docs/en/2/discussion/pending-ui`.

There is also a great Remix Single video about optimistic UI on the Remix YouTube channel: `https://www.youtube.com/watch?v=EdB_nj01C80`.

12
Caching Strategies

"There are only two hard things in computer science: cache invalidation and naming things." – Phil Karlton

Caching can significantly enhance a website's performance by eliminating or shortening network roundtrips and reusing previously stored data and content. However, caching is also hard to get right. As usual, Remix provides a thin abstraction layer on top of the web platform and eases the usage of HTTP caching strategies.

In this chapter, we will learn about different caching strategies and how to utilize them with Remix. This chapter is divided into two sections:

- Working with HTTP caching
- Exploring in-memory caching

First, we will learn about HTTP caching. We will study different HTTP caching headers and see how we can utilize HTTP caching in the browser and with CDNs. Next, we will focus on in-memory caching. We will refer to *Chapter 3, Deployment Targets, Adapters, and Stacks*, to understand when and where we can cache data in memory. We will also discuss using services such as Redis to cache data.

After reading this chapter, you will understand how to utilize caching with Remix to improve the user experience. You will have also practiced working with HTTP headers and know when to use different caching strategies, such as CDN, browser, **entity tags** (**ETags**), and in-memory caching.

Technical requirements

You can find the code for this chapter here: `https://github.com/PacktPublishing/Full-Stack-Web-Development-with-Remix/tree/main/12-caching-strategies`. You can go ahead and use the end solution from the previous chapter. No additional setup steps are required for this chapter.

Working with HTTP caching

The web platform utilizes HTTP headers to control caching behavior. Web clients can read caching directives specified in response headers to reuse previously fetched data. This allows web clients to avoid unnecessary network requests and improve response times. In this section, you will learn about popular HTTP caching headers and strategies and how to use them in Remix. First, we will see how we can define HTTP headers for document responses.

Adding HTTP headers in Remix

Remix's route module API includes a `headers` export that we can use to add HTTP headers to the route's document response. Like the `links` function, the `headers` function is only ever executed on the server.

The `headers` function is called after all `loader` functions and all parent `headers` functions. The `headers` function has access to the `parentsHeaders`, `errorHeaders`, `actionHeaders`, and `loaderHeaders` objects to update document headers based on the headers added via parent `header` functions, loader data responses, action data responses, and error responses. Remix utilizes the most deeply exported `headers` function available and allows you to mix and merge the headers as required.

> **Loader data-based cache control**
>
> Remix's `headers` function receives the `loaderHeaders` parameter, which allows us to specify caching directives for each route based on the loader data for fine-grained cache control.

Now that we have a theoretical understanding of how to apply HTTP headers with Remix, let's run through our BeeRich routes to investigate how to utilize caching.

Caching public pages in shared caches

Public pages without user-specific information can be stored in a shared cache such as a CDN. Adding a CDN in front of your (Remix) web server distributes cached content globally and closer to your users. It reduces the request response time for cached content and the number of requests the web server has to process.

If you aren't sure what a CDN is, the MDN Web Docs provide a great introduction: https://developer.mozilla.org/en-US/docs/Glossary/CDN.

In this section, we will use Remix's `headers` route module API to add HTTP caching headers to our public pages on BeeRich.

BeeRich consists of public and private routes. The public pages are nested inside the _layout segment and include the BeeRich home page (_layout._index.tsx) and the login and signup pages. We can identify that these pages are static and do not depend on user-specific data. We're okay if the user occasionally sees a stale page version. We can specify HTTP headers so that we keep serving a cached version of the page for one hour before requesting a new version.

Let's see what this would look like in action. Add the following headers function export to the _layout.tsx pathless layout route module:

```
import type { HeadersFunction } from '@remix-run/node';

export const headers: HeadersFunction = () => {
  return {
    'Cache-Control': 'public, max-age=3600',
  };
};
```

With these changes, we apply a caching header to all child routes that do not themselves export a headers function. The specified caching header includes a public value and a max-age directive.

The max-age directive defines the number of seconds the available response can be reused before it must be regenerated. This means the nested routes, such as /, /login, and /signup, are now cached for 3,600 seconds (1 hour).

The public value communicates that the response data can be stored in a public cache. We can differentiate between public (shared) and private caches. Private caches exist on web clients (for example, browsers), while shared caches live on proxy services and CDNs. By specifying that a document can be cached publicly, we also allow proxies and CDNs to cache the document for all future requests. This means the cache not only serves one browser (user) but may improve the response times for any subsequent user requests.

Let's investigate this caching behavior:

1. Run npm run dev in the root of the project.
2. Next, open the login page in a new browser window (http://localhost:3000).
3. Open the developer tools of your browser and navigate to the **Network** tab.
4. Make sure you uncheck the **Disable cache** option if it's checked.
5. Now, hard-refresh the page to emulate an initial page load:

Caching Strategies

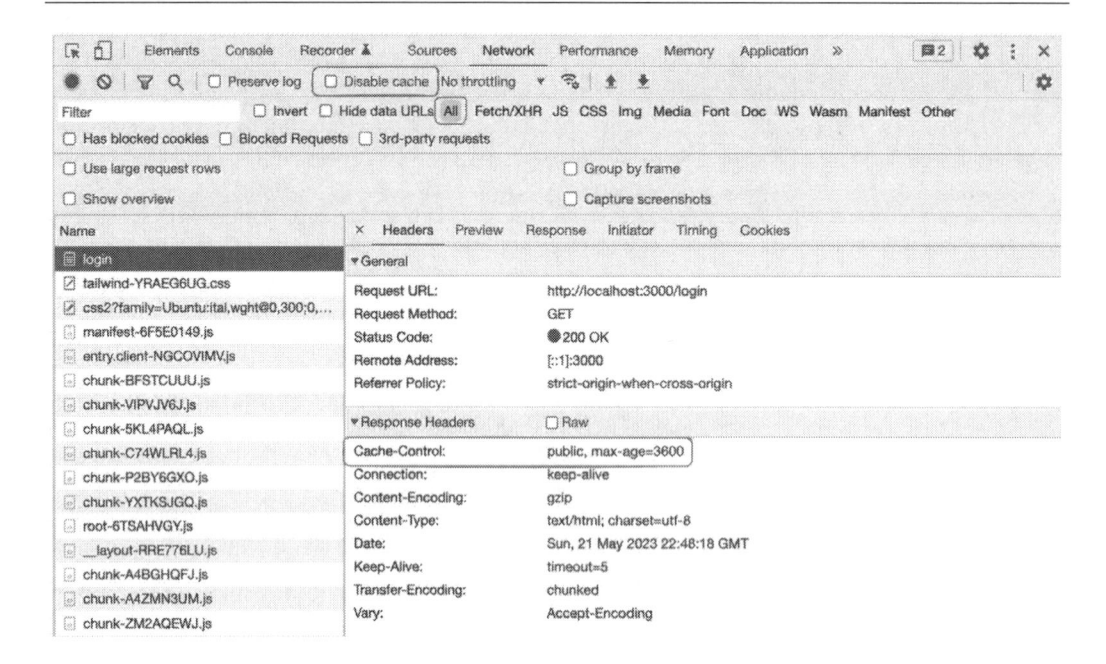

[Screenshot of browser DevTools Network tab showing the login page request with Response Headers including Cache-Control: public, max-age=3600]

Figure 12.1 – Initial page load of the login page

Notice that the specified caching header is returned as part of the response headers.

6. Refresh the page again; you may see that the document was restored from the disk cache. Some browsers disable document request caching headers on localhost for a better developer experience. So, don't worry if you can't seem to make it work on localhost.

Be cautious not to publicly cache documents with user-specific information. While CDNs often automatically remove `Set-Cookie` headers, you likely want to avoid caching altogether when a user session cookie is in the server's response. If you're using a CDN, make sure to cache only for visitors, not logged-in users, to avoid caching conditionally rendered UIs for logged-in users. For example, the navigation bar in `_layout.tsx` shows a Logout button if a user is logged in. Caching this could cause layout shifts when the `Logout` button is replaced by `Log in` and `Sign up` after React hydrates on the client and re-renders the page.

Let's investigate how Remix uses HTTP caching headers for the public assets of our pages.

Understanding Remix's built-in caching

Remix optimizes many of the served assets out of the box. In this section, we will review how Remix utilizes HTTP caching headers on static assets to optimize our app's performance.

Follow the steps from the previous section to open the login page of BeeRich in a browser window. Click on any downloaded JavaScript bundles in the **Network** tab and review the response headers:

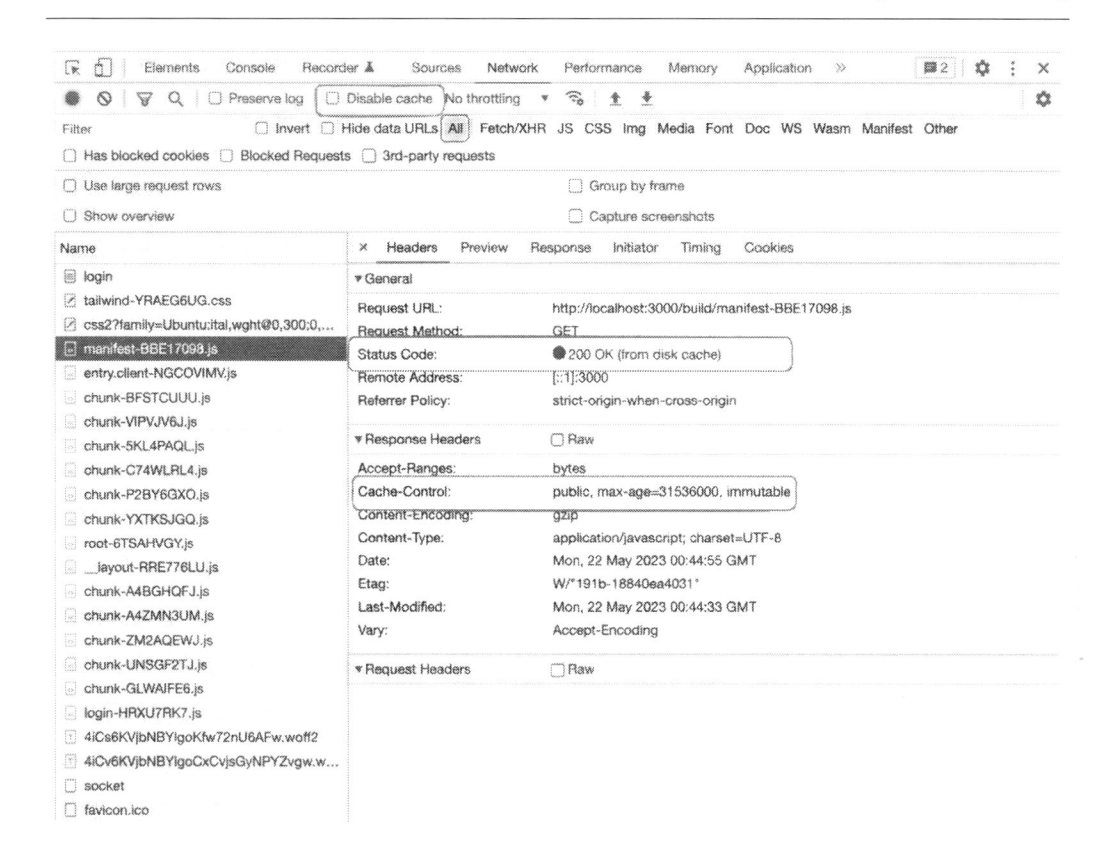

Figure 12.2 – Remix's built-in caching behavior

As visible in *Figure 12.2*, the `manifest-*.js` file was retrieved from the browser's memory or disk cache. Remix adds a cache control header to each JavaScript bundle (`Cache-Control: public, max-age=31536000, immutable`). Each JavaScript bundle is defined to be publicly cached for up to one year – the maximum possible `max-age` value. The `immutable` directive further indicates that the content of the assets never changes, which helps us avoid potential revalidation requests.

Next, review the `tailwind.css` stylesheet from the `root.ts` file's `links` export. Compare the cache control header of the linked stylesheet and the JavaScript bundles. They match!

Finally, review the names of the static assets. Notice that all JavaScript bundles and linked assets include a hash postfix. The hash is computed based on the content of the asset. Any time we update any assets, a new version is created. The hash ensures that there are never two assets with the same name but different content. This allows Remix to allow clients to cache each asset indefinitely.

> **Remix's built-in HTTP caching**
>
> Hash-based filenames of static assets ensure that new versions automatically result in new assets. This allows Remix to add aggressive caching directives to all linked assets returned from the `links` route module API. Remix adds the same directives to all its JavaScript bundles.

The aggressive caching directives used by Remix allow browsers and CDNs to cache all static assets of your Remix app. This can significantly improve performance.

Next, we will discuss how to cache personalized pages and content.

Caching personalized pages in private caches

Controlling HTTP caching is not only about caching responses but also about controlling when not to cache. Remix offers full control over what should be cached by providing access to the `Response` object of each document and data request.

The `dashboard` routes of BeeRich are personalized pages that are made up of user-specific data. User-specific data must not be stored in a shared cache to avoid leakage of private user information. The content on the `dashboard` routes is highly dynamic, and we should only cache it briefly to avoid stale UI states.

Let's utilize the `no-cache` and `private` directives on the `dashboard.tsx` route to apply a default for all `dashboard` routes:

```
import type { HeadersFunction, LoaderFunctionArgs, MetaFunction,
SerializeFrom } from '@remix-run/node';

export const headers: HeadersFunction = () => {
  return {
    'Cache-Control': 'no-cache, private',
  };
};
```

The added cache control header specifies that the HTML documents on the `dashboard` routes can only be cached in private caches (for example, the browser) and that any request should go to the server for revalidation.

Note that the `no-cache` directives still allow the browser to reuse content when using the browser's back and forward buttons. This is different from `no-store`, which forces the browser to fetch new content even during back and forward navigation.

Great – we've now learned how to apply caching headers to document responses. But how about `loader` and `action` data responses?

Caching immutable data responses

In Remix, we can also control HTTP headers for data responses from `loader` and `action` functions. Thus, we can set caching controls not only for documents but also for data responses.

Most of the data in BeeRich is highly dynamic. The invoice and expense data can be edited and must always be fresh. However, this is different for the expense and invoice attachments. Each attachment has a unique filename (identifier), which is part of the request URL. Conclusively, two attachments are never served via the same URL.

Let's update the attachment logic in BeeRich to take advantage of HTTP caching:

1. First, update the `buildFileResponse` function in `app/modules/attachments.server.ts` so that it supports passing in custom headers:

    ```
    export function buildFileResponse(fileName: string, headers =
    new Headers()): Response {
      const localPath = path.join(process.cwd(), 'attachments',
    fileName);
      try {
        const file = fs.readFileSync(localPath);
        headers.append('Content-Type', 'application/octet-stream');
        headers.append('Content-Disposition', `attachment;
    filename="${fileName}"`);
        return new Response(file, { headers });
      } catch (error) {
        console.error(error);
        return new Response('Not Found', { status: 404 });
      }
    }
    ```

    We now allow a `headers` object to be passed in so that HTTP headers can be added to the file response object.

2. Next, update the `loader` function in the `dashboard.expenses.$id.attachments.$.tsx` resource route module:

    ```
    export async function loader({ request, params }:
    LoaderFunctionArgs) {
      const userId = await requireUserId(request);
      const { id } = params;
      const slug = params['*'];
      if (!id || !slug) throw Error('id and slug route parameters
    must be defined');

      const expense = await db.expense.findUnique({ where: { id_
    userId: { id, userId } } });
      if (!expense || !expense.attachment) throw new Response('Not
    ```

Caching Strategies

```
  found', { status: 404 });
    if (slug !== expense.attachment) return redirect(`/dashboard/
expenses/${id}/attachments/${expense.attachment}`);
  const headers = new Headers();
  headers.set('Cache-Control', 'private, max-age=31536000,
immutable');
  return buildFileResponse(expense.attachment, headers);
}
```

Here, we supply a cache-control header to the `buildFileResponse` function, which returns the file download response.

Since we know that the attachment never changes – a new attachment would create a new filename – we apply the `immutable` directive and cache the asset for a year. Because the attachments contain sensitive user information, we set the cache to `private` to avoid shared caching.

3. Start BeeRich by executing `npm run dev` and, in your browser, navigate to an expense details page.

4. Next, download an attachment twice and inspect the second network payload in the **Network** tab:

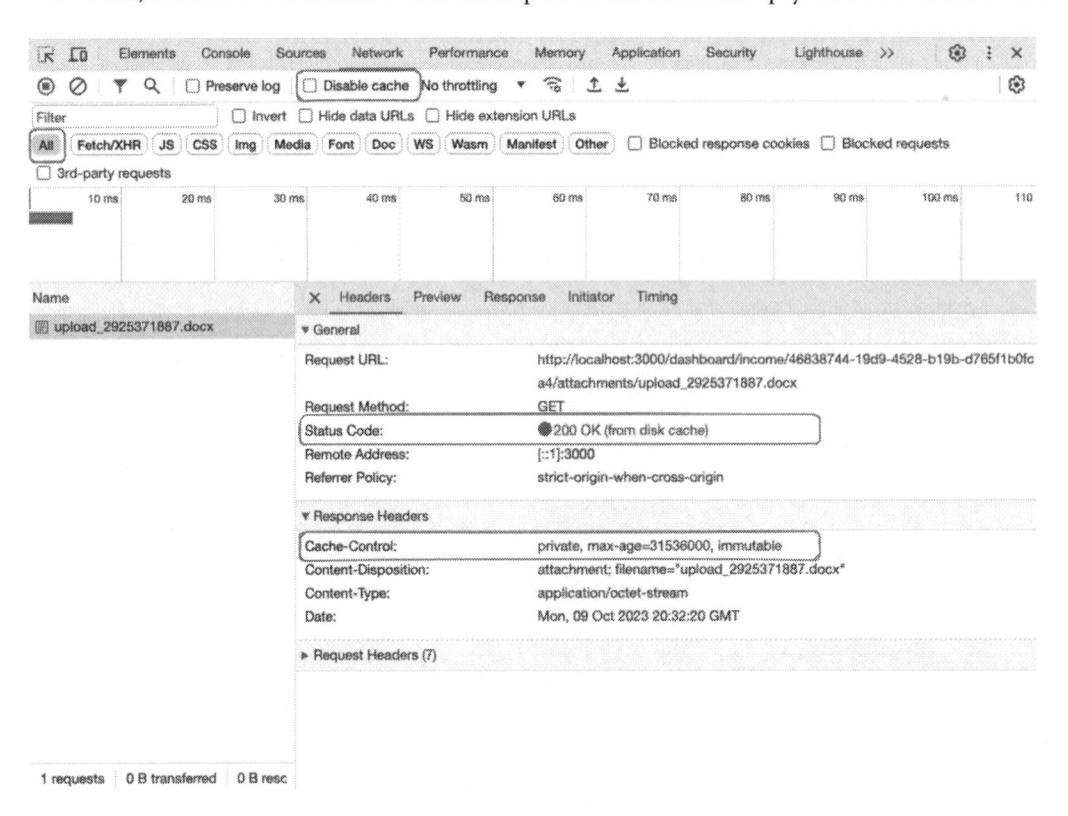

Figure 12.3 – Attachment cached on disk

Great! As visible in *Figure 12.3*, we avoided a request to the web server for the second download request. Instead, the attachment was downloaded from the disk cache of the browser.

Caching is hard, especially when you're trying to cache user-specific data. Can you think of any potential security concerns with the current implementation?

Imagine a user logging in to BeeRich from a public computer to access expense attachments. The user downloads one of the attachments to print it. The user then deletes the attachment from the public computer and logs themselves out from BeeRich. Now, could a malicious actor retrieve the attachment from the browser cache? Potentially.

Copy and paste the **Request URL** property to your attachment from the **Headers Network** tab. Now, log out from BeeRich to be redirected to the login page. Copy and paste the copied request URL into the address bar and hit *Enter*. Since we allow the browser to cache the document on its private disk cache, the request will not go to the resource route where we would authenticate the user. Instead, the browser retrieves the document from the memory or disk cache and serves it to the user, a potential security vulnerability.

In this section, you learned about the potential security risks of leaking user data using private and public cache control directives. We can use a different caching strategy instead of caching private data in the browser cache. Next, we will have a look at entity tags.

Caching dynamic data responses with entity tags

An HTTP request for a document can result in different HTTP responses. A response with status code 200 usually includes an HTTP body containing the requested document – for instance, an HTML document, PDF, or image.

The HTTP request-response flow allows us to authorize user access and potentially turn down requests with 401 (Unauthorized) responses. In the previous section, we cached data in private and shared caches, which cuts the request-response flow short from reaching our server on a cache hit.

In this section, we will explore how to utilize the `ETag` and `If-None-Match` headers so that we can avoid resending full responses but still execute authorization functions on the server.

The `ETag` header may carry a unique identifier (entity tag) for a response, which the client can use to append subsequent requests to the same URL with the `If-None-Match` header. The server can then compute the new response and compare the new tag with the request `If-None-Match` header.

Let's update the `loader` function in the `dashboard.expenses.$id.attachments.$.tsx` resource route module to see how this looks like in action:

```
export async function loader({ request, params }: LoaderFunctionArgs)
{
  const userId = await requireUserId(request);
  const { id } = params;
```

```
    const slug = params['*'];
    if (!id || !slug) throw Error('id and slug route parameters must be defined');

    const expense = await db.expense.findUnique({ where: { id_userId: { id, userId } } });
    if (!expense || !expense.attachment) throw new Response('Not found', { status: 404 });
    if (slug !== expense.attachment) return redirect(`/dashboard/expenses/${id}/attachments/${expense.attachment}`);
    const headers = new Headers();
    headers.set('ETag', expense.attachment);
    if (request.headers.get('If-None-Match') === expense.attachment) {
      return new Response(null, { status: 304, headers });
    }
    return buildFileResponse(expense.attachment, headers);
}
```

We use the attachment identifier as the entity tag and append it to the response headers. If a client requests the same attachment twice, we can access the previously sent `ETag` header through the `If-None-Match` request header.

After authorizing the user in the `loader` function, we can check whether the request contains an `If-None-Match` header. In that case, we can communicate to the client that there has been no change to the response using the 304 status code. The client can then use the cached response body instead of redownloading the attachment.

Investigate the new implementation by repeating the steps from the previous sections to download the same attachment twice. Note that your browser's guest and incognito modes reset caches on each session, which makes them great tools for testing initial page load times:

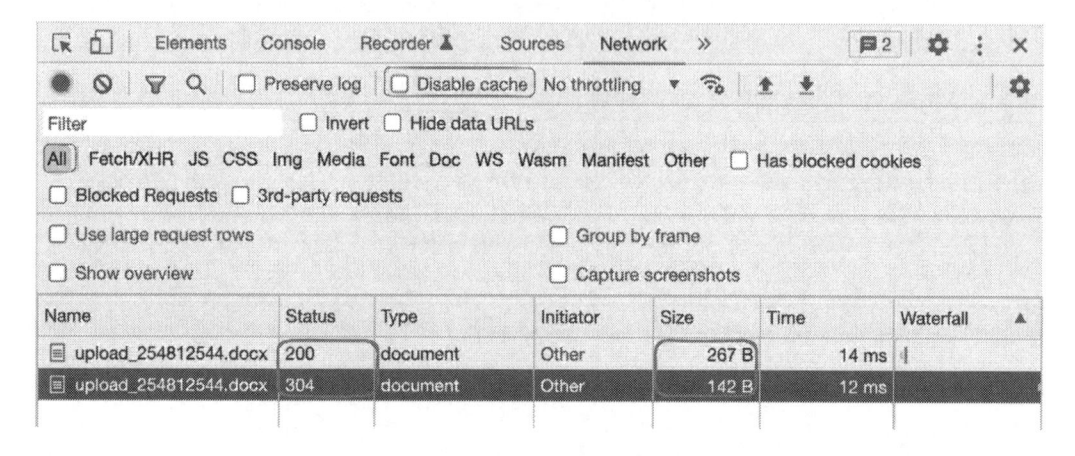

Figure 12.4 – ETag-based caching of attachments

As visible in *Figure 12.4*, any subsequent download of the attachment now triggers a request that receives a 304 response. When inspecting the **Headers** tab, you will see the `ETag` (response) and `If-None-Match` (request) headers.

Finally, copy the **Request URL** property and log out. Now, attempt to access the attachment by navigating to the request URL. Notice that BeeRich redirects to the login page. This is because ETag-based caching triggers a request to the server. The server then checks for the session cookie and redirects accordingly.

ETags come with a different set of trade-offs. When using ETags to revalidate content, we can't avoid the roundtrip to the web server, but we can still avoid downloading the same response body twice. This serves as a good middle ground as we can execute authorization and authentication functions on the server but also improve performance by reusing existing response bodies.

Great! We implemented three HTTP caching strategies in BeeRich: public caching of public pages, no caching for the dynamic dashboard pages, and ETags for private static assets. You also learned how Remix uses HTTP caching for static assets out of the box.

Ensure you update the `dashboard.income.$id.attachments.$.tsx` resource route to take advantage of ETag-based caching for invoice attachments.

HTTP caching has much to offer. In this chapter, you learned about a few common strategies, but there are many more, such as stale-while-revalidate caching strategies. Refer to the *Further reading* section for more information about HTTP caching strategies.

Next, let's discuss how to utilize caching on our Remix server.

Exploring in-memory caching

Caching effectiveness increases the closer the cache is to the users. In-browser caching avoids network requests altogether. CDN-based caching can significantly shorten network requests. However, we may also give up more control over the cache the further it is away from our Remix server.

In this section, we will discuss in-memory caching strategies and learn about the advantages and disadvantages of in-memory caching options.

HTTP caching might not always be the right strategy. For instance, we already discussed privacy issues when caching user-specified information. In some cases, it might make sense to implement a custom caching layer on the web server.

The easiest way is to store computation results or fetched responses in memory on the server itself. However, as we learned in *Chapter 3*, *Deployment Targets, Adapters, and Stacks*, this may not always be possible. Runtime environments such as the edge and serverless may shut down after every request and may not be capable of sharing memory between requests.

In BeeRich, we utilize a long-running Express.js server. Long-running environments are capable of sharing memory between requests. Hence, we can use our server's memory to cache data. Caching data in memory allows us to avoid database queries and downstream fetch requests. Caching data in memory is a great way to improve performance. However, we must also consider memory limitations and overflows.

Alternatively, we can utilize services such as Redis, low-latency in-memory databases, to store computation or fetch results. Utilizing Redis as a cache is also a great solution when running on serverless or edge runtimes, where memory might not be shared between requests.

But what about BeeRich? BeeRich utilizes a SQLite database, which provides very fast responses for simple queries (a few milliseconds). Using Redis would likely not improve the performance as it would introduce a network request to the Redis server.

Unfortunately, in the real world, database and API requests may be much slower. In these cases, it may make sense to cache the results in Redis or in-memory on the server to reuse fetched results and avoid subsequent slow requests.

One great example is our user object. We fetch the user object on every incoming request in the `root.tsx loader` function. We can identify that we read the user object disproportionally more often than updating it. If responses become slow, this may be a good indication to store the user object in an in-memory cache.

In-memory caching requires us to implement custom cache invalidation logic, but it may also improve performance when HTTP caching is not the right tool for the job. Conclusively, adding a service such as Redis could be a good consideration in case our responses become slow, and we identify that slow database or API queries are the root cause.

Summary

In this chapter, you learned about different caching strategies and how to implement them with Remix.

Remix's `headers` route module API export lets us specify HTTP headers for the HTML document on a per-route level. We also have access to `loaderHeaders` and `parentHeaders`, which allows us to merge HTTP headers and specify headers based on the loader data.

You also learned how to cache both document and data requests in Remix. You learned how to use the `Cache-Control` header to specify and prevent caching.

Then, you applied the `private`, `public`, `max-age`, `no-cache`, and `immutable` directives. Additionally, you reviewed how Remix implements HTTP caching for static assets out of the box.

Next, you learned about the privacy concerns of caching user-specific data and how to use ETags to avoid downloading full responses while sending requests to the server where the user authorization can be checked.

Finally, we discussed in-memory caching and using services such as Redis to avoid requests to slow third-party services or databases.

In the next chapter, we will learn about deferring loader data. Like caching, deferring loader data is a great lever to improve the user experience and performance of web applications.

Further reading

You can learn more about CDNs in the MDN Web Docs: `https://developer.mozilla.org/en-US/docs/Glossary/CDN`.

You can also find an overview of HTTP caching concepts in the MDN Web Docs: `https://developer.mozilla.org/en-US/docs/Web/HTTP/Caching`.

The MDN Web Docs also provide detailed information about each HTTP caching header:

- `ETag`: `https://developer.mozilla.org/en-US/docs/Web/HTTP/Headers/ETag`
- `Cache-Control`: `https://developer.mozilla.org/en-US/docs/Web/HTTP/Headers/Cache-Control`

Refer to the Remix documentation for more information about Remix's `headers` route module API: `https://remix.run/docs/en/2/route/headers`.

Ryan Florence recorded two great videos about caching on the Remix YouTube channel. Fun fact – they were the very first videos that were uploaded on the Remix YouTube channel, and they are worth checking out:

- *Remix Run – Introduction to HTTP Caching*: `https://www.youtube.com/watch?v=3XkU_DXcgl0`
- *CDN Caching, Static Site Generation, and Server Side Rendering*: `https://www.youtube.com/watch?v=bfLFHp7Sbkg`

You can also find a great guide for using ETags with Remix on Sergio's blog: `https://sergiodxa.com/articles/use-etags-in-remix`.

13
Deferring Loader Data

Executing data loading on the server can speed up initial page load times and improve core web vitals such as **Largest Contentful Paint** (**LCP**). However, server-side data fetching can also become a bottleneck if a request is particularly slow. For such cases, Remix provides an alternative data-fetching approach.

In this chapter, we will work with Remix's `defer` function and learn how to utilize HTTP and React streaming, React `Suspense`, and Remix's `Await` component to defer slow loader data requests. This chapter is split into two sections:

- Streaming data to the client
- Deferring loader data

First, we will discuss the trade-offs of server-side data fetching and review the requirements for working with Remix's `defer` function. Next, we will utilize Remix's `defer` function in BeeRich and practice working with React `Suspense` and Remix's `Await` component.

After reading this chapter, you will know how to use `defer` to improve the performance of your Remix applications. You will have also learned the requirements for working with HTTP and React streaming. Finally, you will understand the trade-offs of deferring loader data and know when to utilize `defer` in Remix.

Technical requirements

We need to update some code before we can get started with this chapter. Please follow the steps in the `README.md` file in this chapter's folder on GitHub before continuing. You can find the code for this chapter here: `https://github.com/PacktPublishing/Full-Stack-Web-Development-with-Remix/tree/main/13-deferring-loader-data`.

Streaming data to the client

There are several different data-fetching strategies. We can initiate data fetching on the client using client-side `fetch` requests or execute data fetching on the server to take advantage of server-side rendering. We can even fetch data during build time for static site generations. In this section, we will discuss the trade-offs of server-side data fetching and review the requirements of HTTP streaming.

Motivating server-side data fetching and streaming

Remix promotes fetching data on the server using `loader` functions for each route, as opposed to fetching data at the component level. During the initial page load, the `loader` functions are called before React renders on the server. This guarantees that the loader data is available for the server-side rendering step, eliminating the need for client-side data-fetching logic and loading states.

When initiating data fetching on the client, we first need to load the HTML document and then wait for the JavaScript bundles to download and execute before executing the required fetch requests. This results in three client-server roundtrips before the LCP is finalized. In comparison, we can paint the LCP after one client-server roundtrip with server-side data fetching and rendering. Reducing the number of client-server roundtrips almost always results in faster response times and improved core web vitals.

Let's run through an example to understand how server-side data fetching can improve the LCP of the initial page load. Assume we maintain an e-commerce web page for a product. The site shows an image of the product and some additional information about the product, such as the name of the product and its price.

First, let's assume we operate a client-side-only SPA. What happens once a user visits our web page?

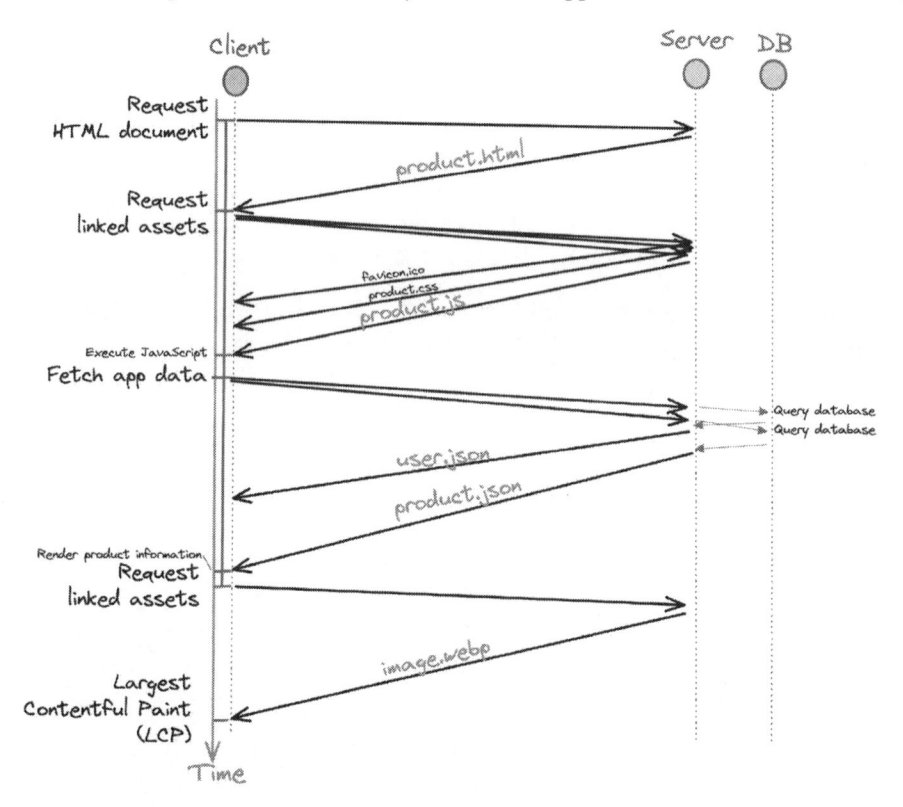

Figure 13.1 – Client-side data-fetching waterfall

As visible in *Figure 13.1*, the following requests are executed from the browser:

- The browser requests the HTML document.
- The browser requests scripts and other assets referenced in the document.
- The React app is running and fetches the product information. The browser executes the fetch requests.
- The React app re-renders with the fetched data, and the browser requests assets linked in the HTML, such as the product images. The downloaded assets are used to paint the LCP.

We execute four subsequent requests to display the product image and finalize the LCP, each request adding to the request waterfall and delaying the LCP.

Now, let's assume we use Remix to render the product page. How many client requests are necessary to finalize the LCP?

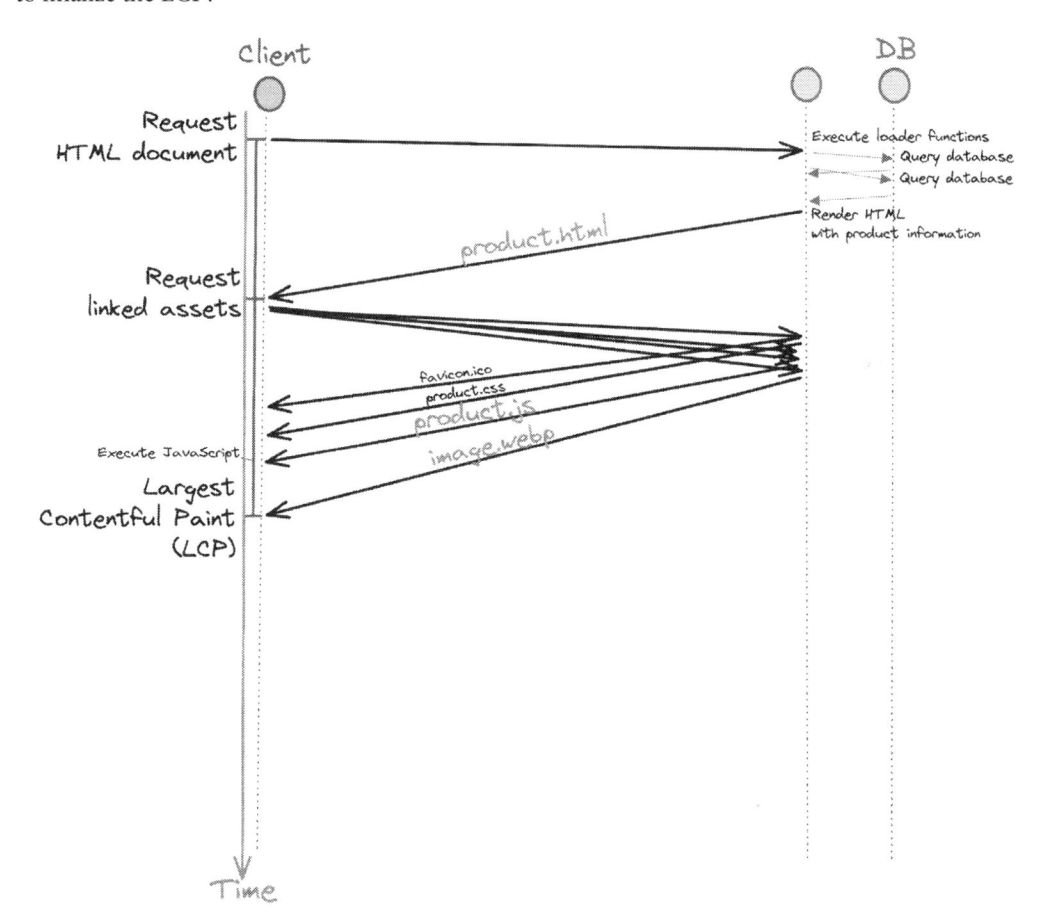

Figure 13.2 – Server-side data-fetching waterfall

As visible in *Figure 13.2*, the following requests are executed from the browser:

- The browser requests the HTML document. The received document already includes the product information and image HTML element.
- The browser requests the product image together with the other linked assets. The downloaded assets are used to paint the LCP.

With server-side data fetching, we only require two client-server roundtrips to render the product page. This is a significant improvement.

What changed? Remix flattens the request waterfall by moving the data fetching to the server. This way, images and other assets can load parallel to the JavaScript bundles.

Unfortunately, this model may not work well when executing particularly slow requests in `loader` functions. Since we wait for all `loader` functions to finish before server-side rendering our React application, a slow request can become a bottleneck for our application and slow down initial page loads. In this case, we might want to look for alternative approaches.

One solution could be fetching the slow request from the client after the initial page has been downloaded from the server. However, this results in the request waterfall outlined earlier – further delaying the slow data response. Luckily, Remix provides a simple set of primitives to defer loading a promise and instead stream the response to the client.

Streaming allows us to send bytes to the client, even if the full response has not been finalized. React provides utilities to stream server-side-rendered content to the client. React will start sending pieces of the rendered content to the client while still awaiting other pieces. With `Suspense`, React can suspend component subtrees from rendering until a promise resolves. Remix builds on React `Suspense` to defer specific loader data requests using the `defer` function and the `Await` component.

Remix `loader` functions fetch data at the route level to avoid network waterfalls. If a request is particularly slow and in danger of becoming a bottleneck, we can pull another lever to defer that request. This is made possible by HTTP streaming and the web streaming API. In the next section, we will discuss the requirements to utilize HTTP streaming with Remix.

Understanding HTTP streaming requirements

Since Remix's `defer` function uses HTTP and React streaming, we can only utilize it on a server environment that supports HTTP streaming responses. In this section, we will discuss the requirements for HTTP streaming and `defer`.

In *Chapter 3, Deployment Targets, Adapters, and Stacks*, we learned how Remix utilizes adapters to run on different JavaScript runtimes and server environments. Some environments, such as traditional serverless environments, may not support streaming responses. This is important to remember when evaluating hosting providers and runtimes.

Fortunately, a growing number of environments do support HTTP streaming, and by default, Remix is set up with React streaming. This is great even without using `defer` as it speeds up the initial document request. With HTTP streaming, the client can start receiving parts of the response without needing to wait for the full response to be finalized.

To find out whether your Remix project is set up with React streaming, you can check the `app/entry.server.tsx` file in your Remix project. Search for the `renderToPipeableStream` function. If it is in use, you can be certain that React streaming is set up. Otherwise, you can follow Remix's `defer` guide to set up React streaming: `https://remix.run/docs/en/2/guides/streaming` (if your runtime and hosting environment supports it).

If you can't locate the `app/entry.server.tsx` file, it may be that you are using Remix's default implementation and that you need to reveal it by executing the `npx remix reveal` command. You can learn more about the `entry.server.tsx` file in *Chapter 2, Creating a New Remix Project*, or in the Remix documentation: `https://remix.run/docs/en/2/file-conventions/entry.server`.

Now that you understand how Remix uses HTTP and React streaming, let's try it out in BeeRich. In the next section, we will practice working with Remix's `defer` function.

Deferring loader data

Not all payloads are equally important to the user. Some data may only appear below the page's fold and is not immediately visible to the user. Other information may not be of primary content of the page but slow down the initial page load. For example, we may want to prioritize displaying the product information for an e-commerce site as fast as possible. However, we might be okay deferring the loading of the comments section to speed up the initial page load time. For this, Remix provides the `defer` and `Await` primitives. In this section, we will utilize Remix's primitives with React `Suspense` in BeeRich to defer specific loader data.

Please review the `README.md` file on GitHub for this chapter if you haven't already: `https://github.com/PacktPublishing/Full-Stack-Web-Development-with-Remix/tree/main/13-deferring-loader-data/bee-rich/README.md`. This file will guide you through setting up the new expense and invoice changelog. Now, let's allow users to see the full history of all changes to their expenses and invoices:

1. Let's start by fetching the changelog data in the `dashboard.expenses.$id._index.tsx` route module's `loader` function:

   ```
   const userId = await requireUserId(request);
   const { id } = params;
   if (!id) throw Error('id route parameter must be defined');
   const expense = await db.expense.findUnique({ where: { id_
   userId: { id, userId } } });
   ```

```
if (!expense) throw new Response('Not found', { status: 404 });
const expenseLogs = await db.expenseLog.findMany({
  orderBy: { createdAt: 'desc' },
  where: { expenseId: id, userId },
});
return json({ expense, expenseLogs });
```

We now also return an `expenseLogs` array.

Note that the current implementation blocks the expense logs query until the expense has been fetched. This increases the initial page load time as we introduce a subsequent database query, something we will fix later.

2. Next, create an `ExpenseLogs` component:

```
import type { ExpenseLog } from '@prisma/client';
import type { ActionFunctionArgs, LoaderFunctionArgs,
  SerializeFrom } from '@remix-run/node';

function ExpenseLogs({ expenseLogs }: { expenseLogs:
  SerializeFrom<ExpenseLog[]> }) {
  return (
    <ul className="space-y-2 max-h-[300px] lg:max-h-max overflow-y-scroll lg:overflow-hidden py--5">
      {expenseLogs.map((expenseLog) => (
        <li key={expenseLog.id}>
          <p>
            <b>
              {`${expenseLog.title} - ${Intl.
                NumberFormat('en-US', {
                  style: 'currency',
                  currency: expenseLog.currencyCode,
                }).format(expenseLog.amount)}`}
            </b>
          </p>
          {expenseLog.description && (
            <p>
              <i>{expenseLog.description}</i>
            </p>
          )}
          <p className="text-sm text-gray-500">
            {`${new Date(expenseLog.createdAt).
              toLocaleDateString()} ${new Date(
                expenseLog.createdAt,
              ).toLocaleTimeString()}`}
          </p>
```

```
        </li>
      ))}
    </ul>
  );
}
```

We will render the component below the expense edit form to display the changelog.

Note that we use the generated `ExpenseLog` type from Prisma for the component's prop type. We wrap it with `SerializeFrom` as loader data is fetched from the server and serialized as JSON while sent over the network.

3. Update the `useLoaderData` call in the route module component to access the `expenseLog` array:

   ```
   const { expense, expenseLogs } = useLoaderData<typeof loader>();
   ```

4. Import our reusable H3 component:

   ```
   import { H2, H3 } from '~/components/headings';
   ```

5. Render the `ExpenseLogs` component below the edit expense form:

   ```
   <section className="my-5 w-full m-auto lg:max-w-3xl flex flex-col items-center justify-center gap-5">
     <H3>Expense History</H3>
     <ExpenseLogs expenseLogs={expenseLogs} />
   </section>
   <FloatingActionLink to="/dashboard/expenses/">Add expense</FloatingActionLink>
   ```

6. Now, run BeeRich on `localhost` to test it out. Execute `npm run dev` and open an expense details page in a browser window.

   The new change history is great, but also not the most important aspect of the page. We render the history below the expense and invoice details on the nested detail routes. Most likely, the information will be rendered below the page's fold.

7. To avoid delaying the initial page load, utilize Remix's `defer` function:

   ```
   import { defer, json, redirect, unstable_parseMultipartFormData } from '@remix-run/node';
   ```

8. Replace the `json` helper in the `loader` function with a `defer` call:

   ```
   return defer({ expense, expenseLogs });
   ```

9. Refresh the page and note that nothing changed. `defer` acts just as `json` when called with resolved data. The magic only starts happening once we `defer` an unresolved `Promise`.

10. Remove the `await` keyword before the `expenseLog.findMany` call:

    ```
    const expenseLogs = db.expenseLog
      .findMany({
        orderBy: { createdAt: 'desc' },
        where: { expenseId: id, userId },
      })
      .then((expense) => expense);
    return defer({ expense, expenseLogs });
    ```

    Passing an unresolved `Promise` to `defer` changes the behavior of the `loader` function. The function now returns without awaiting the `expenseLog` query, and `defer` will make sure to stream the data to the client once resolved.

11. Note that we also chain a `then` call at the end of the query. This is a trick to map `PrismaPromise`, which is returned by `findMany`, to an actual `Promise` object, as Remix's `defer` function requires `Promise` instances.

12. Snap! We broke the page as `expenseLogs` is now of the `Promise` type. We need to update our React code so that it can work with deferred loader data. First, import `Suspense` from React and `Await` from Remix:

    ```
    import {
      Await,
      isRouteErrorResponse,
      useActionData,
      useLoaderData,
      useNavigation,
      useParams,
      useRouteError,
    } from '@remix-run/react';
    import { Suspense } from 'react';
    ```

13. Wrap the ExpenseLogs component with `Suspense` and `Await`:

    ```
    <Suspense fallback="Loading expense history...">
      <Await resolve={expenseLogs} errorElement="There was an error loading the expense history. Please try again.">
        {(resolvedExpenseLogs) => <ExpenseLogs expenseLogs={resolvedExpenseLogs} />}
      </Await>
    </Suspense>
    ```

The new suspense boundary renders the fallback content until Remix resolves the promise on the pending `expenseLogs` request. To inform Remix which promise we are awaiting, we must pass the `expenseLogs` loader data to `Await`. We can also pass `Await` an `errorElement` component in case the promise is rejected.

We pass `Await` a callback function as its child component. Once the promise is resolved, `Await` will call the callback with the resolved data. This ensures that the `ExpenseLogs` component has access to the resolved `expenseLogs` data.

Alternatively, we can access the resolved data by using Remix's `useDeferredValue` hook within the child component.

14. Run BeeRich locally and notice how the initial page load does not include the `expenseLogs` data.

    Note that you may need to delay the `expenseLogs` query for better visibility. Otherwise, the deferred loading might be too fast on localhost to capture.

15. Update the `then` statement of the `expenseLogs` query in the `loader` function:

    ```
    const expenseLogs = db.expenseLog
      .findMany({
        orderBy: { createdAt: 'desc' },
        where: { expenseId: id, userId },
      })
      .then((expense) => new Promise((resolve) => setTimeout(() => resolve(expense), 2000)));
    ```

    Instead of resolving the results immediately, we add a two-second delay using `setTimeout`.

16. Now, inspect the deferred data loading in the UI and the **Network** tab.

    The page first renders without the `expenseLogs` data. Instead, the suspense fallback string is rendered. Once the `expenseLogs` promise resolves, the page re-renders with the `expenseLogs` data.

    Note that `defer` introduces a pending state in the UI. It is important to understand that this impacts the user experience. Introducing loading spinners should be considered a trade off for deferring loader data. We may introduce layout shifts once the data resolves that affect SEO as web crawlers may now parse the fallback UI.

17. Next, optimize the call order in the `loader` function. Move the expense logs query above the expense query:

    ```
    const userId = await requireUserId(request);
    const { id } = params;
    if (!id) throw Error('id route parameter must be defined');
    // Start expense logs query first before we await the expense query
    const expenseLogs = db.expenseLog
    ```

```
      .findMany({
        orderBy: { createdAt: 'desc' },
        where: { expenseId: id, userId },
      })
      .then((expenseLogs) => expenseLogs);
  const expense = await db.expense.findUnique({ where: { id_
userId: { id, userId } } });
  if (!expense) throw new Response('Not found', { status: 404 });
  return defer({ expense, expenseLogs });
```

Since we no longer await the expense logs query, we can start executing it before starting the expense query. This allows us to start the expense logs query as soon as possible.

Note that we also removed the `setTimeout` call. Make sure you throttle the network and re-add the `setTimeout` call if necessary to better investigate the experience.

From this, we can summarize that Remix provides us with a way to defer loader data per request. We can decide for each request whether we want to await or defer in the `loader` function.

Remember that we broke the page before adding `Await` and `Suspense`. It is good practice to first add the `Await` and `Suspense` components to the page before returning promises with `defer` in the `loader` function. This will help you avoid errors while implementing `Await` and `Suspense`.

Practice using `defer` by applying the same changes to the income routes. Copy-paste and adapt the `ExpenseLogs` component into the `dashboard.income.$id._index.tsx` route module. Utilize the component and implement the same `defer`, `Suspense`, and `Await` flow as practiced in this chapter. Use `setTimeout` to test the user experience.

If you want more practice, add a **Revert** button to every expense and invoice log item to revert the expense object to that version. How could you make use of optimistic UI? How do deferring and optimistic UI play together? Review Remix's documentation about `defer` and optimistic UI if you need more guidance.

> **Remix provides levers**
>
> Remix provides levers so that we can optimize the user experience based on our app's requirements. When considering `defer`, it is important to remember that deferred data loading may also degrade the user experience by adding a pending UI and introducing loading spinners.

In this section, you practiced working with Remix's `defer` and `Await` primitives. You now know how to use deferred response data streaming to optimize slow or secondary data requests but are aware that `defer` is a lever that impacts the user experience by introducing pending UIs.

Summary

In this chapter, you learned that Remix supports different data-fetching strategies. Deferring loader data can be utilized to resolve performance bottlenecks in your Remix apps when fetching from slow endpoints. Remix's `defer` function detects unresolved promises in the loader data and streams them to the client once resolved. React `Suspense` and Remix's `Await` component are used to manage the deferred loader data in React.

You also learned that using `defer` requires fallback UIs to communicate loading states. You now understand that using `defer` comes with trade-offs that impact the user experience. On one hand, deferring loader data can speed up the initial document request. On the other hand, using `defer` creates loading UIs, which results in a different user experience.

After reading this chapter, you know that Remix uses React streaming to speed up document requests. However, React and HTTP streaming are not supported on all server runtimes and environments. Conclusively, not all Remix adapters support React streaming. Since Remix's `defer` function takes advantage of React `Suspense` and React streaming, deferring loader data only works when React streaming is supported and set up.

Finally, you practiced deferring loader data by implementing an expense changelog in BeeRich.

In the next chapter, we will extend the changelog implementation and add real-time data responses with **Server-Sent Events (SSE)**.

Further reading

You can read more about the Streams API via MDN Web Docs: `https://developer.mozilla.org/en-US/docs/Web/API/Streams_API`.

The Remix documentation includes a guide for streaming and `defer`: `https://remix.run/docs/en/2/guides/streaming`.

The `defer` function's documentation can be found here: `https://remix.run/docs/en/2/utils/defer`.

In this chapter, we discussed core web vitals. You can read more about core web vitals, such as LCP, here: `https://web.dev/vitals/`.

14
Real Time with Remix

The web platform offers standards and capabilities to send data in real time. With real-time technologies, we can implement chat features and multiplayer UIs for real-time collaboration and interactions. We have seen several apps with real-time features grow in popularity and redefine their product categories, such as Google Docs and Figma. In this chapter, we will learn about real-time UIs with Remix.

This chapter is split into two sections:

- Working with real-time technologies
- Building real-time UIs with Remix

First, we will compare real-time technologies and discuss the requirements for hosting providers and server environments. Next, we will outline implementations with Remix. Finally, we will implement a simple real-time UI in BeeRich by utilizing **Server-Sent Events** (**SSE**).

After reading this chapter, you will understand the requirements for working with real-time technologies in Remix. You will also be able to name the differences between polling, SSE, and WebSocket. Finally, you will know how to work with SSE in Remix.

Technical requirements

You can find the code for this chapter here: `https://github.com/PacktPublishing/Full-Stack-Web-Development-with-Remix/tree/main/14-real-time-with-remix`. No additional setup is required for this chapter.

Working with real-time technologies

The web platform offers different protocols and standards for real-time communication. In this section, we will review different technologies and techniques and discuss the requirements for utilizing them with Remix. We will discuss polling, learn about SSE, and review the WebSocket API. First, let's have a look at polling techniques.

Understanding polling

Polling is a client-pull technique in which the client requests data from the server. Instead of relying on a server to push updates, polling utilizes intervals to check for the latest data from the server.

We can differentiate between short and long polling. Short polling sends requests in time-based intervals to the server. The server responds immediately, either with new data or indicating nothing has changed. With long polling, the server only responds once new data is available, keeping the request unanswered until then. The client sends a new request once the server responds or the request times out.

The advantage of polling is that it does not require the server environment and hosting provider to support WebSockets, HTTP/2, or long-running streaming responses. Polling can be a great compromise when working with server environments and hosting providers that do not support real-time protocols and standards. It is also simpler to implement and potentially a great tool for prototyping.

The disadvantage of polling is its wasteful resource consumption and delayed real-time behavior. Short polling creates many unnecessary requests that yield no new data, while long polling forces the server to handle idle requests until new data is received. Short polling may also delay real-time updates based on the interval retry time.

Next, let's have a look at SSE.

Understanding SSE

SSE is an HTTP-based server push standard and part of the HTML5 spec. SSE requires both a client and a server. The client requests a connection using the `EventSource` API; the server implements an endpoint that returns a stream response with the `text/event-stream` media type.

The stream response creates a one-way communication line from the server to the client. This allows the server to send events to the client without the need for the client to use polling.

The advantage of SSE is reduced resource consumption. The client does not need to send unnecessary requests to the server. Instead, the server only sends events to the client once an update is available.

The disadvantage of SSE is the long-running HTTP connection, which needs to be maintained by the server. Additionally, SSE only provides a one-way communication line. The client is not able to send messages to the server. Finally, HTTP/1 only allows servers to maintain six concurrent connections at a time. Luckily, most server environments support HTTP/2, but the HTTP/1 limitation may still be relevant, depending on your hosting provider.

Understanding WebSocket

WebSocket is a communication protocol that's implemented through the web's WebSocket API and creates a persistent two-way communication line. Unlike SSE and polling solutions, WebSocket operates directly on TCP rather than HTTP.

Once a WebSocket connection has been established, both parties (for example, the browser and the server) can send and receive messages simultaneously. Since the protocol operates on TCP, it can transfer not only UTF-8-encoded data but also binary data, making it a performant lower-level protocol.

The advantage of WebSocket connections is their two-way communication channel and the increased performance from using TCP directly. However, WebSocket connections are not supported by all hosting providers and JavaScript runtimes as they require long-running servers. The WebSocket API is also the most complex to implement and utilize, requiring the setup of a WebSocket server.

All three techniques enable us to implement real-time capabilities. Polling lets us build multiplayer UIs, even if our server environment does not support streaming responses or setting up WebSocket servers. SSE provides a simpler way for the server to send events and data to the client. The WebSocket API is a lower-level protocol that allows us to create bi-directional communication channels capable of creating performant and scalable multiplayer UIs.

Now that you understand the differences between polling, SSE, and the WebSocket API, we can implement a real-time UI in BeeRich. In the next section, we will do just that.

Building real-time UIs with Remix

BeeRich uses Remix's Express.js adapter and runs on a long-running server. As such, BeeRich can take advantage of polling, SSE, and the WebSocket API to implement real-time features.

Short polling is simple to set up. We can implement short polling in Remix by using Remix's `useRevalidator` hook:

```
import { useEffect } from 'react';
import { useRevalidator } from '@remix-run/react';

function Component() {
  const { revalidate } = useRevalidator();
  useEffect(() => {
    const interval = setInterval(revalidate, 4000);
    return () => {
      clearInterval(interval);
    };
  }, [revalidate]);
}
```

The `revalidate` function of the `useRevalidator` hook triggers a `loader` revalidation. This allows us to refetch all loader data, similar to how Remix refetches all loader data after executing an `action` function.

Since the WebSocket protocol is TCP-based, we would need to create the WebSocket server and endpoint outside of our Remix application using the `server.js` file at the root of our project or using a different server environment altogether. This is doable but outside the scope of this book. Instead, we will review how to use SSE with Remix.

Remix's `loader` and `action` functions can create HTTP-based resource routes. We can implement an SSE endpoint on a long-running server environment by using a `loader` function to return a stream response with the `text/event-stream` media type.

We aim to inform all devices and open browser tabs that are logged in with the same user of expense and invoice data changes. We also want to revalidate the UI whenever such a change is detected. Let's get started:

1. First, create a new `server-sent-events` folder in `app/modules/`.
2. Next, create an `events.server.ts` file in the new folder and add the following code:

   ```
   import { EventEmitter } from 'events';

   declare global {
     // eslint-disable-next-line no-var
     var emitter: EventEmitter;
   }

   global.emitter = global.emitter || new EventEmitter();

   export const emitter = global.emitter;
   ```

   We use the `EventEmitter` API from Node.js and declare a globally accessible event emitter for our server environment. The `EventEmitter` object can be used to listen to and emit events. We will utilize the `emit` function in our `action` functions to communicate data changes to the server-sent event connection handler code.

   Note that the `EventEmitter` API has nothing to do with SSE but provides a neat way for event-based communication in our Node.js server environment.

3. Now, implement an `eventStream` helper function in `events.server.ts`:

   ```
   export type SendEvent = (event: string, data: string) => void;
   export type OnSetup = (send: SendEvent) => OnClose;
   export type OnClose = () => void;

   export function eventStream(request: Request, onSetup: OnSetup)
   {
     const stream = new ReadableStream({
       start(controller) {
   ```

```
          const encoder = new TextEncoder();

          const send: SendEvent = (event, data) => {
            controller.enqueue(encoder.encode(`event: ${event}\n`));
            controller.enqueue(encoder.encode(`data: ${data}\n\n`));
          };

          const onClose = onSetup(send);

          let closed = false;
          const close = () => {
            if (closed) return;
            closed = true;
            onClose();
            request.signal.removeEventListener('abort', close);
            controller.close();
          };

          request.signal.addEventListener('abort', close);
          if (request.signal.aborted) {
            close();
            return;
          }
        },
      });

      return new Response(stream, {
        headers: {
          'Cache-Control': 'no-store, no-transform',
          Connection: 'keep-alive',
          'Content-Type': 'text/event-stream',
        },
      });
    }
```

The `eventStream` function creates a new `ReadableStream` object. The stream object contains a `start` function. In `start`, we define the `send` function, which is responsible for adding events to the stream that will be sent to the client. The code also includes logic to correctly close the stream. Finally, the function returns an event stream `Response` using the `ReadableStream` object as the response body.

4. Next, implement the endpoint responsible for delivering the event stream response. Create a new /sse.tsx route in the /routes folder:

   ```
   import type { LoaderFunctionArgs } from '@remix-run/node';

   import type { OnSetup } from '~/modules/server-sent-events/
   events.server';
   import { emitter, eventStream } from '~/modules/server-sent-
   events/events.server';
   import { requireUserId } from '~/modules/session/session.
   server';

   export async function loader({ request }: LoaderFunctionArgs) {
     const userId = await requireUserId(request);

     const onSetup: OnSetup = (send) => {
       function handler() {
         send('server-change', `Data change for ${userId}`);
       }
       emitter.addListener(userId, handler);
       return () => {
         emitter.removeListener(userId, handler);
       };
     };

     return eventStream(request, onSetup);
   }
   ```

   This isn't a lot a lot of code considering that we implement an endpoint capable of sending real-time events. First, we ensure the request comes from an authenticated user (requireUserId). Next, we implement a helper function that we will pass to eventStream. This helper function uses our EventEmitter object to listen to events on the server. emitter listens for events that match the userId property of the authenticated user and triggers a new sever-sent event using the event stream once such event is received.

5. Next, add the global emitter object to all expense and invoice action functions. Whenever an action succeeds, we want to emit the server-change event on the server and trigger a new event to all connected clients:

   ```
   emitter.emit(userId);
   ```

6. For instance, in the action function of the dashboard.expenses._index.tsx route module, add the event emitter call before returning the redirect. This ensures the event is only emitted after the action has succeeded and the database has been updated:

   ```
   emitter.emit(userId);
   return redirect(`/dashboard/expenses/${expense.id}`);
   ```

We set the `emitter` object on the global object and can access it on the server without importing it. However, you can also import it if you like:

```
import { emitter } from '~/modules/server-sent-events/events.server';
```

7. After adding the `emit` function call to the expense and invoice creation actions, add `emit` function calls to the `handleDelete`, `handleUpdate`, and `handleRemoveAttachment` functions in the `dashboard.expenses.$id._index.tsx` route module. Again, call `emit` after the data mutation has succeeded to avoid race conditions.

8. Make sure you also apply the same changes to the invoice `action` functions. You can always review the final implementation in the solution folder of this chapter.

9. Let's turn our attention to the client environment. Add a new `event-source.tsx` file in the `app/modules/server-sent-events` folder and implement the event stream connection request:

```
import { useRevalidator } from '@remix-run/react';
import { useEffect } from 'react';

export function useEventSource() {
  const { revalidate } = useRevalidator();

  useEffect(() => {
    function handler(event: MessageEvent) {
      console.log(`Received server event [${new Date().toLocaleTimeString()}]`, event.data);
      revalidate();
    }

    const eventSource = new EventSource('/sse');
    eventSource.addEventListener('server-change', handler);

    return () => {
      eventSource.removeEventListener('server-change', handler);
      eventSource.close();
    };
  }, [revalidate]);
}
```

We use Remix's `revalidate` function to revalidate all loader data once a server-sent event is received. The hook uses the `EventSource` API to connect to the `/sse` route, where we implemented our event stream `loader` function. The hook then adds an event listener to listen for `server-change` events – an arbitrary event name we specified in the `loader` code.

10. Finally, import the new hook in the `dashboard.tsx` route module and call the hook in the route module component:

    ```
    import { useEventSource } from '~/modules/server-sent-events/event-source';

    export default function Component() {
      const { firstExpense, firstInvoice } = useLoaderData<typeof loader>();
      useEventSource();
      //...
    }
    ```

    Just like that, we set up a connection using the `EventSource` API and SSE standard.

    Whenever the user navigates to a dashboard route, we now initiate a request to the `/sse` endpoint. The endpoint authenticates the user and returns a streaming response. The server further listens for events from `action` functions using the `EventEmitter` API. Once the same user calls an `action` function (for example, by submitting a form), the `action` function emits an event that is then handled by the `loader` code of the streaming response. The `handler` function is executed on the server and sends a `server-change` event to all connected clients of the same user. The clients receive the event and initiate a loader revalidation.

11. Run the application locally by calling `npm run dev` in a terminal.

12. Test the implementation by opening BeeRich in two or more tabs. You can also run BeeRich in several browsers to investigate the real-time behavior. Log in as the same user and update and delete invoices and expenses. Do you see how the expense history grows with every change in real time? Can you see the UI update across the different windows and tabs?

Great work! Just like that, we can implement real-time UIs in Remix. However, the current implementation has one notable issue: the client that calls the `action` function revalidates its UI twice – one time using Remix's built-in revalidation step and once after receiving the server-sent event. This puts an extra burden on the server and the user's network bandwidth. Do you have an idea of how we could avoid the double revalidation?

Consider implementing this yourself to practice working with SSE in Remix! Maybe you can use a unique connection identifier to avoid the server-sent event revalidation in the browser tab that mutates the data. You could add the identifier to the server-sent event payload and compare it with a local version stored on the client. Alternatively, you could use Remix's `shouldRevalidate` route module API to avoid Remix's built-in revalidation after `action` function calls that trigger the server-sent events. Refer to the Remix documentation for more information about the `shouldRevalidate` function: `https://remix.run/docs/en/2/route/should-revalidate#shouldrevalidate`.

In this section, you implemented an SSE endpoint in BeeRich to revalidate loader data whenever the user mutates data in an `action` function across different tabs, browsers, and devices.

Summary

In this chapter, you learned about real-time technologies and techniques and how to use them in Remix.

First, we discussed polling, SSE, and the WebSocket API and compared their advantages and disadvantages. Polling is the easiest to set up. A simple polling implementation does not require changes on the server. SSE provides a one-way communication line using the HTTP protocol, while WebSocket connections use TCP and are bi-directional.

Second, you learned about server requirements for SSE and WebSocket. You now understand that SSE requires support for streaming responses, while WebSocket servers can only run on long-running servers.

Finally, we implemented a real-time UI in BeeRich by utilizing SEE. We implemented a new endpoint and associated React hook using the `EventSource` API. Since Remix's `loader` functions return HTTP `Response` objects, we can implement the server-sent event endpoint in Remix using a resource route.

In the next chapter, we will learn more about session management and discuss advanced session management patterns with Remix.

Further reading

You can read more about SSE and WebSocket in the MDN Web Docs:

- `https://developer.mozilla.org/en-US/docs/Web/API/Server-sent_events`
- `https://developer.mozilla.org/en-US/docs/Web/API/Websockets_API`

Here is a great talk from Remix Conf 2023 about SSE by Alex Anderson: `https://www.youtube.com/watch?v=cAYHw_dP-Lc`.

Sergio Xalambrí wrote an article on how to set up Remix with socket.io to create a WebSocket connection: `https://sergiodxa.com/articles/use-remix-with-socket-io`.

15
Advanced Session Management

Session management is crucial to building good user experiences. Persisting session data can increase the user's experience and productivity by remembering user settings, selections, and preferences.

We learned how to manage user sessions in *Chapter 8*, *Session Management*. In this chapter, we will work on advanced session management patterns.

This chapter is split into two sections:

- Managing visitor sessions
- Implementing pagination

First, we will implement visitor sessions and use Remix's cookie helper to redirect the user to the right page after login or signup. Next, we will learn how to add pagination with Remix and Prisma. We will practice pagination by applying it to the expense and invoice lists in BeeRich.

After reading this chapter, you will know how to use cookies to persist arbitrary session data in Remix. You will also understand the difference between Remix's session cookie and cookie helpers. Additionally, you'll learn when to store session data in a cookie versus in a database. Finally, you will understand how to implement pagination with Remix.

Technical requirements

You can find the code for this chapter here: `https://github.com/PacktPublishing/Full-Stack-Web-Development-with-Remix/tree/main/15-advanced-session-management`. No extra setup is required for this chapter.

Managing visitor sessions

In *Chapter 8*, *Session Management*, we used Remix's session cookie helpers to implement a login and signup flow. In this section, we will use Remix's cookie helper to persist additional session data.

You might remember from *Chapter 8, Session Management*, that cookies are added on the server to an HTTP response using the **Set-Cookie** header. Once received, the browser attaches the cookie to all subsequent HTTP requests using the **Cookie** header.

In Remix, we can access incoming HTTP requests in our `loader` and `action` functions. In our loaders and actions, we can use Remix's cookie helper functions to parse the cookie data from the request headers and use it to improve the user experience.

In BeeRich, we already utilize a cookie to handle the authentication of our users. However, there are plenty of other use cases for cookies.

Consider the following advanced use case: we aim to offer visitors a taste of our app's functionality without requiring an account. Visitors should be able to directly interact with the content. At some point, the visitor decides to create an account. Now, we want to ensure that the data associated with the visitor is transferred to the new user account. How can we make this work?

Depending on the use case, session data can be persisted using local storage, cookies, memory, or databases. We could store all generated data directly in local storage or a cookie and only commit it to the database once the user account has been created. However, this only works if the data is not meant to be visible to other users.

What if we want to treat the visitor-generated content like the content of any other user? First, we must assign the visitor a unique identifier that can be tracked across different page transitions. Whenever the visitor triggers a mutation, we associate the persisted data with the unique identifier. Once the visitor signs up, we migrate all data associated with the visitor identifier to the new user account.

Generating a unique session identifier is a common pattern when handling sessions, and storing it in a cookie is a great way to ensure we have access to the identifier on the server. This example illustrates how powerful cookies are. Cookies can be utilized to implement complex user interfaces and features. However, cookies can also be used to persist short-living session data.

Let's practice working with Remix's cookie helpers by implementing a redirect flow after login and signup in BeeRich. If a user attempts to visit a dashboard page without authorization, we currently redirect to the login page. Once the user logs in or signs up, we navigate the user to `/dashboard`. We now want to update this logic and navigate the user to the initially requested dashboard page.

We'll start by creating a visitor cookie:

1. Create a `visitors.server.ts` file in `app/modules`.
2. Next, import `createCookie` from Remix and create a `visitorCookie` object:

   ```
   import { createCookie } from '@remix-run/node';

   const visitorCookie = createCookie('visitor-cookie', {
     maxAge: 60 * 5, // 5 minutes
   });
   ```

The `createCookie` function receives a cookie name parameter and a configuration object. A list of possible configuration options can be found in the Remix documentation: https://remix.run/docs/en/2/utils/cookies#createcookie.

Rember that Remix offers both a cookie helper utility and a session cookie helper utility. Refer to `session.server.ts`, where we utilize Remix's `createCookieSessionStorage` function. `createCookieSessionStorage` provides three functions:

- `getSession`
- `commitSession`
- `destroySession`

In comparison, Remix's `createCookie` function only provides two functions: `parse` and `serialize`.

Session cookies are one of many implementations of Remix's session abstraction. On the other hand, `createCookie` provides a simple helper to read (`parse`) and write (`serialize`) a cookie to and from cookie headers.

We use Remix's session helpers to implement user session flows, while `createCookie` is a utility for reading and writing to and from cookies.

3. Next, define the type of data that we will store in the visitor cookie:

   ```
   type VisitorCookieData = {
     redirectUrl?: string;
   };
   ```

   Our goal is to persist the URL the visitor wants to visit before we redirect them to the login page.

   For instance, imagine a user is logged in and working on the dashboard of BeeRich. The user then returns a few days later and wants to continue managing their finances with BeeRich. Since the session has expired, BeeRich redirects the user to the login page. So far, we've navigated the user back to the dashboard after a successful login but do not remember where exactly the user left off. Let's change that!

4. In `visitors.server.ts`, create a function to get the cookie data from a request:

   ```
   export async function getVisitorCookieData(request: Request):
   Promise<VisitorCookieData> {
     const cookieHeader = request.headers.get('Cookie');
     const cookie = await visitorCookie.parse(cookieHeader);
     return cookie && cookie.redirectUrl ? cookie : { redirectUrl:
   undefined };
   }
   ```

   We use the cookie object to parse the `Cookie` header and extract the visitor cookie data.

5. Similarly, create a function to write the visitor cookie data to the `Set-Cookie` header:

   ```
   export async function setVisitorCookieData(data:
   VisitorCookieData, headers = new Headers()): Promise<Headers> {
     const cookie = await visitorCookie.serialize(data);
     headers.append('Set-Cookie', cookie);
     return headers;
   }
   ```

6. With these utilities in place, we can read the cookie data on incoming requests and write the cookie to the response when the user is redirected to login.

7. Import `setVisitorCookieData` in `app/modules/session/session.server.ts`:

   ```
   import { setVisitorCookieData } from '~/modules/session/session.server.ts';
   ```

8. Next, update the `requireUserId` function to add the visitor cookie when redirecting to log in:

   ```
   export async function requireUserId(request: Request) {
     const session = await getUserSession(request);
     const userId = session.get('userId');
     if (!userId || typeof userId !== 'string') {
       const headers = await setVisitorCookieData({ redirectUrl: request.url });
       throw redirect('/login', { headers });
     }
     return userId;
   }
   ```

   Note that we utilize the `url` property on the `Request` object to access the URL the user wanted to visit before the redirect.

9. Next, open the `_layout.login.tsx` route module and import the `getVisitorCookieData` function:

   ```
   import { getVisitorCookieData } from '~/modules/visitors.server';
   ```

10. Update the `_layout.login.tsx` route module's `action` function so that it reads `redirectUrl` from the visitor cookie:

    ```
    try {
      const user = await loginUser({ email, password });
      const { redirectUrl } = await getVisitorCookieData(request);
      return redirect(redirectUrl || '/dashboard', {
        headers: await createUserSession(user),
      });
    } catch (error: any) {
    ```

```
        return json({ error: error?.message || 'Something went wrong.'
    });
}
```

By default, the user is now redirected to the previously requested URL. If no redirect happened, then the user is navigated to /dashboard instead.

11. Test the implementation by running BeeRich locally.
12. Start by logging in and visiting a route on the dashboard. For instance, navigate to an expense details page. Copy the URL from the URL bar for easy access and log out from BeeRich.
13. Now, enter the copied URL into the URL bar. Since we are logged out, we are redirected to log in.
14. Next, log in to your account and notice the redirect back to the requested dashboard page.
15. Play around with the implementation a bit more. Notice that it doesn't matter how often you leave the login page, close the browser tab, or reload it. For the five minutes before the cookie expires, the cookie persists and remembers the user's latest requested URL.

Great job! Would the same flow also make sense for signup? In BeeRich, not as much, as all dashboard URLs are account specific. However, imagine an application where you can invite your coworkers to collaborate. You may share an invite link for a project. A coworker joining for the first time would then be redirected to log in but navigate to sign up to create a new account. From there, we could take advantage of the visitor cookie to read the invite URL and navigate the new user to the collaborative project.

Practice working with the visitor cookie by implementing the same flow on the signup page. Follow the implementation from the _layout.login.tsx action function and read the visitor cookie data in the _layout.signup.tsx action function to navigate the user accordingly.

In this section, you practiced working with Remix's createCookie helper and learned more about advanced session management implementations. You now know the difference between Remix's session cookie and cookie utilities. Next, we will implement pagination with Remix.

Implementing pagination

Pagination is an important pattern when working with large and user-generated lists of objects. Pagination divides the content into separate pages and thereby limits the number of objects that must be loaded for a given page. Pagination aims to reduce load times and improve performance.

In this section, we will implement pagination in BeeRich for expenses and invoices:

1. First, open the dashboard.expenses.tsx route module and define a constant for the page size:

    ```
    const PAGE_SIZE = 10;
    ```

    The page size defines the number of expenses we will show at once in the expenses overview list. To see more expenses, the user has to navigate to the next page.

2. Update the `loader` function in `dashboard.expenses.tsx` and access a new search parameter named `page`:

   ```
   const userId = await requireUserId(request);
   const url = new URL(request.url);
   const searchString = url.searchParams.get('q');
   const pageNumberString = url.searchParams.get('page');
   const pageNumber = pageNumberString ? Number(pageNumberString) : 1;
   ```

   We will use a search parameter to track the current page the user is on. Every time the user clicks **Next** to navigate to the next page, we will increment the page search parameter by 1. Every time the user clicks **Previous**, we will decrement the parameter by 1.

3. Import Prisma from `@prisma/client`.

   ```
   import type { Prisma } from '@prisma/client';
   ```

4. Now, update the expenses database query so that it only queries a total of 10 expenses for the current page, skipping all previous pages:

   ```
   const where: Prisma.ExpenseWhereInput = {
     userId,
     title: {
       contains: searchString ? searchString : '',
     },
   };
   const [count, expenses] = await db.$transaction([
     db.expense.count({ where }),
     db.expense.findMany({
       orderBy: { createdAt: 'desc' },
       take: PAGE_SIZE,
       skip: (pageNumber - 1) * PAGE_SIZE,
       where,
     }),
   ]);
   ```

   Note that we replaced the expense query with two simultaneous queries: one to fetch the expenses and one to count all user expenses for the current search query. We will utilize the count of expenses to determine whether we should hide or disable the pagination **Next** and **Previous** buttons.

   We execute the queries with Prisma's `$transaction` utility instead of `Promise.all` for the additional performance benefit of making one big call to the database instead of two.

5. Update the `loader` function's return statement so that it returns both the expenses list and the count:

   ```
   return json({ count, expenses });
   ```

6. Update the `useLoaderData` call so that it reads the updated loader data:

   ```
   const { count, expenses } = useLoaderData<typeof loader>();
   ```

7. In the route module component, use the `useSearchParams` hook to read the `page` query parameter:

   ```
   const [searchParams] = useSearchParams();
   const searchQuery = searchParams.get('q') || '';
   const pageNumber = searchParams.get('page') ?
     Number(searchParams.get('page')) : 1;
   const isOnFirstPage = pageNumber === 1;
   const showPagination = count > PAGE_SIZE || !isOnFirstPage;
   ```

   We utilize `showPagination` to either show or hide the pagination buttons.

8. Add the following form below the expenses list (`<ul>...</ul>`):

   ```
   {showPagination && (
     <Form method="GET" action={location.pathname}
       className="flex justify-between pb-10">
       <input type="hidden" name="q" value={searchQuery} />
       <Button type="submit" name="page" value={pageNumber - 1}
         disabled={pageNumber === 1}>
         Previous
       </Button>
       <Button type="submit" name="page" value={pageNumber + 1}
         disabled={count <= pageNumber * PAGE_SIZE}>
         Next
       </Button>
     </Form>
   )}
   ```

The form submits an HTTP GET request to the current URL path. This follows the same pattern we already implemented for the `expense-search` feature.

The **Previous** and **Next** buttons submit the form and update the `page` search parameter. Since the form uses GET, the route's `loader` function is called (not its `action`).

We could also use anchor tags instead of a form. Both initiate an HTTP GET request. The reason we decided to use a form here is so that we can utilize HTML button elements. We want to show the **Previous** and **Next** buttons even if they are disabled. Disabling anchor tags may require additional effort to ensure screen reader accessibility, while buttons offer a `disabled` attribute.

Note that we include a hidden input field for the expense search filter parameter called q. This is necessary as we would otherwise reset the search filter when navigating between the different pages. By persisting the filter, the pagination works together with the search functionality and allows us to navigate between different pages of the filtered expenses list.

9. Finally, update the search form to reset the pagination whenever the search filter changes:

```
<Form method="get" action={location.pathname}>
  <input type="hidden" name="page" value={1} />
  <SearchInput name="q" type="search" label="Search by title" defaultValue={searchQuery} key={searchQuery} />
</Form>
```

The number of expenses may change when updating the search filter. Hence, we need to reset the pagination.

10. Run BeeRich locally and play around with the implementation. Notice that the URL is updated on every navigation between the pages.

What happens if an expense is created or deleted?

Remix revalidates all loader data after every mutation. When we add an expense, the `loader` function is called, and the `count` loader data is updated. This ensures that the pagination buttons are added if the expenses exceed the first page. It turns out that the `loader` revalidation fixes stale data issues in almost every chapter of this book!

Similarly, the count value is updated on deletion. However, because we redirect the user back to their current page after deletion, the user may remain on a page without expenses. For instance, if we have 11 expenses and delete the last remaining expense on the second page, the user ends up on an empty page.

This is fine if we keep the pagination **Previous** button on the page so that the user can navigate to the previous page. We ensure this by always showing the pagination buttons if the user is not currently on the first page:

```
const isOnFirstPage = pageNumber === 1;
const showPagination = count > PAGE_SIZE || !isOnFirstPage;
```

It seems like we have all the edge cases covered! Nice work!

Let's take a moment to reflect on our development journey with BeeRich. We have come a long way since kicking off our work on BeeRich. From the ground up, we've built an extensive feature set, including:

- A routing hierarchy with nested routes
- SQLite database integration with multiple schemas
- Forms for managing expenses and income
- User login, signup, and logout flows
- Server-side access authorization
- File upload capabilities
- Pending, optimistic, and real-time UIs
- Various caching techniques

- Deferred data loading with React streaming and Remix's `defer`
- Pagination for expense and invoice lists

Congratulations on completing BeeRich, a full stack web application that fully utilizes Remix and the web platform. Now is your chance to take over BeeRich and keep practicing. You could start by adding the two search parameters: `q` and `page` to more links and redirects to persist them across different user actions and navigations. Or maybe there is something you wanted to change for a while already? Now is the time!

And as always, practice what you have learned in this chapter by implementing the same pagination logic on the income route for the invoices list. Refer to the Prisma and Remix documentation if you get stuck. If you need more guidance, refer

to the implementation on the expense routes.

In this section, we implemented pagination in Remix using URL search parameters. You learned how to carry over search parameters across different form submissions and practiced advanced session management in Remix.

Summary

In this chapter, you learned about advanced session management patterns with Remix and wrapped up your work on BeeRich.

Remix offers a `createCookie` helper function for working with cookie data. The function returns a cookie abstraction for parsing and serializing cookie data to and from request headers.

After reading this chapter, you know how to use `createCookie` to store and access arbitrary user session data in a cookie. You practiced working with cookies by adding a visitor cookie to the login and signup flow in BeeRich that persists the URL the visitor wants to access.

You also learned how to implement a simple pagination feature with Remix and Prisma. Pagination is a pattern that can improve performance and avoid long loading times when working with data lists. Utilizing pagination limits the amount of data that needs to be fetched for each page load.

In the next chapter, we will learn more about deploying Remix applications on the edge.

Further reading

You can find more information about working with search parameters via MDN Web Docs: https://developer.mozilla.org/en-US/docs/Web/API/URL/searchParams.

You can reference the Remix documentation to learn more about the `createCookie` helper function: https://remix.run/docs/en/2/utils/cookies.

You can read more about pagination with Prisma in the Prisma documentation: https://www.prisma.io/docs/concepts/components/prisma-client/pagination.

16
Developing for the Edge

Edge is a multifaceted term that can mean different things in different contexts. It might denote a location, a runtime, or a computing paradigm. You may recall from *Chapter 3*, *Deployment Targets, Adapters, and Stacks*, that Remix can be deployed to various server environments, including edge environments. In this chapter, we will dive deeper into developing for the edge and explore what it means to develop Remix applications that run on edge environments.

The chapter is split into two sections:

- Living on the edge
- Understanding the edge's benefits and limitations

First, we will discuss edge computing and define related concepts. Next, we will consider the benefits and limitations of hosting Remix at the edge.

After reading this chapter, you will understand what it means to deploy to the edge and know what to consider when working with Remix in edge environments. Further, you will know about popular edge providers and be able to discuss the pros, cons, and limitations of the edge as a location and runtime.

Living on the edge

Edge computing is a paradigm that has been around for many years but has picked up steam in association with the **Internet of Things** (**IoT**). The term also found a new meaning in web development when CDNs started offering new JavaScript runtimes to host web applications on the edge. In this section, we will define what it means to run websites on the edge and see what edge development with Remix looks like. First, let's take a step back and understand the different meanings of the term "edge."

Computing at the edge

Edge computing is a paradigm of computer science that contrasts cloud computing. It describes a system architecture where the compute is located as close as possible to its utilization. While cloud computing happens in offsite data centers, edge computing aims to locate computing at the edge of a given network. This is why we often use the term edge to describe a location that contrasts the massive data centers of the cloud.

The goal of edge computing is to reduce round-trip times from the client to the server by moving the server closer to the user. Among other things, edge computing is enabled by the increased availability and reduced cost of computing. Why not compute closer to the user if the computing power is available?

Think about a security camera designed to automatically detect movement and set off an alarm in case of suspicious activity. In a cloud-based setup, the camera sends its video feed to a central data center for analysis. If it detects movement, the central system triggers the building's alarm. On the other hand, with an edge-based architecture, the camera may process the feed right on the device. If it spots movement, the camera itself sends an alert to the building's central server, which then activates the alarm system.

Edge computing requires available computation capabilities on the network's edge, while cloud computing takes advantage of the computation capabilities of centralized data centers. With edge computing, we can decrease response times and network bandwidth by avoiding round trips to the cloud. However, the required computation capabilities must be available. Sometimes, we may need to rethink our application and its runtime to make it lighter and suitable for the edge. This is why we may use the term edge to describe optimized runtime environments for the edge.

To clarify, we won't try to deploy and run Remix on security cameras. Edge computing is a distributed computing paradigm that can be applied to many use cases, such as the Internet of Things. The Internet of Things is one example of edge computing, where smart devices communicate in an edge network without the need to stream the collected data directly to the cloud for processing.

In web development, edge computing takes place in highly geographically distributed data centers that heavily increase proximity to users compared to the centralized data centers of traditional cloud computing offerings. Next, let's review today's edge offerings for web apps.

Running web apps on the edge

CDNs have served content on the edge of the internet for decades. Conclusively, edge computing is not a new concept within web development. What's cutting-edge (pun intended) is the ability to host dynamic web applications on the edge.

Traditionally, CDNs are used to deliver static content, including web page assets (HTML, CSS, and JavaScript files) and media files (images and videos). CDNs maintain geographically distributed data centers in as many locations as possible and are optimized for reliability, scale, and performance. This makes CDNs perfect not just for caching and serving static content but also for acting as edge computing providers.

In recent years, CDNs have expanded their scope to handle dynamic content and offer web application hosting services. Popular CDNs that offer edge runtimes are Cloudflare and Fastly. Additionally, a growing list of hosting providers, such as Netlify and Vercel, partner with CDNs to offer edge environments through their hosting platforms.

Remix is one of the first web frameworks to support deploying and running on the edge. As you know from the previous chapters of this book, Remix was developed with various runtime environment requirements in mind. In the next section, we will learn more about today's edge hosting providers.

Remixing the edge

In theory, Remix can run on any server that can execute JavaScript. This is possible because Remix utilizes an adapter architecture. Remix uses adapters to translate requests and responses between the native server runtime and Remix. This allows Remix to work together with various web server libraries and runtimes. In this section, we will review how to deploy Remix at the edge.

Remix maintains official adapters for many popular deployment targets, but the adapter architecture also allows the community to build adapters for any environment. At the time of writing, there are Remix templates for the following edge and edge-like deployment targets:

- Cloudflare Pages
- Cloudflare Workers
- Deno Deploy
- Fastly Compute@Edge
- Netlify Edge Functions
- Fly.io
- Vercel Edge Functions

Deploying Remix to the edge is as easy as picking an edge template and deploying it to the associated provider service. Try it out by running the following command:

```
npx create-remix@2 --template remix-run/remix/templates/
cloudflare-workers
```

Follow the instructions of the `create-remix` script and then open the bootstrapped README.md file. The README.md will guide you through deploying the app to Cloudflare Workers. Just like that, you deployed to the edge with Remix.

Note that there are differences between the listed edge and edge-like deployment targets. CDNs utilize lightweight JavaScript runtimes that are not compatible with Node.js. Edge-like deployment targets such as Deno Deploy and Fly.io provide regional distribution but may offer less proximity than their

CDN counterparts. You can refer to *Chapter 3, Deployment Targets, Adapters, and Stacks*, to learn more about Remix's different deployment targets and their runtimes and environments.

In this section, you learned that edge computing is a distributed computing paradigm and understood how it differs from cloud computing. You further reviewed available edge deployment targets for Remix and deployed a Remix app to the edge. You also learned how serving from the edge can improve response times. Maybe you're wondering why we didn't build BeeRich to run on the edge. In the next section, we will consider the limitations of running at the edge and discuss further pros and cons.

Understanding the edge's benefits and limitations

In the previous section, you learned that edge computing is about performance. By moving the compute closer to the user, we can reduce response times and, consequently, improve the user experience. Let's dive deeper and learn more about the edge's pros and cons.

Edge environments follow a serverless programming model. Each incoming request starts up a new edge function. The function runs the web application (our Remix app) to fulfill the request and shuts down afterward. The serverless programming model makes edge environments highly scalable but also increases the complexity of the associated system architecture as it limits what can be done within the web application.

Serverless execution avoids wasting computing power on idle applications. However, serverless also reduces the capabilities of web applications to short-lived functions that shut down after handling an incoming request. For example, serverless functions cannot be used for long-running tasks, such as maintaining server-sent event endpoints or WebSocket servers.

Like most serverless environments, edge functions also do not have access to a filesystem and cannot write and read files. This requires us to utilize a remote service to store files. Additionally, edge functions do not offer long-living application states that can be shared between different requests. This prevents us from caching data or managing user sessions in memory.

Edge providers utilize lightweight runtimes to make web applications less computation-intensive. Most of today's CDN-based edge runtimes operate on V8 isolates, isolated contexts within the V8 engine. Booting up a V8 isolate is faster than booting up containers or virtual machines. This makes edge applications handle a request within milliseconds. Most traditional serverless functions suffer from cold start times of several hundred milliseconds to start after being dormant for a while. Edge functions do not suffer from the same cold start problem.

Most edge-native runtimes, such as workerd from Cloudflare, are designed with web standards in mind but do not support executing Node.js standard libraries. This makes them incompatible with Node.js. Conclusively, we can only use npm packages if these packages do not use Node.js standard libraries internally. This may or may not be an issue, depending on the use case of the application, but it certainly is a point to consider.

The big advantage the edge has over traditional web hosting is global distribution. Most server and serverless environments do not automatically distribute applications across different regions, at least not without additional configuration overhead and costs. Edge computing allows us to distribute web applications globally with minimal configuration efforts and significantly lower price points. However, geographical distribution also increases the complexity of the associated system architecture.

Regional distribution only decreases response times if it decreases the total round-trip time behind a request. Refer to *Figure 13.2* in *Chapter 13, Deferring Loader Data*, where we illustrated how Remix reduces response times by removing client-server round trips. Instead of doing fetch requests from the client to the server, we can execute `loader` functions on the document request and query the closely located database. Notice that in *Figure 13.2*, the round-trip time from the server to the database is very small. We assume that the database is closely located to the server – for instance, in the same cloud region, data center, or even on the same. *Figure 16.1* illustrates how the response time may increase if the database is distant from the server:

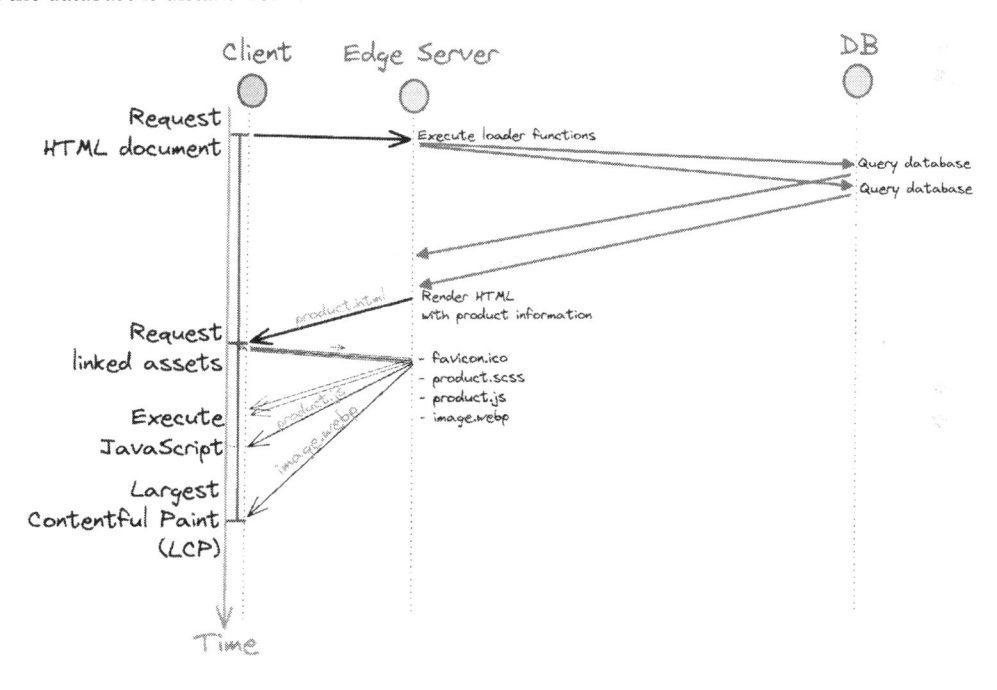

Figure 16.1 – Edge response waterfall with distant database

By moving the server close to the user, we may be able to reduce client-server round trips. However, each client-server round trip might trigger several server-database round trips. If these round trips increase due to the distance between the server and the database, we may decrease performance overall.

Figure 16.1 assumes we make two separate database queries to fulfill the document request. As we can see, we further assume that we can make both database requests in parallel. However, sometimes, we may need to make subsequent requests. Notice how such requests would further delay the response time.

The performance of today's web applications heavily depends on the distance between the server and the database. In cloud data centers and regions, databases are usually close to the web servers. However, to accomplish proximity between the server and the database on the edge, we must distribute our database.

Geographically distributed database offerings exist and CDNs have also started to offer distributed key-value and SQL databases, but it is important to consider the costs and complexity of a globally distributed system architecture.

You may notice a pattern here. Edge functions provide computational and geographical scalability but introduce additional complexity. You must weigh the discussed benefits and considerations carefully when evaluating the edge for a project.

Let's wrap up by doing a short thought experiment. What pieces of BeeRich would require a rework to make BeeRich run on an edge environment? For edge-like environments such as Fly.io or Deno Deploy, not many. However, for true edge environments such as Cloudflare Workers and Pages, we would need to make signification changes:

- SQLite databases run on the same machine and require filesystem access. SQLite is not supported by edge runtimes. We would need to use a different database.

- The expense and invoice attachment file upload feature would require a rework. We currently use the server's filesystem. We would need to use a third-party file storage service or build a custom one.

- The real-time update feature would require a rework. We currently use a server-sent events endpoint to update clients about data changes. Server-sent events require long-running connections that are not supported by edge runtimes. We must deploy the server-sent events endpoint to a different long-running server.

This example illustrates that long-running servers support simpler application designs, while serverless edge runtimes introduce limitations due to their scalable and performance-driven nature.

In this section, you learned about the benefits and limitations of the edge. We also discussed what is not possible in edge environments. Equipped with these considerations, you can now evaluate whether moving to the edge is worthwhile for a given project.

Summary

In this chapter, you learned about the edge as a computing paradigm, a location, and a runtime. You now understand that edge computing contrasts cloud computing and aims to move the compute as close as possible to the users to reduce response times.

You further learned that CDNs can serve as the edge of the internet. Running Remix on the edge moves the web server much closer to the user compared to the regionally centralized data centers of the cloud.

Remix offers adapters for several edge deployment targets, and you practiced deploying to the edge by using Remix's `create-remix` script. You now understand how easy it is to set up a Remix application on the edge.

We discussed both the benefits and limitations of the edge as a deployment target. You now understand that the edge follows a serverless programming model, which makes it highly scalable but also introduces complexity. Edge runtimes use lightweight container technologies to optimize for geographical distribution and performance. Geographical distribution introduces additional considerations, such as the distance to the databases.

Finally, you learned what cannot be done on the edge, such as accessing the filesystem, sharing application states in memory across requests, and handling long-running tasks and connections.

In the next and last chapter, we will review what we have learned. We will further touch upon some final topics, such as migration strategies and Remix's versioning.

Further reading

Review the Remix documentation for a list of official and community adapters: `https://remix.run/docs/en/2/other-api/adapter`.

You can find more information about Fastly's Remix adapter here: `https://www.fastly.com/blog/host-your-remix-app-on-fastly-compute-edge`.

Refer to this article to learn how to deploy your Remix application to Netlify's edge functions: `https://www.netlify.com/blog/how-to-use-remix-framework-with-edge-functions/`.

If you want to learn more about edge environments, have a look at Cloudflare's learning resources: `https://developers.cloudflare.com/workers/learning/how-workers-works/`.

17
Migration and Upgrade Strategies

Throughout this book, we've explored many aspects of web development with Remix. You learned how to use Remix to unlock the full potential of the web platform, and you thoroughly practiced developing full stack applications by building BeeRich. In this last chapter, we will talk about migration and upgrade strategies.

The chapter is split into two sections:

- Migrating to Remix
- Keeping Remix apps up to date

First, we will discuss how to migrate to Remix. Different applications may require different migration strategies with varying efforts. We will look at non-React, React, and React Router apps and create a migration strategy for each. Next, we will learn how major version upgrades are rolled out in Remix. We will introduce you to Remix's future flags and discuss how future flags enable us to gradually upgrade Remix apps.

After reading this chapter, you will know different migration strategies for Remix. You will understand how to run Remix side by side with an existing legacy application and how React Router can be used to prepare your code base for a migration. Further, you will know how Remix can be integrated within a wider system architecture. Finally, you will learn how to gradually upgrade your Remix application with future flags.

Migrating to Remix

Migrations are never easy. Moving an existing code base to a new framework comes with difficulties and may involve a lot of refactoring. Remix is no exception, but some strategies may make a migration less painful, depending on the existing application architecture. In this section, we will discuss different migration strategies for Remix. Let's start by reviewing a migration from a non-React app.

Migrating non-React apps to Remix

Migrating from a non-React app to Remix is a challenging task and may be very time-consuming, depending on the size of the existing application. The complexity of a migration usually increases with ongoing feature development. Most of the time, we may be unable to freeze feature development and bug fixes while migrating. This results in having to migrate existing code and features to Remix while also having to implement new features in both the old and new applications.

One solution may be to run the new and old applications side by side. By doing so, we can keep our legacy application alive while ramping up our Remix application. Step by step, we may be able to move more and more code to Remix.

For instance, we can host the new Remix application on a subdomain and implement new pages and flows in Remix. Using a subdomain, we can share existing cookies between the two applications.

The migration process could look like this:

1. Create a new Remix application.
2. Register the Remix application on a subdomain to share cookies.
3. Re-implement reusable components in React.
4. Recreate the page layout, footer, and navbar in Remix.
5. Develop new pages and flows in Remix.
6. Migrate existing pages incrementally to Remix.

By developing new pages in Remix, we avoid having to implement new features in both the old and new applications. Instead, we can route users back and forth between the two applications. We can use cookies and the URL to share application states.

Running both applications side by side still requires us to do some work up front, such as re-implementing reusable components and page layout in React, but we can avoid having to make a complete switch before being able to run Remix in production.

If we already use React, then the migration should be easier.

Migrating from a React app

We can reuse bigger parts of our existing code base if we maintain a React application. However, if we are currently using a different React framework, such as Gatsby or Next.js, then migrating may still require us to run the legacy app and Remix app side by side in production.

Migrating from another React meta framework

Different React frameworks utilize different routing conventions, primitives, and component APIs. Migrating from another meta framework may allow us to reuse existing React components but may still require refactoring.

The migration process from a different React framework could look like this:

1. Create a new Remix application.
2. Register the Remix application on a subdomain to share cookies.
3. Copy, paste, and adapt reusable components.
4. Copy, paste, and adapt the page layout, footer, and navbar.
5. Develop new pages and flows in Remix.
6. Migrate existing pages incrementally to Remix.

We may need to refactor existing components to use Remix's primitives and utilities. For instance, we want to refactor existing anchor tags to use Remix's `Link` and `NavLink` components. Conclusively, it may be best to copy code to Remix and refactor it from there. This requires us to maintain duplicate code across the legacy and Remix apps.

It becomes easier if we run a client-side-only React application without a framework. Let's review how to migrate a client-only React app to Remix.

Migrating from a client-only React app

If we maintain Create React App or a Vite React app (client-only), we might have an easier time migrating to Remix, especially if the application already utilizes React Router.

On the client, Remix runs a client-side React application, and most of the React code and client-side fetch requests will work the same way in Remix as they did before. Hence, we can run the existing app on the client side inside Remix. From there, we can incrementally refactor pieces from the client-side-only app to Remix routes.

The migration process from a client-only React app could look like this:

1. Create a new Remix application.
2. Move the existing app inside the new Remix app.
3. Render the existing app in the `index` route.
4. Copy and adapt the page layout, footer, and navbar.
5. Develop new pages and flows in Remix.
6. Migrate existing pages incrementally to Remix.

We may still need to copy and paste existing components to create Remix-compatible versions. However, at least for now, we can do so in the same code base.

Migrating becomes much easier if we use React Router as the client-side routing solution.

Migrating from React Router

Remix was created by Michael Jackson and Ryan Florence, the creators of React Router. Remix has been heavily inspired and influenced by the development and maintenance of React Router over the years.

React Router is a library for client-side routing in React. Since Remix's development, the Remix team has also worked on releasing React Router version 6, which aligns React Router's API with that of Remix. Remix and React Router have since been refactored to build upon the same baseline router package.

When looking through the API documentation of React Router version 6, you may notice many familiar concepts such as the `loader` and `action` functions, many familiar hooks such as `useLoaderData`, `useActionData`, `useNavigation`, `useSearchParams`, `useFetcher` and `useLocation`, and familiar components such as `Form` and `Link`.

React Router's `loader` and `action` functions are executed on the client, not the server, as React Router is a client-side routing solution. However, React Router uses the same navigation, data loading, and revalidation flow as Remix, which allows us to build React Router apps with the same mental model, conventions, and primitives. This makes migrating from React Router version 6 to Remix easier.

We can derive the following migration process for client-only React applications:

1. Migrate to React Router version 6.
2. Iteratively refactor code to use React Router's primitives and conventions, most importantly the `loader` and `action` functions.
3. Migrate from React Router version 6 to Remix.

First, we need to migrate to React Router version 6. We can follow the existing migration guides on the React Router documentation.

Once we use React Router version 6, we can refactor the code iteratively over time. We will refactor existing fetch requests to React Router's `loader` and `action` functions and utilize React Router's `Link` and `Form` components to implement navigations and mutations – just like with Remix. This also allows us to utilize React Router's life cycle hooks, such as `useNavigation` and `useFetcher`, to implement pending states and optimistic UI.

In contrast to Remix, React Router does not use a file-based routing convention. If we want to utilize Remix's file-based routing convention – or any other routing convention – then we might want to start defining it already in the client-side application. For instance, it may be helpful to move route components into a new `routes/` folder and to co-locate the `loader` and `action` functions together with the React Router route components, matching Remix's route file convention.

At some point, we will have to make the switch and move the app over to Remix. The closer we bring the application to Remix's routing convention and data flow, the better. However, there is no need to refactor everything to the `loader` and `action` functions before making the migration, even though it would be helpful.

We can render the client-side React Router routes within Remix, as discussed in the previous section. Naturally, this is not as effective as moving the routes over to Remix, but for bigger applications, this may be a valid option to ensure a timely migration.

You can read more about an incremental migration from React Router version 6 to Remix in the Remix documentation: `https://remix.run/docs/en/main/guides/migrating-react-router-app`.

Now that we have discussed a strategy to migrate the client-side code, let's review the backend code.

Working with a backend application

Remix's `loader` and `action` functions run on the server. We can use them to read and write directly from and to a database and implement webhooks and server-sent event endpoints with resource routes. We can use Remix to implement standalone full stack applications that do not require additional backend applications. In this section, we will discuss how Remix fits into a bigger system architecture and how we can utilize Remix when there are downstream backend applications.

In bigger application architectures, there might be more systems between a frontend application and a database. In this case, Remix will serve as the web server for our frontend.

Let's review the code example from *Chapter 1*:

```
export async function action({ request }) {
  const userId = await requireUserSession(request);
  const form = await request.formData();
  const title = form.get("title");
  return createExpense({ userId, title });
}

export async function loader({ request }) {
  const userId = await requireUserSession(request);
  return getExpenses(userId);
}

export default function ExpensesPage() {
  const expenses = useLoaderData();
  const { state } = useTransition();
  const isSubmitting = state === "submitting";
  return ( <>
```

```
      <h1>Expenses</h1>
      {expenses.map((project) => (
        <Link to={expense.id}>{expense.title}</Link>
      ))}
      <h2>Add expense</h2>
      <Form method="post">
        <input name="title" />
        <button type="submit" disabled={isSubmitting}>
          {isSubmitting ? "Adding..." : "Add"}
        </button>
</Form> </>
);  }
```

On incoming requests, the `loader` function fetches a list of expenses. The route component renders both an expense list and an expense form, which on submit posts to the same route's `action` function.

Note how we call the `createExpense` and `getExpense` helper functions in the `loader` and `action` functions. We could implement these functions to read and write from and to a database. However, we could also implement the functions to `fetch` from downstream backend services.

Similarly, we could implement `requireUserSession` to send a request to a downstream authentication service, instead of implementing the authentication code within our Remix app. Conclusively, Remix can also be used to forward requests to backend applications and implement the **Backend for Frontend** (BFF) pattern.

> **Backend for Frontend**
>
> The BFF pattern specifies a software architecture where each frontend has a dedicated backend that is used to tailor content for the specific needs of the frontend application. The backend then forwards or orchestrates requests to more generic downstream services.

We don't need to migrate our backend application to Remix simultaneously with our frontend application. Instead, we can forward requests from the frontend to the legacy backend application. We can then gradually migrate the backend code into Remix's `loader` and `action` functions. Alternatively, we can also maintain the backend application together with the Remix app. In bigger system architectures, it may be desirable to use Remix only as a web server and use generic backend services to implement REST APIs that can be reused across different clients.

In this section, you learned how to migrate different applications to Remix. You now understand how to use Remix as a BFF. In the next section, you will learn how to keep your Remix app up to date.

Keeping Remix apps up to date

Remix, like every framework, undergoes constant maintenance and development. Bigger updates are introduced as major releases that can include breaking changes. Upgrading to a newer major version can require refactoring, and especially for bigger applications, this can be a painful chore. Remix aims to make upgrading to major versions as painless as possible. In this section, we will see how we can gradually migrate to newer major versions in Remix.

Like most open source projects, Remix uses semantic versioning to denote its patches and updates. Semantic versioning provides a way to document three different kinds of changes in a definitive hierarchy:

1. `2.x.x`: Changes that increment the first digit are major releases that include breaking changes
2. `x.1.x`: Changes incrementing the middle digit are minor releases that introduce new features but remain backward-compatible
3. `x.x.1`: Changes that increment the last digit are bug fixes and dependency patches that remain backward-compatible

A new major release breaks backward compatibility, meaning you must update existing code to upgrade to the major version. This can be a painful process. Luckily, the Remix team provides future flags to avoid all-at-once upgrade processes.

Future flags are Boolean flags that we can specify in the `remix.config.js` file:

```js
/** @type {import('@remix-run/dev').AppConfig} */
module.exports = {
  future: {
    v2_errorBoundary: true,
    v2_meta: true,
    v2_routeConvention: true,
  },
};
```

Whenever the Remix team finalizes a feature of a new major version, it also releases the feature in the previous major version, hidden behind a future flag. This means we can start using the new features in the previous version before the next major version is released. By utilizing the future flags, we can gradually (feature by feature) refactor our code.

The Remix team distinguishes two kinds of future flags:

- Unstable flags
- Version flags

Unstable future flags (`unstable_`) are used for features where the API is still under active development and may be up to change. These features are unstable, and the API might be removed or changed in future releases.

Once an unstable feature is stable, the feature may either be introduced in a minor version update or transformed into a version future flag (`vX_`). Version-based feature flags enable stable API changes in the current Remix version. Enabling a version-based feature flag allows developers to prepare for the next major version update. For instance, the `v2_meta` future flag is used to enable the updated meta-function API of Remix v2 in Remix v1.

Future flags allow the Remix team to iterate on Remix's primitives and conventions and release new features, one by one, in the current major version. This also allows the team to receive early feedback and identify potential issues and bugs as early as possible.

Future flags do not remove the need to refactor existing code on existing changes, but they allow gradual refactoring that can be stretched out over time.

Summary

In this chapter, we discussed different migration strategies for Remix. You learned strategies to migrate a non-React, React, and React Router application to Remix.

For bigger migrations, you can run the new Remix app and the old legacy application side by side in production. You can build new pages in Remix while incrementally moving features from the old application to Remix. Using a subdomain for your new Remix app, you can share UI state using cookies.

You now understand that React Router and Remix use the same baseline routing implementation. Thus, migration from React Router applications to Remix is easier, as you can incrementally prepare your React Router app by taking advantage of the shared primitives and conventions. This allows you to reuse much of the code between a React Router and Remix app without further refactoring.

After reading this chapter, you now understand how to use Remix as a BFF to forward and orchestrate requests to downstream services. You know that Remix can be used independently and as a part of a wider system architecture. When migrating to Remix, you can focus on migrating your frontend code while forwarding all requests from Remix's `action` and `loader` functions to the existing backend applications.

Finally, you learned about Remix's future flags system. Remix offers future flags to unlock features of upcoming major versions in the current ones. This allows gradual upgrades on a per-feature basis and avoids painful migrations that require updating all code at once.

Over the last 17 chapters, you studied many concepts to build full stack applications with Remix. As a React developer, Remix provides a lot of great primitives, conventions, and levers to let you unlock the full potential of the web platform. Due to Remix's philosophy of embracing the web platform, you not only practiced how to work with Remix but also learned about many web standards and concepts, such as the web Fetch API, progressive enhancement, HTTP caching headers, and HTTP cookies.

Remix is truly a full stack framework for the web, and by following the exercises in this book, you were introduced to many aspects of full stack web development, such as request-response flows, user authentication, session management, data revalidation, and implementing progressive, optimistic, and real-time UIs. I am excited to see what you will build next. Happy coding!

Further reading

The Remix documentation includes a guide on how to migrate from React Router to Remix: `https://remix.run/docs/en/main/guides/migrating-react-router-app`.

The Remix documentation further includes an article by Pedro Cattori that documents how to migrate from webpack to Remix: `https://remix.run/blog/migrate-from-webpack`.

Refer to Remix's release log to stay up to date with Remix's releases: `https://github.com/remix-run/remix/releases`.

Sergio Xalambrí wrote an article on how to run Next.js side by side with Remix for an incremental migration: `https://sergiodxa.com/articles/run-next-and-remix-on-the-same-server`.

You can find Remix's roadmap on GitHub: `https://github.com/orgs/remix-run/projects/5`. You can also find roadmap planning meetings on YouTube: `https://www.youtube.com/c/Remix-Run/videos`.

You can find more information about semantic versioning here: `https://semver.org/`.

Learn more about Remix's future flag approach in this blog post by Matt Brophy: `https://remix.run/blog/future-flags`.

You can read more about Remix as a BFF in the Remix documentation: `https://remix.run/docs/en/main/guides/bff`.

Index

A

action data
　working with　114-117
adapters　24
　switching between　42-44
asset manifest　54
assets
　exposing, with loader functions　187, 188
　handling　180

B

backend application, Remix
　working with　283, 284
Backend for Frontend (BFF) pattern　284
BeeRich　47, 57
　testing, on slow 3G networks　110, 111
　working with　47, 48
Blues stack　45

C

caching　225
　HTTP caching　226
　in-memory caching　235, 236
client-only React app
　migrating, to Remix　281

concurrent mutations
　form, adding to list　117-120
　handling　117
　multiple pending states, supporting　120
　pending deletion states, indicating　120-123
conventions　9
Cumulative Layout Shifts (CLS)　10

D

dashboard pages, BeeRich
　composing, with nested routing　57-62
data
　prefetching　111-113
data fetching　84
　data loading, in parallel　92-97
　dynamic data, fetching in
　　parameterized routes　89-92
　on route level　84-88
data mutations　97
　with JavaScript　103-105
　without JavaScript　97-103
data streaming, to client　239
　HTTP streaming requirements　242
　server-side data fetching　240-242
　server-side data streaming　240-242

declarative way 102
defer function 243
deployment target
   selecting 36-41
dynamic routing
   route parameters, using 63

E

edge 271
   benefits 274-276
   limitations 274-276
   remixing 273
   web apps, running 272
edge computing 271
error handling
   page not found (404) errors, handling 142, 143
esbuild
   using 11

F

file-based routing 54
   working with 52-54
files
   forwarding, to third-party services 210
   loading, into memory 197-199
   processing, on server 197
file uploads 191
fonts
   handling 180

G

global meta tags
   declaring 174

graceful degradation 108
Grunge stack 45

H

Hello World! Remix App
   creating 16-18
hosting environment
   selecting 38-40
HTTP caching
   dynamic data responses, caching with entity tags 233-235
   HTTP headers, adding in Remix 226
   immutable data responses, caching 231-233
   personalized pages, caching in private caches 230
   public pages, caching in shared caches 226-228
   Remix's built-in caching 228-230
   working with 226
HTTP streaming
   requirements 242

I

images
   handling 180
   working with 187
Indie stack 45
in-memory caching
   exploring 235
Internet of Things (IoT) 271

J

JavaScript runtime
   selecting 37, 38

L

Largest Contentful Paint (LCP) 239
layout sharing 65
   parent layout routes, using 65-67
   pathless layout routes, using 67-69
levers 10
linked resources
   prefetching 185, 186
links
   managing 181-183
loader data
   deferring 243-248

M

meta exports
   nesting 176
meta functions
   exploring 174-176
   loader data, using 177, 178
   matches data, using 178-180
meta tags 173
   global meta tags, declaring 174
   using, in Remix 173
multipart form data
   using, in Remix 192-197

N

navigations
   handling 69
   handling, with Remix's link
     components 69-72
   page transitions, indicating 73-75
   user, redirecting from server 75-78
nested error handling 134-137

nested routing
   pages, composing with 57-62
Node Package Execute 16
non-React apps
   migrating, to Remix 280
npx command 16

O

Open Web Platform 4
optimistic UI 215
   client and server states, synchronizing 216
   client and server states,
     synchronizing in Remix 217
   considering 216
   rollbacks, communicating 216
optimistic UI updates, in Remix 217
   attachment, removing 222, 223
   expense, creating 217, 218
   expense, deleting 220-222
   expense, updating 218, 219

P

page not found (404) errors
   handling 142, 143
pagination 265
   implementing 265-268
parameterized route segment 63
   using 63-65
parent layout routes 61
   using 65-67
pathless layout routes
   using 67-69
polling 252
prefetching, Remix
   enabling 112, 113

primitives 9
progressive enhancement 97, 108
progressive enhancement, Remix 108
    experience enhancing, with JavaScript 109
    testing, on slow 3G networks 110, 111
    working, without JavaScript 108, 109

R

React app
    migrating, to Remix 280
React meta framework
    migrating, to Remix 281
React Router 282
    migrating, to Remix 282, 283
    reference link 283
real-time technologies
    polling 252
    SSEs 252
    WebSockets 252
    working with 251
real-time UIs
    building, with Remix 253-258
Remix 4
    asset manifest, compiling 11
    backend application, working with 283, 284
    command-line interface (CLI) 11
    file-based routing, working with 52-54
    full-stack framework 5, 6
    images, working with 187
    limitations 12, 13
    linked resources, prefetching 185, 186
    migrating, from client-only React app 281
    migrating, from React app 280
    migrating, from React meta framework 281
    migrating, from React Router 282, 283
    migrating to 279
    multipart form data, using 192-197

    navigations, handling 69
    non-React apps, migrating to 280
    philosophy 7, 8
    progressive enhancement 108
    responsibilities 10
    route file-naming conventions 52
    route module exports 56, 57
    route modules, creating 54-56
    route modules, working with 52
    stylesheet 184
    styling 184
    web framework 4, 5
Remix App
    bundles 23, 24
    client and server environment 22
    client-side app code 25, 26
    files and folder structure 18-22
    Hello World!, creating 16-18
    server-side app code 25, 26
    support, looking for 31
    troubleshooting 27
    updating 285, 286
Remix App Server 16
Remix components
    compiler 11
    router 11
    runtime 12
Remix Discord server
    reference link 31
Remix's link components
    navigating with 69-72
Remix stacks
    Blues stack 45
    custom templates, working with 46, 47
    Grunge stack 45
    Indie stack 45
    official stacks, working with 45, 46
    using 45

Remix's upload handler helper functions
  using 199-208
Requests for Comments (RFCs) 7
resource route 54
  for authorizing access 208-210
root error boundary
  unexpected errors, handling with 130-133
route-level data fetching 84-88
route modules
  creating 54-56
  exports 56, 57
  working with 52
route parameters
  using, for dynamic routing 63
route-scoped stylesheets 184

S

Search Engine Optimization (SEO) 173
search parameters
  forms, submitting
    programmatically 151, 152
  reading, in loader functions 146, 147
  updating, with form submissions 148-150
  working with 146
Server-Sent Events (SSE) 251, 252
  advantage 252
  disadvantage 252
session management 145, 261
  pagination, implementing 265-268
  visitor sessions, managing 262-265
single-page applications (SPAs) 5
Slow 3G 110
splat routes 65
  creating 65
static assets
  working with 180
stylesheets
  handling 180

T

third-party services
  files forwarding to 210
thrown responses, handling 137, 138
  exception handling, with error
    boundaries 138, 139
  resilient experience, creating 140, 141
Time to First Byte (TTFB) 10
troubleshooting, Remix App 27
  console and network tabs 28
  error message, trusting 28
  issue, searching on Google 30
  line, locating 28
  server, restarting 29
  time or runtime, building 28

U

UI route 54
unexpected errors
  client error, invoking 129
  dealing with 128
  handling, with root error boundary 130-133
  nested error handling 134-137
  server error, invoking 128, 129
upload handler helper functions, Remix
  using 199-208
useLoaderData 117
user access
  authorizing, with resource routes 208-210
user data authentication
  cookie data, accessing on server 162, 163
  enforcing, on server 166-171
  user data on client, working with 164-166
user sessions creation, with cookies 153
  Remix's session helpers,
    working with 153-155

session, deleting during logout 160-162
user login flow, adding 158-160
user registration flow, adding 155-158

V

visitor sessions
managing 262-265

W

WebSockets 252
advantage 253
World Wide Web Consortium (W3C) 4

‹packt›

www.packtpub.com

Subscribe to our online digital library for full access to over 7,000 books and videos, as well as industry leading tools to help you plan your personal development and advance your career. For more information, please visit our website.

Why subscribe?

- Spend less time learning and more time coding with practical eBooks and Videos from over 4,000 industry professionals
- Improve your learning with Skill Plans built especially for you
- Get a free eBook or video every month
- Fully searchable for easy access to vital information
- Copy and paste, print, and bookmark content

Did you know that Packt offers eBook versions of every book published, with PDF and ePub files available? You can upgrade to the eBook version at packtpub.com and as a print book customer, you are entitled to a discount on the eBook copy. Get in touch with us at customercare@packtpub.com for more details.

At www.packtpub.com, you can also read a collection of free technical articles, sign up for a range of free newsletters, and receive exclusive discounts and offers on Packt books and eBooks.

Other Books You May Enjoy

If you enjoyed this book, you may be interested in these other books by Packt:

Building Micro Frontends with React 18

Vinci J Rufus

ISBN: 978-1-80461-096-1

- Discover two primary patterns for building micro frontends
- Explore how to set up monorepos for efficient team collaboration
- Deal with complexities such as routing and sharing state between different micro frontends
- Understand how module federation works and use it to build micro frontends
- Find out how to deploy micro frontends to cloud platforms
- Figure out how to build the right development experience for teams

React 18 Design Patterns and Best Practices, 4e

Carlos Santana Roldán

ISBN: 978-1-80323-310-9

- Get familiar with the new React 18 and Node 19 features
- Explore TypeScript's basic and advanced capabilities
- Make components communicate with each other by applying various patterns and techniques
- Dive into MonoRepo architecture
- Use server-side rendering to make applications load faster
- Write a comprehensive set of tests to create robust and maintainable code
- Build high-performing applications by styling and optimizing React components

Packt is searching for authors like you

If you're interested in becoming an author for Packt, please visit `authors.packtpub.com` and apply today. We have worked with thousands of developers and tech professionals, just like you, to help them share their insight with the global tech community. You can make a general application, apply for a specific hot topic that we are recruiting an author for, or submit your own idea.

Share Your Thoughts

Now you've finished *Full Stack Web Development with Remix*, we'd love to hear your thoughts! Scan the QR code below to go straight to the Amazon review page for this book and share your feedback or leave a review on the site that you purchased it from.

`https://packt.link/r/1-801-07529-8`

Your review is important to us and the tech community and will help us make sure we're delivering excellent quality content.

Download a free PDF copy of this book

Thanks for purchasing this book!

Do you like to read on the go but are unable to carry your print books everywhere? Is your eBook purchase not compatible with the device of your choice?

Don't worry, now with every Packt book you get a DRM-free PDF version of that book at no cost.

Read anywhere, any place, on any device. Search, copy, and paste code from your favorite technical books directly into your application.

The perks don't stop there, you can get exclusive access to discounts, newsletters, and great free content in your inbox daily

Follow these simple steps to get the benefits:

1. Scan the QR code or visit the link below

https://packt.link/free-ebook/9781801075299

2. Submit your proof of purchase
3. That's it! We'll send your free PDF and other benefits to your email directly

Printed in Poland
by Amazon Fulfillment
Poland Sp. z o.o., Wrocław